CAPACITY EXPANSION

Analysis of Simple Models
with Applications

John Freidenfelds
Bell System

NORTH HOLLAND
New York • Oxford

Elsevier North Holland, Inc.
52 Vanderbilt Avenue, New York, New York 10017

Sole distributors outside the USA and Canada:
Elsevier Science Publishers
P.O. Box 211, 1000 AE Amsterdam, The Netherlands

Library of Congress Cataloging in Publication Data

Freidenfelds, John.
    Capacity expansion: analysis of simple models with applications.

    Includes bibliographies and index.
    1. Industrial capacity—Mathematical models.
    I. Title.
HD69.C3F73   658.5'038   80-25079
ISBN 0-444-00562-5

Desk Editor   Danielle Ponsolle
Design   Edmée Froment
Designer   Glen Burris
Production Manager   Joanne Jay
Compositor   Science Typographers, Inc.
Printer   Haddon Craftsmen

Manufactured in the United States of America

To Cecil Bo

Contents

Foreword

Economic progress and investments in capacity expansion go hand in hand: the capital and technology embodied in new capacity are driving forces behind economic growth and development. Thus, it is not surprising that capacity expansion decisions draw attention from a wide range of disciplines. Economists are particularly interested in the implications of such decisions for the planning of economic development and the structure of industries. Managers are concerned with the formulation of specific investment proposals for capacity expansion within their own enterprises. Operations research analysts tend to focus on mathematical models that can aid the process of deciding among capacity expansion alternatives. Engineers must recognize the interaction between economic considerations and the technological design choices inherent in capacity expansion. All of these groups should find much value in John Freidenfelds's excellent introduction to capacity expansion models and their applications.

The models explored here offer valuable insights into the nature of capacity expansion choices. For example, why should expansion be carried out in discrete steps rather than as a gradual, continuous process? The answer is found in the relationship between economies-of-scale in capacity investment and the time-value of investment capital. Thus, one finds an economic rationale for specifying expansion in the form of distinct "projects" rather than as a gradual investment process. The models also reveal how changes in underlying economic parameters, such as the discount rate or the cost of capacity shortages, influence the expansion decision.

From these models, one may learn a great deal about approaches for selecting a best decision from many alternatives. Operations research methods such as dynamic programming often are presented in a dry, rather abstract manner. Here application brings life to the approaches, and even those trained in such methods will find new perspectives. The exposition of the methods develops a philosophy of problem solving, and the principles that emerge are useful for providing solutions to much more complicated situations than those represented by the original models.

Capacity expansion models have found use in many settings, including the process industries, electric power generation, transportation, water resources, and communications. A taste of applications in all these areas appears here, but I find particularly appropriate the focus on models and applications from the communications field. There is an impressive history of capacity expansion models and calculations in communications, dating back at least to the 1927 *Handbook of Outside Plant Engineering Practices* of the American Telephone and Telegraph Company. The applications are rich in structure and variety, and they are drawn together for the first time in this book.

Often one thinks of investments in terms of portfolios of stocks and bonds or deeds to real estate. But these investments involve only claims on physical assets, and making such investments frequently represents no more than an exchange of claims that has little direct influence on the creation of real capital assets. Although models for this type of paper, or financial, investment have been analyzed extensively elsewhere, they receive little attention here. Instead, the emphasis is on models for the real capital investment decisions involved in establishment of new productive capacity. I hope that this book will bring these investment models to a prominence equal to those that involve purely financial investments.

University of California, Los Angeles   Donald Erlenkotter

Acknowledgments

The author's technical work in this area and the writing of this manuscript were done while he was a Member of Technical Staff at Bell Telephone Laboratories. Their support and encouragement are gratefully acknowledged. Further work on the manuscript, including preparation of the figures, was done at AT&T.

This book draws on a great deal of work done at Bell Laboratories and AT&T. Some of the people who have been involved are:

B.S. Abrams, J. Albers, R.W. Amory, W.N. Bell, S. Blum, I.O. Bohachevsky, A.D. Braley, R.C. Carlson, V.P. Chaudhary, H.S. Edwards, H.T. Freedman, F.J. Gratzer, P.A. Gresh, A.D. Hall, H.Z. Hardaway, R.G. Hinderliter, R.B. Hirsch, D.R. Hortberg, W.M. Hubbard, A.J. Kalotay, M.J. Karson, M.D. Kennedy, W.L.G. Koontz, E.P. Klein, M.J. Krone, P.B. Linhart, N.G. Long, D.B. Luber, H. Luss, B.L. Marsh, W.H. Marshall Jr., C.D. McLaughlin, J.P. Moreland, J. Opacic, T. Pecsvaradi, J.M. Rodgers, R.S. Shipley, F.W. Sinden, R.A. Skoog, R.L. Smith, H. Southworth, R.A. Sutton, C.E. Warren, T.W. Wylonis.

PART I

BACKGROUND

Chapter 1

Introduction

Capacity expansion decisions are made daily by various agencies of the government, by businesses, and to some extent by private individuals. Some are large decisions, such as the construction of a major dam; others are small, such as the purchase of an additional stamping machine. Some are made following months or even years of study and deliberation, while others seem to be made with no study at all. These decisions, large and small, add up to a massive commitment of capital. The efficient commitment of that capital depends on making good decisions in individual capacity expansion undertakings.

This book is dedicated to the proposition that capacity expansion investment decisions can be improved through the use of mathematical models. By making many simplifying assumptions, we obtain models that can be analyzed readily. The analysis of such simple capacity expansion models is the subject of most of this book. While real capacity expansion problems are invariably more complex than the ones studied here, these models *do* capture aspects of capacity expansion problems that are important in many applications. Furthermore, as we shall show, an understanding of the simple models is crucial to understanding more complex models.

This chapter tells what the rest of the book is all about. In Section 1.1 we give a quick intuitive idea of what we mean by a *capacity expansion problem*. In Section 1.2 we discuss, at length, various aspects of capacity expansion problems, what we mean by the name, where these problems arise, what we wish to solve for, and so on. Then in Section 1.3 we outline the particular topics to be covered in later chapters.

1.1 A Capacity Expansion Problem

Suppose that the regional school board in a growing community proposes that a high school be built. The board's plan is to make the school large enough to meet the community's needs for the next 15 years at a cost of $10 million. However, it is an election year, and the opposition party claims that this plan is "shortsighted" and "fiscally irresponsible." They point out that with the community's projected growth, another school will have to be built in 15 years for another $10 million. Alternatively, the first school could be made large enough to accommodate all 30 years of growth for $15 million—a savings, claims the opposition, of $5 million!

Is the opposition right? Is there some *other* plan that would be better than either of these proposals? How is one to evaluate such proposals? This is an instance of a *capacity expansion* problem. Problems like this arise in many, many contexts. The capacity of electrical power generating facilities must be augmented as the demand for power increases over time. Transmission cables must be added to serve new customers who want telephone service. Refineries must be built to supply a growing demand for petroleum products.

The situations surrounding decisions about expanding electrical generating capacity, telephone network capacity, or manufacturing capacity are very complex, but they all share some basic features with the school problem outlined above. Typically, it costs less per unit of capacity to install that capacity in large chunks. Such *economy-of-scale* effects result from various underlying characteristics. In the school problem, for example, it is quite plausible that a facility of twice the capacity would cost *less* than twice as much. There are bound to be savings in such items as architect's fees, site preparation, and construction costs if one large building is constructed all at once, rather than two separate smaller projects.

But, is the $15-million school really a better buy than the two $10-million schools? That is an example of the central subject of this book. Although the full answer is a bit more complicated, the choice between the plans boils down to whether the community is willing to *invest* an extra $5 million now to avoid a $10-million expenditure 15 years from now. Recognizing this argument, the incumbent school board members demonstrate the following calculation:

1. Raise $15 million now.
2. Build the $10-million school.
3. Put the extra $5 million in a bank at 5% interest per year.
4. Watch the balance grow, as the interest is compounded.
5. Withdraw the balance of $10.39 million [$5(1.05)^{15}$] in 15 years.
6. Build the other $10-million school at that time.
7. Give the school board members a raise with the leftover $390,000.

One might question precisely how this calculation was done or should be done, but it is surely sufficient to demolish the claim that building a single school is superior by $5 million to building two schools in 15 years. The results of this calculation are identical to comparing the plans according to their *present worth cost*, a subject to be discussed in much more depth in Chapter 2.

1.2 Characteristics of Capacity Expansion Problems

Capacity expansion is the addition of facilities to serve some need. The *capacity expansion problem*, as we shall think of it, is restricted to situations in which the following apply:

1. The cost of the equipment or facilities added exhibits *economies-of-scale* (i.e., their cost is less than proportional to size).
2. *Time* is an important factor. That is, there is a continuing (possibly changing) need for the facilities, and the facilities or equipment added are durable (i.e., they provide service over more than a short time interval).

Capacity expansion problems arise in a myriad of applications:

communications networks

gas and oil pipelines

electrical power generation and transmission

public facilities such as schools, water systems, sewer systems, and roads

manufacturing facilities, including whole factories and individual machines within a factory.

Many different idealized capacity expansion problems can be abstracted from such applications. These are mathematically describable problems that can be related more or less to situations that arise in the applications:

Additional units of a single type of facility are to be deployed periodically as demand increases over time.

Several different types of interdependent facilities are to be added.

There are other costs, such as operating costs that depend on the capacity expansion decisions.

Backlogging some demand or importing services is permitted as an alternative to capacity expansion.

Some existing capacity may have to be replaced due to obsolescence, deterioration, or cost advantages of new equipment.

A finite set of projects is to be undertaken, and the problem is to determine the optimal sequence.

The optimal location of additional facilities is affected by transportation costs.

The link capacities of an interconnected transmission network are to be expanded.

Demand depends on price, which depends on cost, which depends on capacity expansions, which depend on demand.

The primary capacity expansion decisions typically involve the *sizes* of facilities to be added and the *times* at which they should be added. Expansion timing is especially important when, for example, operating costs are significant or importing is allowed. Often the *type* of capacity or the *location* of the capacity to be added are also major concerns. In addition to these primary decisions, there may be dependent secondary decisions involving the optimal *utilization* of the capacity being added. For example, the demand for transmission capacity in the links of a communication network depends on how messages are routed through the network.

All of these concerns—size, time, type, location, and utilization—are what we may call the *operational* aspects of the capacity expansion problem. Parts II and III of this book deal exclusively with these questions. Before we can proceed with the analysis, however, we must also examine what we might call *behavioral* questions. The key concern is, What should be the *decision criterion* (or criteria)? How do we decide which of two capacity expansion plans is better? In this book, we use *present worth*, sometimes also called discounted present value, for choosing between plans. Present worth is widely used in problems of this kind and many people find it intuitively appealing. Since it is such a fundamental assumption, however, we devote a lengthy Chapter 2 to a discussion of why present worth is a reasonable criterion.

In adopting the present worth as our optimization criterion, we do not mean to imply that other factors are unimportant. Our basic contention is that given two capacity expansion plans that provide the same service, the one with the smaller present worth cost is superior. We recognize that there may be extenuating circumstances under which this will not strictly be the case. For example, a politician may have a preference for the larger water project quite independently of economic calculations. Similarly, a business manager may prefer the alternative that makes this year's earnings statement look the best. More generally, it is never possible to model explicitly all aspects of a decision-making situation; judgment inevitably will have to be applied. In such cases, the present worth calculation can give a quantitative measure of how much it would cost to indulge these other considerations.

Another behavioral simplification that we use throughout the book is that demand for the capacity in question can be determined (forecast) *independently* of the capacity expansion decisions. The left-to-right sequence in Figure 1.1 illustrates this schematically. We start with a demand forecast and determine a capacity expansion schedule that results in some pattern of costs over time. A more complete analysis would recognize that these costs influence the prices charged for the service, which, in turn, influence the demand. Strictly speaking, the entire demand/expansion/cost/price problem should be solved simultaneously. Unfortunately, such an approach would be terribly complex. A great many questions arise, for example, with respect to pricing assumptions. Should prices be assumed to vary with the amount of spare capacity? If so, should they be higher when there is more slack capacity (to compensate investors for their extra investment), or less slack capacity (to discourage additional demand and forestall the need for more expansion)? Further complications may come in the form of governmental subsidies to promote a "socially desirable" price structure for some service. An example of this relates to passenger rail service: without subsidy there may not be a price/demand to cover the cost of providing the service, and the whole operation may have to close down.

   We avoid these problems by assuming that a demand forecast can be made without knowledge of the expansion schedule. In many practical problems, this is reasonable because demand is simply not *that* sensitive to price. Also, demand forecasts are difficult to make even for some assumed price structure, without having to estimate sensitivities of the demand in each period with respect to prices in every other period. Furthermore, we shall see that capacity expansion decisions tend to be relatively insensitive to small changes in the demand forecast. Finally, if the demand sensitivity to price *is* deemed important for some applications, the methods presented

Figure 1.1. Interdependence of demand, capacity expansions, and price.

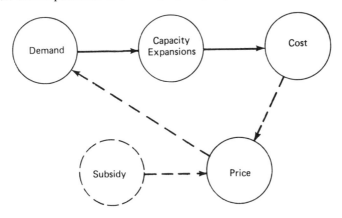

here may still be useful as a suboptimization within a larger optimization procedure.

Of course, it is not possible to treat adequately all of the idealized capacity expansion problems mentioned in this section, especially when one considers the almost endless combinations, such as "interconnected transmission networks with several types of interdependent facilities, with backlogging permitted." Our basic plan is to examine the present worth decision criterion in the remainder of Part I of this book. This is a more general discussion; it is not limited to the *capacity expansion problem* as we have defined it. In Part II, we study simple capacity expansion models. Then, in Part III, we look at some more complex models and show that an understanding of the simple models can be very helpful.

1.3 Overview

Chapter 2 discusses, from several points of view, why one would use present worth as the decision criterion in problems of this kind.

The first three chapters of Part II, Chapters 3, 4, and 5, thoroughly discuss the capacity expansion problem in which a single capacity type is to be added to serve a known deterministic demand. These chapters introduce, in a simple setting, solution methods and approaches that are useful later. Also, examples worked out here are used later in more complex settings.

Chapter 6 shows that if we allow more than one capacity type, the problem becomes significantly more complex. Approximations based on the solution of single-capacity-type expansion problems provide good solutions as well as insight.

Throughout most of the book, we assume a deterministic knowledge of all variables. Chapter 7 is an exception. Here we allow the demand to be described by a certain random process. It turns out that for this random demand process, we can generate an *equivalent deterministic demand* that can be treated as if it were known with certainty.

In Chapters 8 and 9 we explicitly model the effects of what we call congestion costs. These are costs that depend on the amount of slack capacity in the system at a given time. Such costs are shown to arise in the form of minor rearrangements in, for example, certain telephone networks and the operating costs of electrical power generation systems. Congestion costs affect the optimal timing of expansion and may also be a major influence on the optimal size.

The two chapters of Part III deal with more complex problems. Chapter 10 describes a capacity expansion algorithm for a telephone feeder cable network. In this problem there are several different types of capacity. There are four gauges of cable, a coarser gauge being temporarily substitutable for finer gauge; and there are conduit ducts, one of which is used up by each cable addition. Although this problem is specific to the telephone feeder cable network, the solution approach illustrates how one may utilize an understanding of simpler capacity expansion problems to analyze more realistic problems.

Chapter 11 is a compendium of other capacity expansion problems: expansion/replacement, sequencing/location, network expansion, and relation to economic indicators. Descriptions and solutions are necessarily more sketchy in this survey chapter, but they provide a background for further study of capacity expansion problems.

Chapter 2

The Economic Criterion—
Present Worth

This chapter explores the philosophical underpinnings of all that follows. It is *not* a prerequisite to the rest of the book; but, since we will be devoting a good deal of time and energy to solving problems based on present worth cost, it seems only prudent to examine the reasonableness of the criterion. Also, we shall have occasion later to refer to some of the concepts developed here.

If all cash flows—income, expenses, etc.—associated with some decision occurred at the same time, an obvious selection criterion would be net cost. Of course, even in such a simple situation, there could be confounding considerations. There may be various intangible elements not incorporated in the net cost. There could be questions regarding the decision maker's *utility function* if the outcomes are uncertain (more on this in Section 2.3.1).

In the decision problem we shall be examining, cash flows occur at *different points in time*. Clearly, we cannot simply add up costs or income for different years. The fundamental question is, What is the value of a dollar at time t_1 compared to a dollar at time t_2? Another way to put the question is, Suppose you could save a dollar at time t_1, but only if you were willing to spend an additional C dollars at time t_2; for what value(s) of C would this be worthwhile?

The present worth criterion says to evaluate a cash flow with C_1 at time t_1, C_2 at t_2,..., C_n at t_n according to its *present worth*

$$PW \equiv \sum_{i=1}^{n} C_i e^{-rt_i},$$

where r is called the *discounting rate*.[1] The intuitive interpretation is that if we could borrow and lend at the rate r, we could convert any money stream into any other having the same present worth. This follows directly from the fact that if a dollar is invested in an account bearing interest at the rate r compounded continuously, the account will be worth e^{rt} dollars in time t.

A more general formulation would allow the discounting rate to vary over time. We consider such a complication only briefly in connection with our discussion of the proper discounting rate.

Why is the present worth a reasonable criterion? And how do we choose an appropriate discounting rate? These are the (related) major questions we shall explore. Our study will touch on ideas from several fields. Primarily, we shall argue that the firm should accept projects on a present worth basis to ensure its ability to meet all financial obligations. In addition, there is reason to believe that appropriate discounting rates indeed can be found and that these rates are related to fundamental and measurable investment considerations.

2.1 The Revenue Requirements Model[2]

In this section we develop a simple investment model that leads to the present worth as an appropriate investment decision criterion. Since it is much easier, we first examine a situation in which there are no income taxes. We then show that income taxes can be taken into account readily.

2.1.1 Revenue Requirements—Ignoring Income Tax

In this model of investment, we assume that there are three basic elements: (1) the *investors*, who act as bankers lending money and must be paid at the rate r for any outstanding funds; (2) the *firm*, which borrows money from the investors and transforms it into some revenue-producing good to pay the investors back; and (3) the *customers*, who buy the firm's output, supplying the revenues to keep the whole thing going.

We assume that (1) *the investors are indifferent to the particular payback schedule as long as they get a rate of return r* (by this we just mean interest at the rate r on any outstanding balance); (2) the firm is a large going business in the sense that it has loans outstanding and revenues coming in

---

[1] Since we shall be considering continuous time, we also allow cash flows that are given as rates $c(t)$ over time, where $c(t)\,dt$ is the amount of cash flow in the interval t to $t+dt$. In this case,

$$\text{PW} \equiv \int_0^T c(t)e^{-rt}\,dt.$$

The appendix at the end of the chapter briefly discusses the mathematics of money.

[2] This model follows the general philosophy of Linhart, cited at the end of the chapter.

that, on the average, pay the investors their due; and (3) each investment is a small perturbation of the firm's overall financial position. The first assumption says that our criterion will be independent of accounting or dividend payout policies. Only the rate of return on outstanding balance matters. In a regulated firm this corresponds, roughly, with the idea of an allowed return on invested capital. In a competitive firm, this would be the return that is necessary to raise new capital for ventures of this kind. (Section 2.3 discusses risk as an important determinant of the necessary return.) With competition, we do not expect firms consistently to overpay or underpay their investors in the long run.

The second and third assumptions are meant to avoid nonlinearities. For example, in discussing income tax effects, we assume there is enough income to take advantage of future tax deductions. Also, we would like to avoid the question of projects that individually are so large that they would affect drastically the firm's future operations.

What attitude may we expect such a firm to exhibit toward some proposed project for which there may be cash flows at various times?

To start with, what kind of cash flow would just maintain the status quo? Consider, for example, Figure 2.1: spend C_0 now, at time 0, and get back C_1 at time t_1. In this case, the firm would borrow an additional C_0 at time 0. Since it is getting no payback from this project over the interval $(0, t_1)$, at time t_1 it would owe the investors $C_0 e^{rt_1}$, the future worth of C_0 compounded continuously. Thus if $C_1 = C_0 e^{rt_1}$, the overall investment would not change the firm's financial position. If the payback at t_1 were slightly larger, the investment would have a favorable impact, and vice versa if smaller. This observation leads us to call r the firm's *discounting*, or *time value of money*, *rate*. Another way of looking at the same cash flow that gives an identical result is to calculate its present worth at time zero using the discounting rate r:

$$PW = -C_0 e^{-rt_0} + C_1 e^{-rt_1}.$$

Figure 2.1

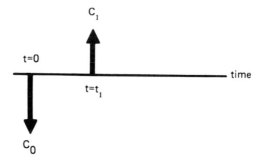

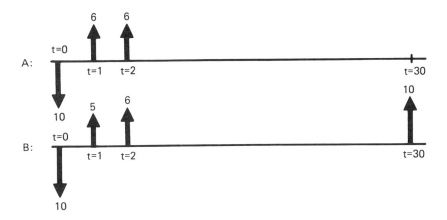

Figure 2.2

The project will have a favorable (or, at least neutral) impact on the firm if and only if the present worth of its cash flow is nonnegative.

The same argument can be extended easily to the general case of cash flows occurring at various times. In fact, we get the even more general observation that *investment A will have a more favorable financial impact on the firm than investment B if and only if the present worth of the cash flow of A is larger than that of B.*

Although the criterion is rather straightforward, some interesting aspects of it can be illustrated with examples. If the notation or calculations are not clear, the reader should consult the appendix at the end of the chapter.

Example 2.1. Consider a situation in which the firm must choose between the following two cash flows (see Figure 2.2). Using $r = 0.1$,

$$PW(A) = -10 + 6e^{-0.1(1)} + 6e^{-0.1(2)} = 0.34,$$

$$PW(B) = -10 + 5e^{-0.1(1)} + 6e^{-0.1(2)} + 10e^{-0.1(30)} = -0.07.$$

Cash flows near the current time have much more impact than cash flows far in the future. //

Example 2.2. Consider the mutually exclusive investments A and B illustrated below in Figure 2.3.[3] In each of these a \$100 initial investment is repaid after a period during which the investment returns a continuous

---

[3]Arrows indicate one-time expenditures, and horizontal lines indicate constant continuous annuities. If this is not clear, see the appendix at the end of the chapter.

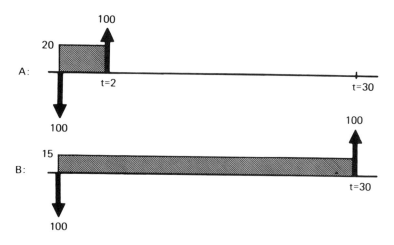

Figure 2.3

annuity. At $r=0.1$,

$$PW(A)= -100+20\left[\frac{1-e^{-0.1(20)}}{0.1}\right]+100e^{-0.1(2)}=\$18.13,$$

$$PW(B)= -100+15\left[\frac{1-e^{-0.1(30)}}{0.1}\right]+100e^{-0.1(30)}=\$47.51.$$

Alternative A is like lending someone money at 20% interest for 2 years, while alternative B is like lending someone money at 15% interest for 30 years;[4] yet B is better. Is this somewhat counterintuitive? We shall return to this example in Section 2.2.2. //

Example 2.3. Consider the cash flow pattern of Figure 2.4. Its present worth at $r=0.1$ is

$$PW= -100+10\left(\frac{1-e^{-0.1T}}{0.1}\right)+100e^{-0.1T}=0.$$

A project that just pays interest at r and returns invested capital makes no present worth impact on the firm. //

A useful notion natural to this model is the idea of *revenue requirements*. If we embark on a spending program, how much revenue must we collect to just cover costs? Consider, for example, a machine that costs \$1,000 now at $t=0$, \$500 to overhaul at $t=5$ years, and is sold for \$100 at $t=10$ years. What kind of revenue stream would be just enough to pay for it? To put

---

[4]That is, a bond with interest continuously paid to the lender.

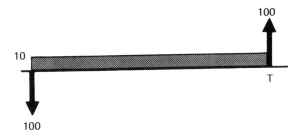

Figure 2.4

the question more precisely, what kind of revenue stream, combined with this expenditure stream, would have a neutral financial impact on the firm? According to the present worth criterion, there will be no financial impact on the firm if

$$PW(\text{cash flow}) = 0,$$

or

$$PW(\text{revenues less costs}) = 0,$$

or

$$PW(\text{revenues}) - PW(\text{costs}) = 0,$$

or

$$PW(\text{revenues}) = PW(\text{costs}).$$

That is, any revenue stream whose present worth equals the present worth of the costs will be sufficient to pay off those costs plus return to investors. A convenient revenue stream to consider is one that is constant over the life[5] of the investment, in which case the revenues required per unit time can be found by applying a standard annuity factor to PW(costs).

Example 2.4 (The machine mentioned above). What are the equivalent constant revenue requirements when $r = 0.1$ and when $r = 0$? (See Figure 2.5.)

$$PW(\text{revenues}) = PW(\text{costs}),$$

$$R\left(\frac{1 - e^{-r10}}{r}\right) = 1{,}000 + 500e^{-r5} - 100e^{-r10}.$$

At $r = 0.1$,

$$6.32R = 1{,}000 + 303 - 37,$$

---

[5] More on investment life in Section 2.6.

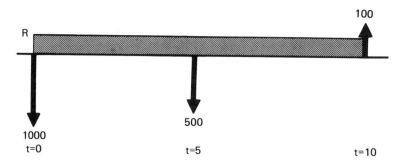

Figure 2.5

or

$$R = 200$$

As $r \to 0$, the present worth of annuity factor in the left-hand side approaches the constant $1/r = 10$, so that

$$10R = 1,000 + 500 - 100,$$

$$R = 140.$$

The \$140/year would only repay the investment, while the \$200/year would also pay a return of 10% on outstanding balance. //

Example 2.5. What if a \$1,000 machine lasts forever (see Figure 2.6)?

$$\text{PW}(\text{revenues}) = \text{PW}(\text{costs}),$$

$$R\left(\frac{1}{r}\right) = 1,000,$$

$$R = 1,000r.$$

In this case, the revenues never repay the investment, but only pay interest on it. //

Figure 2.6

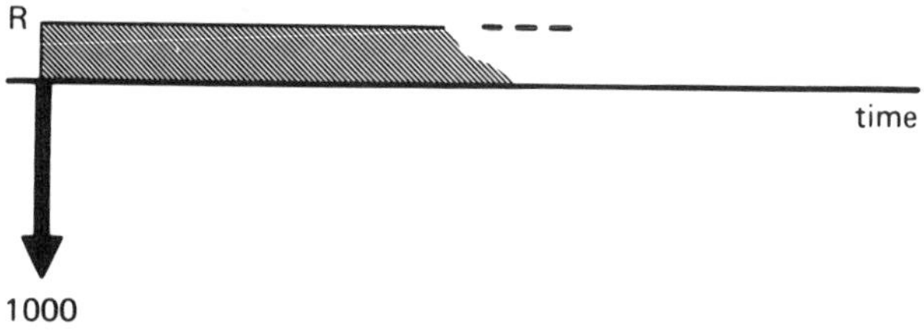

2.1.2 Revenue Requirements—Including Income Tax

We obviously cannot give a complete discussion of income taxes, since volumes have been written on the subject; also, tax laws are changing all the time. Our objective is to illustrate some of the major effects on our investment model.

We start by making a distinction between *expense* dollars and *capital* dollars, since the two are treated differently in terms of income tax. Expenses generally are defined to be those costs of doing business that are paid for on a year-by-year basis—salaries, fuel, raw material. Capital costs, on the other hand, are those expenditures that are allocated over several years—machinery, buildings, equipment. Detailed laws and administrative rulings by the Internal Revenue Service specifically prescribe which expenditures must be expensed and which capitalized. A key distinction between expense and capital is that in calculating the firm's income taxes, expenses are deducted from revenues in the year in which they are incurred, while deductions for capital expenditures must be spread out over several years in the future.

Example 2.6. Suppose a firm has a machine that may be repaired for $1,000 of expense money. Alternatively, the firm may buy a new machine for $1,000 of capital money. Assume that the corporate tax rate is 50% and that the new machine must be depreciated on a straight line over 5 years.[6] That means we can deduct $200 per year for the next 5 years from taxable income. The tax benefit to the firm in the case of the $1,000 expense is 50% of $1,000, or $500, in the first year. In the case of the capital expenditure, the benefit is 50% of $200, or $100 in each of the next 5 years. Although this also adds up to $500, it is less advantageous to the firm, as we shall see, since the money is not available as soon. //

In keeping with our policy of building up to the more complicated situations, we suppose for the moment that the investors are all *equity* holders. That is, all new capital is raised by selling more stock. In practice, the firm typically raises some of its capital by selling bonds, called *debt* as opposed to equity. The reason we need to distinguish between the two at this point is, again, income taxes. Interest paid on bonds is deductible from income for tax purposes.

How would such an all-equity firm evaluate the *expense* stream of Figure 2.7? The firm incurs an additional expense of C_0 at time 0 and reduces its expenses by C_1 at time t_1. Since expenses are tax deductible, the firm ends up with $C_0 - \tau C_0$ less money at time 0 and with $C_1 - \tau C_1$ extra at time t_1 (τ

---

[6]At present, depreciation methods are allowed that accelerate the depreciation—that is, allow more to be charged to earlier years. In addition, tax credits may be obtained in the first year after a new capital expenditure. The reader is referred to Smith, cited at the end of the chapter.

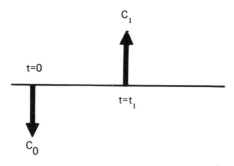

Figure 2.7

is the marginal corporate income tax rate). To make ends meet, the firm must borrow $(1-\tau)C_0$ from its investors at time 0. Thus, at t_1 the firm owes its investors $(1-\tau)C_0e^{rt_1}$. If the venture is to be worth it, the extra cash flow $(1-\tau)C_1$ at time t_1 must at least offset this:

$$(1-\tau)C_1 \geq e^{rt_1}\left[(1-\tau)C_0\right],$$

or

$$-C_0 + C_1e^{-rt_1} \geq 0.$$

Thus we are led to the same present worth criterion as before. In terms of the revenue requirements model, given some flow of expenses over time we might ask, What kind of revenue stream would be sufficient to meet all obligations? It is not difficult to show that

$$\mathrm{PW}\binom{\text{revenues}}{\text{after taxes}} \geq \mathrm{PW}\binom{\text{expenses less}}{\text{income tax deduction}},$$

or

$$(1-\tau)\mathrm{PW}(\text{revenues}) \geq (1-\tau)\mathrm{PW}(\text{expenses}),$$

or

$$\mathrm{PW}(\text{revenues}) \geq \mathrm{PW}(\text{expenses}).$$

This should not be surprising, since changes in revenue have exactly the same impact on the firm's financial position as changes in expense.

Next, consider the same all-equity firm contemplating a *capital* expenditure (as defined by the people who collect income taxes). As discussed earlier, the financial impact of a capital expenditure on the firm is spread over several years. Thus spending C now looks like Figure 2.8, where $I_1,\ldots, I_T$ are the income tax reductions obtained in future years due to depreciating C, plus investment tax credits, and so forth. A useful way to evaluate such a cash flow is to calculate the revenues required to just meet

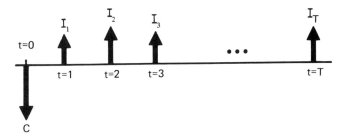

Figure 2.8

all obligations:

$$PW\left(\begin{array}{c}\text{revenues}\\\text{after taxes}\end{array}\right) \geq PW\left(\begin{array}{c}\text{capital spent}\\\text{less income tax advantage}\end{array}\right),$$

or

$$(1-\tau)PW(\text{revenues}) \geq C - PW\left(\begin{array}{c}\text{income tax}\\\text{advantage}\end{array}\right),$$

or

$$PW(\text{revenues}) \geq \frac{1}{1-\tau}\left[C - PW\left(\begin{array}{c}\text{income tax}\\\text{advantage}\end{array}\right)\right].$$

Example 2.7. In Example 2.6 we considered the options of repairing a machine for $1,000 of expense money or buying a new one for $1,000 of capital money. What are the revenue requirements for the two options using $r=0.1$, $r=0$?

For the expensed option,

$$PW(\text{revenues}) = PW(\text{expense}) = \$1,000.$$

For the capitalized option,

$$PW(\text{revenues}) = \frac{1}{1-0.5}\left[1,000 - PW\left(\begin{array}{c}\$100/\text{year for}\\5\text{ years}\end{array}\right)\right].$$

Using $r=0.1$,

$$PW(\text{revenues}) = 2\left[1,000 - 100(e^{-0.1} + e^{-0.2} + e^{-0.3} + e^{-0.4} + e^{-0.5})\right]$$
$$= \$1,252.$$

Using $r=0$,

$$PW(\text{revenues}) = \frac{1}{1-0.5}(1,000 - 500) = \$1,000.$$

This confirms the statement of Example 2.6 that it is better to get the tax deduction right away ($252 better in this case). Of course, if there were no time value of money ($r=0$), the two options would be identical, since they both have the same total tax advantage. //

What this result means in practical terms is that *we cannot just directly add capital and expense costs*. We *can* add the present worth of revenues required for a capital expenditure with expense costs, since both are expressed in commensurate terms. This leads us to define *the present worth cost associated with a capital expenditure* including income tax effects as the present worth of revenues required.

We now introduce the last complication we shall consider in connection with income taxes. Suppose the firm actually gets money from two types of investors, equity holders and debt holders. Since the debt holders have a prior claim on assets of the firm (they get paid first if something goes wrong), their investment is less risky,[7] and so they are generally compensated at some rate r_d that is less than the rate r_e paid to equity holders. We assume that the firm holds debt and equity obligations in some proportion $\rho=\text{debt}/(\text{debt}+\text{equity})$. In assessing the marginal impact of some cash flow on the firm, we assume that the debt ratio must stay constant. This is not to say that the debt ratio in fact never changes, or even that it *should* stay constant. If the debt ratio does change, however, that change in what is termed the "financial structure of the firm" would have an economic impact that would be hard to evaluate. We thus assume that in order to be financially attractive, a project must meet all of its cash flow obligations (repayment of capital, return to investors, taxes, etc.) and leave the debt ratio unchanged. This is not a severe restriction, since most large firms usually exhibit a rather stable debt ratio.

In the following analysis, it will be convenient for expository purposes to assume that all cash flows occur at integral values of time and to replace the future worth factor e^{rt} by $(1+r)^t$.[8]

Consider again an expense flow, as shown in Figure 2.9. As before, we assume that the firm borrows $(1-\tau)C_0$ from its investors at time $t=0$ to make up the temporary deficit after taxes. This time, however, it borrows debt and equity in the proportion ρ, so that at $t=1$ it owes its investors

$$(1+r_d)\rho[(1-\tau)C_0]+(1+r_e)(1-\rho)[(1-\tau)C_0], \qquad (**)$$

which can be rewritten

$$(1+r_c)[(1-\tau)C_0],$$

where $r_c \equiv \rho r_d +(1-\rho)r_e$ is the composite or overall return paid to investors for each dollar of outstanding obligation. Previously, we would have

---

[7]More on risk and return in Section 2.3.

[8]Strictly speaking, we need to use a different discouting rate for discrete cash flows—see the appendix at the end of the chapter.

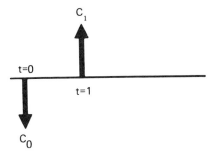

Figure 2.9

required for this case

$$[(1-\tau)C_1] \geq (1+r_c)[(1-\tau)C_0].$$

Now, however, we also would like to take into account the tax deductibility of interest payments on debt. Assuming that the interest payment indicated by the first term of Equation $(**)$ is actually paid, we get a tax advantage in year 1 of $\tau \rho r_d[(1-\tau)C_0]$; and so, to break even we require

$$[(1-\tau)C_1] + \tau \rho r_d[(1-\tau)C_0] \geq (1+r_c)[(1-\tau)C_0],$$

or

$$C_1 \geq (1+r_x)C_0,$$

or

$$-C_0 + C_1(1+r_x)^{-1} \geq 0,$$

where $r_x \equiv r_c - \tau \rho r_d$ is called the *tax-adjusted composite cost of money*. Thus, as before, the project is acceptable if the present worth of cash flows is positive, but with the tax-adjusted composite rate used as the time value of money. It can be shown that this result holds in general for the firm we have postulated. That is, the firm will just be able to meet all of the obligations associated with a cash flow provided the present worth of the cash flow is nonnegative, using the tax-adjusted composite cost of money. Also, even though we have derived the adjusted rate for a discrete time model, we shall use it in the continuous compounding case as well.

2.1.3 Summary—How to Do Cost Studies in Light of the Revenue Requirements Model

1. Choose the alternative that maximizes the present worth of revenues less costs.
2. In an environment including income taxes, *do not simply add capital and expense costs.* A convenient way of making the two commensurate is to replace a capital expenditure C with its present worth

of revenue requirement:

$$PW(\text{revenues}) = \left(\frac{1}{1-\tau}\right)\left[C - PW\left(\begin{array}{c}\text{income tax}\\\text{advantages}\end{array}\right)\right],$$

where τ is the marginal corporate income tax rate and PW(income tax advantages) is the present worth of tax reductions in future years due to allowed depreciation, investment tax credit, and so forth.

3. Use the tax-adjusted composite cost of capital (as long as interest payments are deductible from income for tax purposes):

$$r_x \equiv (1-\rho)r_e + \rho(1-\tau)r_d,$$

where

r_d is return to debt holders

r_e is return to equity holders

ρ is debt ratio: debt/(debt + equity).

Example 2.8. Consider a firm described by the following parameters:

r_d is 0.05 (interest on debt)

r_e is 0.133 (return to equity holders)

ρ is 0.40 (ratio of debt to debt plus equity)

τ is 0.50 (marginal income tax rate).

Since we shall be doing present worth studies, we calculate

$$r_x = (1 - 0.40)(0.133) + (0.40)(1 - 0.5)(0.05) = 0.09.$$

Suppose the motor pool department is concerned with capital expenditures that are treated identically for tax purposes (e.g., suppose all motor vehicles are depreciated identically). In particular, for each capital dollar spent at time $t = 0$, the firm is allowed to deduct from its taxable income: $0.4 at $t = 1$ year; $0.3 at $t = 2$ years; $0.2 at $t = 3$ years; and $0.1 at $t = 4$ years.[9] At the 50% tax rate, these lead to a tax advantage of $0.2, $0.15, $0.1, and $0.05 at the four times. In addition, the firm is allowed an investment tax credit of $0.1 at $t = 1$ year for each dollar of capital spent at $t = 0$.[10] The present worth of these tax advantages is

$$(0.2 + 0.1)e^{-(0.09)1} + 0.15e^{-(0.09)2} + 0.1e^{-(0.09)3} + 0.05e^{-(0.09)4} = 0.509,$$

so the present worth cost of each dollar of capital expenditure (i.e., the

---

[9] This is an accelerated depreciation scheme currently allowed by the government. (Zero salvage is assumed.)

[10] An investment tax credit is allowed by the government in some years to make capital expenditures more attractive and thereby stimulate the national economy.

present worth of revenue required) is

$$PW = \frac{1}{1-0.5}(\$1-0.509) = \$0.98.$$

Thus in this case we actually would *prefer* to spend a capital dollar if it had the same effect as an expense dollar. It is interesting to note that without the 10% tax credit the result would have been $PW = (1-0.418)/(1-0.5) = \$1.17.$ //

Example 2.9. The motor pool is considering the purchase of a $10,000 vehicle that will reduce its operating expenses by $2,600/year over 5 years. Is it worth it? What if the investment tax credit is revoked? The total present worth in the first instance is

$$PW = PW\left(\begin{array}{c}\text{expense}\\\text{saved}\end{array}\right) - PW\left(\begin{array}{c}\text{capital}\\\text{cost}\end{array}\right)$$

$$= (2,600)\left[\frac{1-e^{-(0.09)5}}{0.09}\right] - (0.98)(10,000)$$

$$= \$668,$$

and so the investment pays. If the investment tax credit is not allowed,

$$PW = (2,600)\frac{1-e^{-(0.09)5}}{0.09} - (1.17)(10,000)$$

$$= -\$1,220,$$

and the investment does not pay. //

An important thing to note from these examples is that once we have decided on an appropriate discounting rate and have calculated the present worth cost of each capital expenditure including tax effects, we can proceed without further explicit mention of taxes. In the interest of simplicity, our sample calculations therefore will avoid tax calculations except as necessary to illustrate some point.

2.2 Other Views of the Problem

Although we will view the investment problem principally according to the revenue requirements model of Section 2.1, some other ways of looking at it help to shed further light on the problem.

2.2.1 Mathematical Optimization Approach[11]

Here, we try to reduce the investment problem to some bare essentials and see what we can learn about it. Suppose there are N different kinds of

---

[11] The development here follows that of H. Martin Weingartner, cited at the end of the chapter.

investment opportunities, each characterized by a cash flow over fixed periods $t = 0, 1, \ldots, T$. That is, opportunity or project j has net cash outflows c_{tj} for $t = 0, 1, \ldots, T$, where $c_{tj} < 0$ means the project is absorbing funds in period t. For example, $c_{0j} = -1,000$; $c_{tj} = 100$, $t = 1, \ldots, T$, is a project that requires an initial investment of \$1,000 and then returns \$100/year for the rest of the study period. Suppose the firm can accept any desired number x_j, $j = 1, \ldots, N$, of any of the projects. For mathematical simplicity, we suppose that x_j can be any nonnegative number. Thus we allow the firm to take on fractions of projects[12] (i.e., the same fraction of all of the project's cash flows). Suppose, furthermore, that the firm's only relation to the larger world outside these investment projects is a prespecified set of incremental funds d_t, $t = 0, 1, \ldots, T$, made available to it in each period (or withdrawn if $d_t < 0$). Under these circumstances it seems reasonable to postulate that the firm will choose projects so as to maximize its total cash position at the end of the horizon (remember, all inflows and outflows are prespecified a priori):

$$\text{maximize} \quad \sum_{j=1}^{N} \sum_{t=0}^{T} c_{tj} x_j$$

$$\text{subject to} \quad \sum_{j=1}^{N} \sum_{i=0}^{t} c_{ij} x_j + \sum_{i=0}^{t} d_i \geq 0, \qquad t = 0, 1, \ldots, T,$$

where the project scales, x_j, are nonnegative, and may also be bounded above. The constraints require that the firm limit itself to projects that will allow it to remain solvent in each period. (All surpluses are simply carried forward to the next period.)

For an optimization problem in this form, it can be shown that there exist nonnegative multipliers λ_t, sometimes called dual variables or shadow prices, such that the solution of the original constrained problem is identical to the solution of the unconstrained (except for bounds on the variables x_j) problem

$$\text{maximize} \quad L(x, \lambda) \equiv \sum_{j=1}^{N} \sum_{t=0}^{T} c_{tj} x_j + \sum_{t=0}^{T} \lambda_t \left(\sum_{j=1}^{N} \sum_{i=0}^{t} c_{ij} x_j + \sum_{i=0}^{t} d_i \right).$$

Given the values of the dual multipliers λ_t, we can determine which projects are acceptable (i.e., have nonzero x_j) by examining the derivatives

$$\frac{\partial L}{\partial x_j} = \sum_{t=0}^{T} c_{tj} + \sum_{t=0}^{T} \lambda_t \sum_{i=0}^{t} c_{ij}$$

$$= \sum_{t=0}^{T} \left(1 + \sum_{i=t}^{T} \lambda_i \right) c_{tj}.$$

---

[12] That is, we treat project *scale* as a continuous variable. Section 2.9 discusses, for a special case, the complexities that arise when only a discrete number of project scales is available.

If the derivative is negative, the corresponding x_j must be at its lower limit, zero; that is, project j is unacceptable. Thus the solution is made up entirely of projects for which the derivative is zero or positive. (Those for which it is strictly positive will have x_j at their upper limit.)

In general, it is not possible to determine the values of the multipliers without solving the original optimization problem. However, it turns out that we can infer their values for some interesting special cases. We proceed by rewriting the acceptance criterion as

$$c_{0j} + \left(\frac{1}{1+r_0}\right)c_{1j} + \left(\frac{1}{1+r_0}\right)\left(\frac{1}{1+r_1}\right)c_{2j}$$

$$+ \cdots + \left[\left(\frac{1}{1+r_0}\right) \cdots \left(\frac{1}{1+r_{T-1}}\right)\right]c_{Tj} \geq 0,$$

where

$$\frac{1}{1+r_t} \equiv \frac{1+\sum_{i=t+1}^{T}\lambda_i}{1+\sum_{i=t}^{T}\lambda_i}, \qquad t = 0, 1, \ldots, T-1.$$

Since the λ_t are nonnegative, so are the r_t. Thus we can interpret them as time-varying interest rates, and the acceptance criterion as a present worth calculation.

To reinforce the interpretation of the r_t as interest rates, we suppose that one of the projects available to the firm is to borrow a dollar at time t and repay $1+r$ dollars at time $t+1$. According to the acceptance criterion, this project will be used by the firm if

$$\left(\frac{1}{1+r_0} \cdots \frac{1}{1+r_{t-1}}\right)(1) + \left(\frac{1}{1+r_0} \cdots \frac{1}{1+r_{t-1}} \cdot \frac{1}{1+r_t}\right)[-(1+r)] \geq 0,$$

which reduces to

$$r_t \geq r.$$

Thus the firm should borrow if its internal interest rate r_t exceeds the borrowing interest rate r. Furthermore, if r_t is strictly larger than r, the firm must be borrowing as much as it can in that period (the corresponding x_j must be at its upper limit). Similarly, if r_t is strictly less than r, the firm must be borrowing as little as it can in that period (the corresponding x_j must be at its lower limit). Now, if there are *no limits* on the amount of borrowing (negative x_j would actually correspond to lending in period t at interest rate r), then we must have $r_t = r$. Thus, *if such borrowing and lending opportunities are available in every period, the project acceptance criterion reduces to the usual present worth.*

If the firm *is* borrowing up to its limit in some period, these observations indicate that the effect on project selection will be identical to having a *higher* discounting rate in that period. The interpretation is that in such constrained periods, the firm's "true" cost of capital is an opportunity cost associated with projects that are available to the firm.

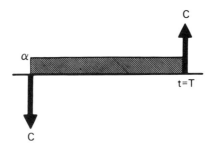

Figure 2.10

2.2.2 The Internal Rate of Return

A concept related to the present worth criterion is the internal rate of return (IROR). Given a cash flow over time, c_0 at time t_0, c_1 at time $t_1,\ldots,$ we define its IROR as that discounting rate r_* that makes its present worth equal zero:[13]

$$\sum_i c_i e^{-r_* t_i} = 0.$$

Of course, depending on the particular values of the c_i and t_i, it is possible to have no real[14] solution, one solution, or multiple solutions. The intuitive interpretation of the IROR is that it is the "rate at which your money grows" if you undertake the project in question. More precisely, if you could deposit in, and withdraw from, a bank account that earns r_* interest, you would just break even with this cash flow. Some examples show what can happen.

Example 2.10. Calculate the IROR for the cash flow shown in Figure 2.10. Set

$$0 = PW = -C + \alpha\left(\frac{1 - e^{-r_* T}}{r_*}\right) + Ce^{-r_* T},$$

or

$$r_* = \alpha/C.$$

This is just the case of borrowing C, paying α interest per unit time, and then paying back C at the end. //

---

[13]In discrete time compounding, replace e^{-r_*} by $1/(1+r_*)$—see the appendix to this chapter.

[14]As opposed to imaginary or complex roots, which have no economic interpretation to my knowledge.

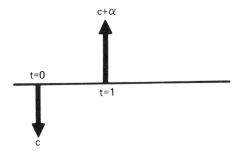

Figure 2.11

Example 2.11. Calculate the IROR using discrete compounding for the cash flow of Figure 2.11. Set

$$0 = PW = -c + (c+\alpha)\left(\frac{1}{1+r_*}\right)$$

or

$$r_* = \alpha/c.$$

Here again, r_* corresponds precisely to what we think of as interest on unpaid balance. //

Example 2.12. Calculate the IROR for the following cash flow when $a = 2.5$, $b = -1.6$ (see Figure 2.12). Set $0 = PW = -1 + \beta a + \beta^2 b$, where $\beta \equiv e^{-r_*}$; then

$$\beta = \frac{-a \pm \sqrt{a^2 + 4b}}{2b}.$$

In this case, $a^2 + 4b = -0.015 < 0$, so no real root exists. //

Figure 2.12

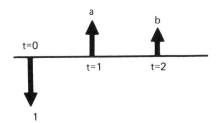

Example 2.13. Calculate the IROR in Example 2.12 when $a = 2.5$, $b = -1.53$. Using the formula of Example 2.12,

$$\beta = 0.935 \qquad \text{and} \qquad \beta = 0.699,$$

so

$$-r_* = \ln(0.935) \qquad \text{and} \qquad -r_* = \ln(0.699),$$

or

$$r_* = 0.067 \qquad \text{and} \qquad r_* = 0.358.$$

In this example there are two real solutions. For interest rates lower than 0.067, the project looks bad because its total undiscounted cash flow is negative (try $r = 0$). Between 0.067 and 0.358, it turns out that the negative impact of b is reduced more than the positive impact of a, making the project look attractive. Above 0.358, the negative cash flow at zero dominates the other two. //

Why would one want to use an indicator such as IROR, which is hard to calculate and, what is more important, can be difficult to interpret (as seen by the examples above, for which there was either no root or multiple roots). One reason for its use is that the decision maker may feel uncomfortable in specifying his cost of money. Even if he knows the interest on the latest bond issue and has a history of equity return, he may feel that the firm cannot *really* get all of the money it needs at that rate. This suggests a relation to our optimization model of Section 2.2.1. According to that model, if the firm *is* constrained in the amount of money it can raise, then some internally determined discounting rate higher than the cost of money may be appropriate.[15] In fact, suppose the firm modeled in Section 2.2.1 found itself consistently unable to undertake projects with IROR less than some value r_* for lack of funds. Suppose also that $r_* > r$, the external cost of money, and think of simple projects such as those illustrated in Examples 2.10 and 2.11 rather than 2.12 and 2.13 in order to avoid interpretational difficulties. If it is operating optimally according to the model of Section 2.2.1, *the firm's discounting rate for evaluating projects will turn out to be r_* rather than r.*

Notice that this result does *not* say that the firm should select projects or select among alternatives for a project by maximizing the IROR. It *does* suggest that the *proper discounting rate for calculating present worth cost, and the lowest acceptable IROR should be approximately equal.* Our position for the remainder of the book will be that the IROR is a useful intuitive concept that helps us to establish an appropriate discounting rate, but that

---

[15] In Section 2.2.1 we actually got a time-varying cost of money.

project evaluations should be done on the basis of present worth at a fixed discounting rate.

Before leaving the subject, we shall discuss a common misconception about IROR. It is sometimes stated that IROR is a measure of profitability, and therefore, obviously, should be maximized. Also, why should some discounting rate determined externally to this project influence the proper decision for *this project*? That is, why should we not simply select the most profitable (as measured by IROR) choice in each instance and thereby get the most profitable overall solution? Mathematically, the answer is that IROR is simply not additive in that fashion even if we ignore problems with nonexistent or multiple roots. Intuitively, perhaps we can get a better idea by reexamining the two cash flows of Example 2.11.

Example 2.14. Consider the mutually exclusive choices shown in Figure 2.13. At $r = 0.1$, PW(A) = \$18.13 and PW(B) = \$47.51. From Example 2.10, IROR(A) = 0.20, IROR(B) = 0.15. //

Example 2.14 shows that present worth and IROR indeed can rank alternatives differently. Which is the "proper" ranking? One intuitive way to look at the situation is to consider two investors, one who chooses A and the other B. During the first 2 years, A earns \$20 interest per year while B earns \$15. At $t = 2$, the investor in A gets his original investment back, while B has another 28 years to run. Which investor is better off? Does the answer depend on what the investor's monetary needs are in the first few years? If the investors are firms whose cost of money is 10%, the answers are clear. Firm A has \$140 (ignoring reinvestment of the \$40 interest paid during the interval), while firm B has \$30 plus an investment with

$$PW = 15 \left[\frac{1 - e^{-0.1(28)}}{0.1} \right] + 100 e^{-0.1(28)} = \$147.$$

Figure 2.13

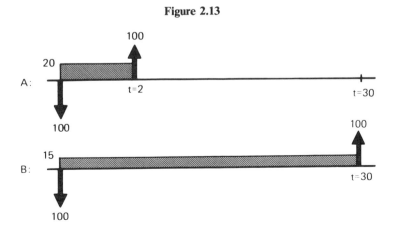

This means that, in addition to the $30 in hand, for example, firm B could borrow $147 from its investors and pay it back with 10% interest out of its remaining investment. That is, *firm B is better off than firm A independently of when it needs the funds.*[16] Another way of seeing the difference between A and B starting at $t = 2$ is to consider the reinvestment opportunities for the $100 returned to A. Supposing that the 10% cost of money represents the IROR at which additional investment projects are available, we cannot expect to obtain any additional present worth from investing the $100 (see Example 2.3).

The conclusion is that the external cost of money and the overall investment opportunities available to the firm are highly relevant in choosing among investment alternatives and that present worth is the better way to rank alternatives.

2.2.3 An Axiomatic Development

Here we summarize a considerably different approach to developing an investment decision criterion.[17] We abstract the decision-making process and very carefully specify some desirable properties of a good decision rule. It turns out that if these properties are to be satisfied, decisions must be made by a present worth criterion. This does not prove, of course, that present worth is the right criterion; it proves only that if the decision rule is to have the specified properties, it must rank cash flows in a manner identical to some present worth formula.

We define the *investment space* as the set of all possible cash flows over $t = 0, 1, \ldots, T$, that is, real $(T + 1)$-dimensional vectors

$$c = (c_0, c_1, \ldots, c_T).$$

We would like to specify a decision rule or investment criterion over this space. That is, we would like to define a preference ordering over all possible pairs of cash flows. Given any pair of cash flow vectors, p, q, let $p R q$ denote "p is preferred or indifferent to q." Taken to be part of the definition of a preference ordering are the following two properties.

1. (*Completeness*) Given any two cash flows p, q, we can always make a choice—either $p R q$ or $q R p$ or both.
2. (*Transitivity*) Given any three cash flows p, q, s, if $p R q$ and $q R s$, then $p R s$.

---

[16] This is an example of what Hirschleifer calls the "separation of production and consumption."

[17] From a classical paper by A. C. Williams and J. I. Nassar, cited at the end of this chapter.

Next, we list the desirable properties of such a preference ordering.

Axiom 2.1 (Continuity). If cash flow p is preferred to cash flow q, then for sufficiently small $\varepsilon_t > 0$, $t = 0, \ldots, T$, cash flow $p - \varepsilon$ is preferred to q. That is, the criterion should not be schizophrenic with respect to small changes in the cash flow.

Axiom 2.2 (Greed). If cash flow p is greater than or equal to q in every period and is strictly greater in some period, then cash flow p is preferred to cash flow q.

Axiom 2.3 (Impatience). If cash flow p is identical to cash flow q except that in some period t a certain amount of cash flow obtained by p is not obtained by q until period $t + 1$, then p is preferred to q. That is, it is better to have money sooner.

Axiom 2.4 (Marginal consistency). Cash flow p is preferred to cash flow q if and only if the difference cash flow $p - q \equiv (p_0 - q_0, \ldots, p_T - q_T)$ is preferred to the zero cash flow.

Williams and Nassar, in their paper cited at the end of this chapter, show the following.

Theorem 2.1. *The only preference orderings that satisfy Axioms 2.1–2.4 are those given by a present worth formula with positive interest rates (possibly different for different time periods). That is, the cash flows should be evaluated by a decision rule of the form*

$$\text{Value}(c) = c_0 + \left(\frac{1}{1+r_0}\right) c_1$$

$$+ \left(\frac{1}{1+r_0}\right)\left(\frac{1}{1+r_1}\right) c_2 + \cdots + \left[\left(\frac{1}{1+r_0}\right) \cdots \left(\frac{1}{1+r_{T-1}}\right)\right] c_T$$

with some positive r_t, $t = 0, \ldots, T-1$.

Of course, this does not tell us what values the interest rates should take on—any positive interest rates would yield an investment criterion that is consistent with the axioms. Thus for example, the investment criterion of maximizing present worth discussed in Section 2.1 *is* consistent with the axioms, while maximizing IROR *is not*. (It is not a complete preference ordering, as evidenced by instances of nonexistent or multiple roots—see Examples 2.12 and 2.13.)

Another axiom leads to a further restriction on the form of the investment criterion:

Axiom 2.5 (Temporal consistency). Let

$$p = (p_0, p_1, \ldots, p_{T-1}, 0), \qquad p' = (0, p_0, p_1, \ldots, p_{T-1}),$$

$$q = (q_0, q_1, \ldots, q_{T-1}, 0), \qquad q' = (0, q_0, q_1, \ldots, q_{T-1}).$$

Then if p is preferred to q, p' is preferred to q'. That is, two opportunities have the same relative ranking "no matter when those opportunities come along."

Theorem 2.2. *With Axiom 2.5 added to the list, the r_t, $t = 0, \ldots, T-1$, of Theorem 2.1 must be identical. That is, the only investment criterion consistent with all of the axioms is the standard present worth:*

$$\text{Value}(c) = \sum_t \left(\frac{1}{1+r} \right)^t c_t.$$

Axiom 2.5 is a very interesting one in that we often make such an assumption implicitly, as we have done in Section 2.1, for example. We return to this question of stability over time in Section 2.3 on uncertainty, and especially in Section 2.4 on price inflation.

2.3 Uncertainty and the Cost of Money

All of our models so far have assumed a world of perfect certainty and have examined the value of money over time. Here we discuss the effects we might expect from uncertainty, using essentially a static (or one-period) model.

First, we explore a utility theory formulation which assumes that individual decision makers are risk averse. According to such a model, a risky investment is worth less to the investor than its expected value. If investors are able to share the outcomes of many statistically independent risky investments, however, the worth of an investment does approach its expected value. The key assumption is independence.

We then present a simple model of investor behavior that is basically consistent with the utility theory approach, but that allows us to take the statistical *dependence* of investments into account. The *capital asset pricing model* argues that we must expect to compensate investors for the systematic, or market-correlated portion, of risk (but not the unsystematic or uncorrelated portion). This leads to a risk-dependent discounting rate for present worth studies. We argue, however, that for practical purposes, it would probably be best to use a single discounting rate that reflects the overall systematic risk taken on by the firm's investors or perhaps recognizes *different risks* for different divisions of the firm or for broad classes of investment projects.

2.3.1 Attitude Toward Risk—Utility Theory[18]

How does risk or uncertainty in the outcome affect the value of an asset? We would like to use some simple measure such as the expected value, but is that consistent with a reasonable individual's choice behavior?

Example 2.15. Suppose you are the holder of a lottery ticket. Several elimination drawings have been held and you are in the fortunate position of being one of two remaining entrants. You thus have a 50% chance of winning $1 million or winning nothing on the next draw. How much would you sell your ticket for? //

The expected value of the lottery in Example 2.15 is $500,000. For many decision makers, however, $500,000 is *not* a good representation of the value of the lottery in the sense that many decision makers would be willing to take far less (e.g., $80,000?) rather than face a 50% chance of getting nothing at all. The problem, then, is that in a decision-making situation with uncertain outcomes, the decision maker cannot always compare alternative courses of action on the basis of the expected value of outcomes.

An elegant solution to this problem is to generate a utility function *u* defined over all possible outcomes such that the expected value of the *utility* of the possible outcomes *is* an appropriate representation of the value of an uncertain prospect. Such a utility function is empirically determined to reflect the decision maker's attitudes toward taking risks. It turns out that a set of fairly mild axioms about choice behavior (analogous to those of Section 2.2.3) guarantees the existence of such a utility function and that the utility function is unique only to within an additive and a multiplicative constant.

Figure 2.14 shows an example of a utility function that could have been measured for some individual. Only the portion of the curve between $0 and $1 million is shown, and the utilities of $0 and $1 million have been set arbitrarily at zero and one, respectively. (The scale is not important.) The utility function is constructed so that the following holds. If x is a random variable (lottery) whose possible outcomes are between $0 and $1 million, and if the decision maker is indifferent to obtaining the known amount $\hat{x}$ or the unknown random amount x, then

$$u(\hat{x}) = E[u(x)],$$

---

[18]As developed by Howard Raiffa and others.

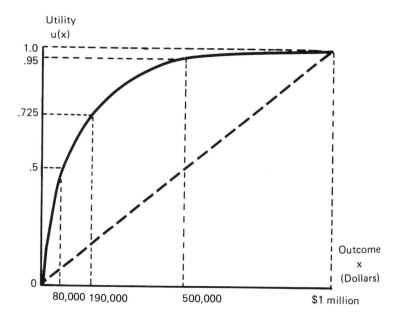

Figure 2.14. A utility function for outcomes between $0 and $1 million.

where $E(\cdot)$ denotes the expected value. Thus the utility function (e.g., the curve in Figure 2.14) can be used to find the certainty equivalent $\hat{x}$ for any random outcome x by the formula

$$\hat{x} = u^{-1}\{E[u(x)]\}.$$

Example 2.16. For the decision maker whose utility function is shown in Figure 2.14, what is the value of the 50–50 lottery between $0 and $1 million? In this case, x is a random variable that is $0 with probability 0.5 and $1 million with probability 0.5, so that

$$E[u(x)] = 0.5(0) + 0.5(1) = 0.5.$$

The certainty equivalent value $\hat{x}$ for this lottery is determined by

$$u(\hat{x}) = 0.5,$$

or, as shown in Figure 2.14, $\hat{x} = \$80,000$.

As another example, we calculate the certainty equivalent of a lottery whose outcomes are

$$x = \begin{cases} \$0 & \text{with probability } \tfrac{1}{4} \\ \$500,000 & \text{with probability } \tfrac{1}{2} \\ \$1 \text{ million} & \text{with probability } \tfrac{1}{4}. \end{cases}$$

From Figure 2.14 the utility values of the three possible outcomes are 0, 0.95, and 1, respectively. Thus,

$$u(\hat{x}) = E[u(x)] = \tfrac{1}{4}(0) + \tfrac{1}{2}(0.95) + \tfrac{1}{4}(1) = 0.725,$$

and we read from Figure 2.14 that $\hat{x} = \$190,000$. //

It is not difficult to check that if u is concave, as shown in Figure 2.14, then $\hat{x} \le \bar{x}$, where $\bar{x}$ is the expected value of x. If this condition holds, the decision maker is called *risk averse*. Intuitively, a risk-averse decision maker is one who will not gamble unless he is given favorable odds. *We will assume that investors are generally risk-averse individuals.* This is not to say that some of them would not gamble occasionally despite bad odds. The popularity of state lotteries indicates, for example, that people sometimes are willing to risk small amounts for a *very* low probability of high gains. We do not see, however, serious business ventures that involve the purchase of lottery tickets. If the utility curve turns out to be actually a straight line, then, for some constants, α and β,

$$u(\hat{x}) = \alpha + \beta\hat{x} = E(\alpha + \beta x) = \alpha + \beta\bar{x},$$

or

$$\hat{x} = \bar{x}.$$

(The value of the lottery is just its expected outcome.) In that case we say that the decision maker is *risk neutral*. According to utility theory, it is only the risk-neutral decision maker who should make decisions according to the expected value of the outcome; all others should use the expected value of the utility of the outcome.

Having briefly sketched some of the main ideas of utility theory, we shall now argue that in many practical decision-making situations, its importance is less than it would at first appear.

Example 2.17. Suppose that Figure 2.14 is the utility function for the decision maker of Example 2.15. Suppose further that this decision maker finds another person holding an identical lottery ticket (50–50 chance at $0 or $1 million) for a *different*, independent lottery and that he negotiates an even splitting of all proceeds of both lotteries between himself and the other ticket holder. In effect, our decision maker would be holding a lottery whose possible outcomes are

$0   (both lose)   probability $= \tfrac{1}{4}$,

$500,000   (only one wins)   probability $= \tfrac{1}{2}$,

$1 million   (both win)   probability $= \tfrac{1}{4}$.

We have already determined in Example 2.16 that our decision maker's certainty-equivalent value for this lottery is $190,000, compared to $80,000 for the single lottery. The shared lottery is much more valuable to the decision maker, even though the expected value of its outcome is still $500,000 as before. //

If the decision maker of Example 2.17 could find more individuals with identical, but statistically independent, lotteries with whom to share the risk, eventually he could increase the value of his share of the outcome to the expected value of $500,000. Intuitively, this simply says that if the individual's share is the average of a sufficiently large number of independent outcomes, that average will be very near the expected value.

This result tells us that *if the uncertain outcomes of many independent lotteries can be shared, the expected value of the outcome is a good representation of the value of a lottery*. Risk sharing is the rule in practice. In a business firm, for example, the individual decision maker's rewards are generally determined not just by the outcomes of his decisions, but by how well the firm as a whole does. On a broader scale, the owners of a firm usually have holdings in other firms as well. In governmental decisions, we might say that all taxpayers (or all *consumers* if you count price inflation resulting from government decisions) share the risks.

Does this mean that we simply should base our decisions on expected value and forget about the effect of the nonlinear utility curve? Not quite!

Example 2.18. Suppose the two lotteries of Example 2.17 are completely *dependent*. (1) What if the outcomes of both necessarily are identical (e.g., both are based on the outcome of the same coin toss)? In that case the pooling of the lotteries gains nothing for the decision makers. (2) What if the outcomes necessarily are opposite (e.g., both tickets are the only tickets for the same lottery—one wins and the other loses)? In that case, the shared outcome to each decision maker is $500,000 for certain. //

Examples 2.18(1) and 2.18(2) illustrate detrimental and beneficial dependencies. More generally, we could think of many uncertain outcomes being positively correlated—for example, if the economy does well, product x will sell briskly, but so will other products.

The capital asset pricing model in the next section explicitly includes the possibility of statistical dependence between investments. It explores the overall effects we may expect when many individuals interact through a market mechanism to share the risk.

2.3.2 The Capital Asset Pricing Model[19]

Why does the American Speculation Corporation have to pay its investors a return of over 20%/year to attract new capital, while the Ye Olde Utility Corporation supports a rather large capital budget paying less than 10%?

---

[19]The presentation follows that of Modigliani and Pogue's review, cited at the end of this chapter, of work by Markowitz, Sharpe, Jensen, and others.

Many businessmen intuitively would explain the difference in terms of the "risks" involved. American Speculation is a new company whose future is not at all assured. It goes for really big gains—uranium mines, musical hoolahoops, palm oil futures, and the like. Ye Olde Utility, on the other hand, has not missed a dividend in its 82 years of existence. It has a steady base of customers dependent on it for service; and it has solid plans for its next 15 years of operations.

The capital asset pricing model has been developed in an attempt to quantify such intuitive observations about risk. In this model one views the cost of money from the investor's standpoint. What kind of risk does he see? What kind of average return is required to entice him to invest? To focus on the risk aspect of the situation, we consider a single-period investment. If the value of some security (e.g., stock or bond) at time 0 is V_0 and at time 1 is V_1, we say that the return to the investor is

$$R = \frac{V_1 - V_0}{V_0}.$$

[Note that this corresponds with the usual notion of interest since $V_1 = V_0(1 + R)$.] The investor naturally prefers securities with larger R. Unfortunately, since the investor must make his choice at time 0, the value at time 1, and hence the return, is unknown to him. In terms of the utility theory formulation of Section 2.3.1, the investment is a lottery whose outcome will be the return R. Assuming that the investor is risk averse, the value of the lottery to him will be something less than its expected return $E(R)$. We further assume that *the investor's attitude toward the risk involved can be adequately inferred from the variance of the return* $\text{Var}(R)$. Of course, for a given $E(R)$, the investor prefers a lower $\text{Var}(R)$.

Suppose there are a large number of such investors and a market in which investments (securities) can be freely traded. We would expect the higher-risk securities to have sufficiently higher expected return to make them attractive to investors. In fact, we would expect the market to adjust security prices until all *equally risky enterprises earn the same expected return*. We have to be careful, however, in reasonably modeling the risk as it actually affects most investors. Most investors hold portfolios of diversified securities—that is, they own several very different securities at the same time. The purpose of such diversification is to reduce risk, and therefore, it is crucial that the existence of portfolios be taken into account in our model. We have found already in our study of the utility theory model in Section 2.3.1 that the combination of a sufficient number of independent gambles essentially would eliminate the risk to investors. We also found, however, that this elimination of risk was not necessarily possible when the gambles were dependent.

In the current context, the dependence between returns on various securities most clearly manifests itself in terms of prices tending to change with the market. A convenient way of modeling this phenomenon is to assume that the return on a given security has a *systematic* portion that is directly related to some average return for all securities that we shall call the *market return* R_m; and an *unsystematic* or random portion that is uncorrelated with other securities. More precisely, we write,

$$R = \alpha + \beta(R_m - R_f) + \varepsilon,$$

where

R is the return for some individual security (a random variable)

α is the expected value of unsystematic return (a constant)

β is a measure of the degree of correlation with other securities[20] (a constant)

R_m is the market return (a random variable)

R_f is the return on "riskless" securities such as government bonds (a constant)

ε is the unsystematic return less its mean (a zero-mean random variable that is independent of R_m and of the ε of any other securities).

The expected value and variance of the return are, respectively,

$$E(R) = \alpha + \beta[E(R_m) - R_f],$$

$$\mathrm{Var}(R) = \beta^2 \mathrm{Var}(R_m) + \mathrm{Var}(\varepsilon).$$

What expected return and variance would an investor face if he diversified his holdings among N such securities? Suppose that he invested in the proportion x_j in security $j, j = 1, \ldots, N$, where the x_j are positive and sum to one, and that the return on security j is given by

$$R^j = \alpha^j + \beta^j[R_m - R_f] + \varepsilon^j.$$

The portfolio return is

$$R_p = \sum_{j=1}^{N} x_j R^j = \sum_{j=1}^{N} x_j \alpha^j + \left[\sum_{j=1}^{N} x_j \beta^j\right][R_m - R_f] + \sum_{j=1}^{N} x_j \varepsilon^j,$$

or

$$R_p = \alpha_p + \beta_p[R_m - R_f] + \sum_{j=1}^{N} x_j \varepsilon^j,$$

---

[20] More specifically, it can be shown that

$$\beta = \mathrm{Covar}(R, R_m)/\mathrm{Var}(R_m).$$

where

$$\alpha_p \equiv \sum_{j=1}^{N} x_j \alpha^j$$ is the average of the expected values of unsystematic return for the portfolio

$$\beta_p \equiv \sum_{j=1}^{N} x_j \beta^j$$ is the average beta coefficient of the portfolio.

The expected value and variance of the portfolio return are

$$E(R_p) = \alpha_p + \beta_p \left[E(R_m) - R_f \right],$$

$$\text{Var}(R_p) = \beta_p^2 \text{Var}(R_m) + \sum_{j=1}^{N} x_j^2 \text{Var}(\varepsilon^j).$$

We are now in a position to see that the unsystematic portion of the variance (i.e., the second term) becomes small with large N. Note that this corresponds to eliminating risk by diversifying among independent investments (Section 2.3.1 on utility theory). Consider the case of N securities with identical $\text{Var}(\varepsilon^j) = \text{Var}(\varepsilon)$ and $x_j = 1/N, j = 1, \ldots, N$. Then

$$\text{Var}(R_p) = \beta_p^2 \text{Var}(R_m) + \sum_{j=1}^{N} \frac{1}{N^2} \text{Var}(\varepsilon)$$

$$= \beta_p^2 \text{Var}(R_m) + \frac{1}{N} \text{Var}(\varepsilon)$$

$$\approx \beta_p^2 \text{Var}(R_m) \quad \text{for large } N.$$

The implication of this observation is that investors really only care about a security's *systematic risk* as measured by its beta coefficient. Since we have assumed that equally risky enterprises (i.e., identical beta) have identical expected return, it must be that α_p, the average value of unsystematic return, is the same for all portfolios. Furthermore, if we look at a portfolio whose return is identical to that of the market (i.e., $R_p = R_m$), we get $\beta_p = 1$ and $\alpha_p = R_f$.

Putting all of this together, we have the so-called *capital asset pricing model*:

$$R = R_f + \beta(R_m - R_f) + \varepsilon,$$

$$E(R) = R_f + \beta \left[E(R_m) - R_f \right],$$

$$\text{Var}(R) = \beta^2 \text{Var}(R_m) + \text{Var}(\varepsilon).$$

This holds for combinations, or portfolios, of securities as well when the portfolio average beta is used. This model says that a security's expected return is entirely determined by its beta.

Example 2.19. $\beta > 1$. This is a security that tends to follow the market, but with larger swings. Construction company stocks may exhibit such behavior. //

Example 2.20. $0 < \beta < 1$. This is a security that follows the market but changes more moderately. Utility stocks may be examples. //

Example 2.21. $\beta = 0$. This is a security that is independent of the market. Relatively riskless government securities would fall into this category, but the category theoretically may contain also securities involving considerable risk so long as that risk is uncorrelated with the market (i.e., is unsystematic). //

Example 2.22. $\beta < 0$. This is a security whose value changes tend to be opposite those of the market as a whole. Its expected return would be lower than that of risk-free securities. A possible example would be gold stocks, whose value may go up as investors try to protect themselves in a declining market. //

The main point of the capital asset pricing model is that the cost of money to a firm should be expected to depend on the risk perceived by its investors and that the most important component of that risk is the market-correlated, or systematic, risk. Furthermore, since the return to a firm's investors can be viewed as the sum of the returns of all projects undertaken by the firm, the firm's systematic risk coefficient (beta) is a combination of the systematic risks of all projects. Thus, if a project is to pay its way, it must provide a sufficient expected return to the investors to compensate for its contribution to the systematic risk. By relating this to the revenue requirements model of Section 2.1, we see that the capital asset pricing model suggests that *each project should be evaluated using a discounting rate that reflects the cost of money associated with that projects' contribution to the systematic risk.* From a practical standpoint, this would involve estimating a correlation between the forecasted project return and the market (recall that this is essentially the definition of beta) and translating that into an expected return through the capital asset pricing model.

Such a detailed procedure undoubtedly would impute more precision to the model than is warranted at this time. In fact, the capital asset pricing model is clearly a simple one and cannot be considered complete by any means. For example, the model does not distinguish between debt financing and equity financing. It suggests that investors taking similar risks should get similar expected returns regardless of the financial instrument. In that case, why should the firm not shift almost entirely to debt financing? It would presumably pay its investors the same overall return, but would reap the income tax advantage of being able to deduct more interest paid on debt from its income (see Section 2.1.2). Also, there are questions about using the *single-period* investment model to evaluate projects that have cash flows in *many periods* into the future. Thus, in reality the capital asset pricing model and beta measurements can serve only as added guidance when considering risk in the basically *judgmental* process of estimating the cost of money for a firm, or a division of the firm, or perhaps some broad class of projects. It probably would not be practical to try measuring betas for individual projects.

2.3.3 Uncertainty and an Effective Cost of Money[21]

There is another context in which uncertainty is sometimes said to affect the cost of money. We would like to distinguish that concept from the concept involved in the capital asset pricing model. Consider the situation in which a dollar is to be spent at time t, its present worth cost being e^{-rt}. If the time t is a random variable (independent of the market—see Section 2.3.2) we shall be interested in the expected value of present worth cost $E(e^{-rt})$.[22] One way to see the effect of uncertainty in this situation is to observe[23] that

$$e^{-r\bar{t}} \leq E(e^{-rt}),$$

where $\bar{t} \equiv E(t)$, the expected value of t. This inequality says that *the present worth cost of an expenditure occurring at the nonrandom time $\bar{t}$ is less than if t is the mean and there is some distribution of possible times around $\bar{t}$.* If we wished to use the expected time in our calculations (or in our mental models), we could define an *effective discounting rate* r_*, which takes the uncertainty into account by

$$e^{-r_* \bar{t}} = E(e^{-rt}),$$

or

$$r_* = -(1/\bar{t})\ln E(e^{-rt}).$$

By the preceding inequality, $r_* \leq r$; and so we can say that uncertainty has the same effect as lowering the discounting rate. We shall not have occasion to use this effective discounting rate. We note that its use would entail discounting different expenditures at different effective rates, since r_* depends on the probability distribution of t.

---

[21]This section is only of technical interest and may be omitted on first reading. It introduces an idea used extensively in Chapter 7.

[22]Note that this is the Laplace transform of the random variable t evaluated at the discounting rate.

[23]This holds for any probability distribution—it is a consequence of Jensen's inequality. (See any standard probability text.)

We shall find use in Chapter 7, however, for a slight variant of this idea. Instead of defining an effective interest rate, we define an effective *time* $\hat{t}$ such that if we assume the expenditure occurs at $\hat{t}$, we get the same present worth as the expected present worth in the random case, or

$$e^{-r\hat{t}} = E(e^{-rt}),$$

$$\hat{t} = -\frac{1}{r} \ln E(e^{-rt}).$$

By the same inequality as before, $\hat{t}$ always will be less than the expected value $\bar{t}$.

To recapitulate, if some cash flow is anticipated to occur at the random time t, we shall get precisely the same expected present worth if we assume that it will occur with certainty at time $\hat{t}$. This formulation gives us the advantage of using a single discounting rate. We can combine this cost at $\hat{t}$ with other cash flows at $\hat{t}$ and treat the whole problem as a deterministic one.

Example 2.23. When machine A breaks, we shall have to spend $1.00 to repair it. Suppose it will break with probability $\frac{1}{2}$ at $t_1 = 0$ and probability $\frac{1}{2}$ at $t_2 = 4$ years.

(1) What is the expected cost? What is the effective time $\hat{t}$? Use $r = 0.1$:

$$\bar{t} = \tfrac{1}{2}(0) + \tfrac{1}{2}(4) = 2,$$

$$E(\text{present worth cost}) = \$1.00\left[\tfrac{1}{2}e^{-0.1(0)} + \tfrac{1}{2}e^{-0.1(4)}\right] = \$0.84,$$

$$\hat{t} = -\frac{1}{0.1}\ln(0.84) = 1.80 \text{ years},$$

$$r_* = -\tfrac{1}{2}\ln(0.84) = 0.090.$$

(2) What if $t_2 = \infty$ (i.e., 50% chance of never breaking)? Then

$$\bar{t} = \tfrac{1}{2}(0) + \tfrac{1}{2}(\infty) = \infty,$$

$$E(\text{present worth cost}) = \$1.00\left[\tfrac{1}{2}e^{-0.1(0)} + \tfrac{1}{2}(0)\right] = \$0.50,$$

$$\hat{t} = -\frac{1}{0.1}\ln(0.50) = 6.93 \text{ years},$$

$$r_* = \text{indeterminate in this case.}$$

Thus in case (1) we can treat the machine as if it had a deterministic life of 1.80 years; and in case (2), 6.93 years. //

In conclusion, if a cash flow occurs at some random time, we can treat it as if it will occur with certainty at $\hat{t}$ for purposes of calculating expected present worth cost. Furthermore, this effective deterministic time $\hat{t}$ will never exceed the expected value of the time of occurrence of the cash flow. Although alternatively we could view the uncertainty modeled here as having an effect on the discounting rate (at least when the expected time is finite), we shall not do so.

2.4 The Effect of Price Inflation

For most economic studies, we are interested in the cost of money *in the future*. We show that the cost of money can be expected to consist of a relatively stable "real" component plus the price inflation rate. In economic studies the price inflation of expenditures and the inflation component of the discounting rate tend to cancel one another, reducing the impact of poor estimates of price inflation.

2.4.1 Price Inflation and the Cost of Money

A major factor in the cost of money is the prospect of price changes. If prices change by 10%, an investor must earn 10% just to maintain his purchasing power. In this section we describe studies[24] suggesting that the cost of money can be viewed roughly as the sum of a relatively stable "real" return plus a compensation for price inflation. These studies have been done on low-risk securities such as government or high-quality corporate bonds. In terms of the capital asset pricing model of Section 2.3.1, we are trying to determine the relation between the risk-free return and price inflation. Of course, with uncertain prospects for price inflation every investment takes on an element of risk, and a precise definition of risk-free investment becomes elusive.

The studies reported here are based on the simple observation that interest rates tend to rise and fall as price inflation rates rise and fall. The underlying model is that investors require a real[25] return plus some amount to compensate for price inflation. Since the interest on debt is determined before the actual inflation is known, the inflation compensation portion of the return must reflect the investors' expectations about future inflation. In order to test this hypothesis and to estimate the real cost of debt, it is assumed that investors predict future inflation from past observations in the same manner as a statistical regression model. This is clearly an approximation, since investors' expectations about inflation could change independently of past predictions following major shifts in government policies, outbreak of war, and so forth. In this model inflation is measured by changes in the consumer price index (CPI). The consumer index rather than, say, an industrial price index is used because it is assumed that

---

[24] Using methodology developed by the Federal Reserve Bank of St. Louis.

[25] In keeping with economic jargon, we use *real* to designate constant purchasing power, as in *real gross national product* (GNP).

investors ultimately are interested in using their returns to purchase consumer goods.

A statistical model that has been used for this purpose is known in the trade as a "polynomial distributed lag regression" on corporate AAA bond yields versus percentage change in the CPI. The regression equation is

$$r_t = \hat{r}_d + \sum_{i=0}^{T} \hat{\alpha}_i CPI_{t-i} + \varepsilon,$$

where

t indexes time (by month in this case) running over some reasonable interval, such as 15 years

r_t is the nominal interest rate in period t (i.e., not adjusted for inflation)

$\hat{r}_d$ is a parameter to be estimated—the real interest on debt

$\hat{\alpha}_i$ is a coefficient to be estimated that indicates how strongly a change in CPI in period $t-i$ will affect the interest rate in period t

T is the lag memory—CPI changes more than T periods in the past are assumed not to affect current return ($T=48$ months was used)

ε is an error term—if the model is correct and sufficient data is included, it goes to 0.

What is meant by a *regression on r_t versus CPI_t* is that, given observed values of r_t and CPI_t, the parameters $\hat{r}_d$ and $\hat{\alpha}_i$ are selected to minimize the sum over t of the error ε squared, where the error for each t is determined by the regression equation. *Distributed lag* means that r_t is allowed in the model to depend on a number of past values of the CPI, and *polynomial* means that the coefficients $\hat{\alpha}_t$ are restricted in a particular way in the values they are allowed to take on. When a large lag time is used, some restriction is necessary to make a statistically significant estimate. (A statistician would say that it is used to reduce the degrees of freedom in the model.) In these studies, the coefficients α_t were assumed to satisfy a second-order polynomial,

$$\alpha_t = a_1 + a_2 t + a_3 t^2,$$

so that even though there are $T+1=49$ α, only three parameters, a_1, a_2, and a_3, actually are estimated.

Application of this model to the 1961–1978 period yields the results shown in Figure 2.15. While the nominal return has risen dramatically during most of that period, the assumption of a constant real return has resulted in only a moderate error in most periods. Some of that error is probably due to changes in the real return with changes in the business cycle; and some of it is due to statistical or measurement error.

These results hold two important lessons for doing cost studies. First, cost of money (at least the debt portion) is strongly related to price

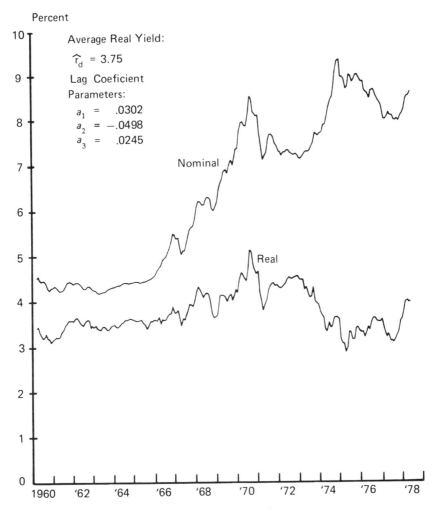

Percent

Average Real Yield:

$\widehat{r}_d$ = 3.75

Lag Coeficient
Parameters:

a_1 =   .0302
a_2 = −.0498
a_3 =   .0245

Nominal

Real

Figure 2.15. Yield of AAA corporate debt.

inflation. That fact must be taken into account when we estimate cost of money and prices of equipment or services in the future. Second, it is not too bad an approximation (and often, perhaps, the best we can do) to assume that the cost of money in the future will have a constant real component plus a component to make up for price inflation.

2.4.2 Price Inflation and Present Worth

If the cost of money is related to price inflation as postulated in Section 2.4.1, its effects tend to cancel in present worth studies. To see this, suppose that the inflation rate is γ and the cost of money is $r+\gamma$, where r is the real component. Let $c(t)$ be some cash flow expressed in constant or real dollars (e.g., purchases expressed in dollars of year zero). Then the expenditure expressed in dollars of the year of purchase would be $c(t)e^{\gamma t}$, and the present worth is

$$PW = \int_0^\infty c(t)e^{\gamma t}e^{-(r+\gamma)t}\,dt = \int_0^\infty c(t)e^{-rt}\,dt.$$

That is, *the present worth can be calculated using only the real discounting rate, provided the cash flow is expressed in real dollars.*

It thus appears that the inflation rate has been completely eliminated from the picture. This is not really true, since we need to make assumptions about the inflation rate in order to be able to express the cash flow $c(t)$ in real dollars. For example, income tax depreciation and investment tax credit are based on historical purchase cost. The following example illustrates how the assumed inflation rate affects the real cash flows associated with income tax benefits.

Example 2.24. In Example 2.8 we calculated an income tax advantage for years 1, 2, 3, and 4 of $0.3, $0.15, $0.1, and $0.05, respectively, for each capital dollar spent in year 0. What would be the value of these tax advantages in real dollars of year 0 assuming inflation rates of $\gamma = 0.02$, 0.06, and 0.12? Their real dollar value declines at the rate γ, so that the tax advantage becomes $0.3e^{-\gamma}$, $0.15e^{-2\gamma}$, $0.1e^{-3\gamma}$, and $0.05e^{-4\gamma}$ in each year as shown below. //

γ	Year 1	Year 2	Year 3	Year 4
0	0.300	0.150	0.100	0.050
0.02	0.294	0.144	0.094	0.046
0.06	0.283	0.133	0.084	0.039
0.12	0.266	0.118	0.070	0.031

Another effect of price inflation is that the income tax deduction for interest paid on debt is allowed on the entire real plus inflation amount (i.e., on the interest actually paid). This makes it necessary for us to recalculate the tax-adjusted discounting rate derived in Section 2.1.3. There we found

$$r_x' = \rho r_d' + (1-\rho)r_e' - \tau \rho r_d',$$

where primes have been added to all rates to indicate that they are not real (inflation adjusted). If we now assume that

$$r_e' = r_e + \gamma,$$
$$r_d' = r_d + \gamma,$$

the tax-adjusted rate becomes

$$r'_x = \rho r_d + (1-\rho)r_e + \gamma - \tau\rho r_d - \tau\rho\gamma,$$

or

$$r'_x = r_x - \tau\rho\gamma + \gamma.$$

Thus, if cash flows are expressed in real dollars, they should be discounted at the rate

$$r = r_x - \tau\rho\gamma.$$

Example 2.25. Do the problem of Examples 2.8 and 2.9 assuming inflation rates of $\gamma = 0.02$, 0.06, and 0.12. At $\gamma = 0.02$,

$$r = r_x - \tau\rho\gamma = 0.09 - (0.5)(0.5)(0.02) = 0.085,$$

and so for each capital dollar,

$$PW\left(\begin{array}{c}\text{income tax}\\\text{advantage}\end{array}\right) = (0.294)e^{-0.085} + (0.144)e^{-(0.085)2}$$

$$+ (0.094)e^{-(0.085)3} + (0.046)e^{-(0.085)4} = 0.497,$$

$$PW\left(\begin{array}{c}\text{capital}\\\text{cost}\end{array}\right) = \frac{1}{1-\tau}(1 - 0.497) = 1.006.$$

Similarly, for the other inflation rates, we get the following.

γ	r	$PW\left(\begin{array}{c}\text{income tax}\\\text{advantage}\end{array}\right)$	$PW\left(\begin{array}{c}\text{capital}\\\text{cost}\end{array}\right)$
0	0.090	0.509	0.980
0.02	0.085	0.497	1.006
0.06	0.075	0.473	1.054
0.12	0.060	0.438	1.124

Assuming that the $2,600/year savings in operating cost is given in real dollars (of year 0 purchasing power), at $\gamma = 0.02$

$$PW\left(\begin{array}{c}\text{expense}\\\text{saved}\end{array}\right) = 2,600\frac{1 - e^{-(0.085)5}}{0.085} = \$10,591,$$

and so the total present worth cost is

$$PW = PW\left(\begin{array}{c}\text{expense}\\\text{saved}\end{array}\right) - PW\left(\begin{array}{c}\text{capital}\\\text{cost}\end{array}\right)$$

$$= 10,591 - (1.006)(10,000) = \$531.$$

Similarly, for the other inflation rates, we get the following.

γ	$PW\left(\begin{array}{c}\text{expense}\\\text{saved}\end{array}\right)$	$PW\left(\begin{array}{c}\text{capital}\\\text{cost}\end{array}\right)$	total PW
0	10,478	9,800	678
0.02	10,591	10,060	531
0.06	10,840	10,540	300
0.12	11,231	11,240	−9

Thus, for moderate inflation rates, there is only a moderate impact on the total present worth. The overall effect as inflation increases is that the discount rate falls, and so PW(expense saved) rises; at the same time, the real tax benefits decrease enough to make PW(capital cost) rise. In this case, their difference, the total PW, decreases slowly until the project becomes unattractive at an inflation rate of about $\gamma = 0.12$. //

To sum up, we can treat inflation in our cost studies as follows:

1. Express all cash flows in real dollars (of year 0 purchasing power), keeping in mind, for example, that income tax deductions are calculated from historical cost.
2. Use the discounting rate

$$r = \left[\, \rho r_{\mathrm{d}} + (1-\rho)r_{\mathrm{e}} - \tau \rho r_{\mathrm{d}} \right] - \tau \rho \gamma,$$

where

r_{d} is the real cost of debt (price inflation has been removed)

r_{e} is the real cost of equity

ρ is the debt ratio

τ is the income tax rate

γ is the inflation rate.

2.5 Governmental Decisions

When the government makes decisions that involve cash flows in different time periods, what economic criterion should it use? We shall not attempt to answer what kinds of functions the government should perform. We shall limit ourselves to the evaluation of alternative means.

Example 2.26. Suppose that the government needs the continuing services of a paper shredding machine and that the following machines of equal performance capability are available on the market.

Machine	Cost ($)	Service Life (years)
A	2,000	2
B	3,000	4
C	5,000	8

Suppose, further, that there is a private supplier, using a discounting rate of 15%, who supplies services of this type with very flexible payment plans. The private supplier has basically three ways of providing 8 years of service:

Buy machine A at time $=0,2,4,6$.

Buy machine B at time $=0,4$.

Buy machine C at time $=0$.

The present worth costs (ignoring income taxes, etc.) are

$$PW_A = \$2,000\left[1+e^{-0.15(2)}+e^{-0.15(4)}+e^{-0.15(6)}\right]=\$5,392,$$
$$PW_B = \$3,000\left[1+e^{-0.15(4)}\right]=\$4,646,$$

and

$$PW_C = \$5,000.$$

Clearly, the supplier would favor machine B. In fact, the supplier could provide shredding service on various payment plans (using the 4-year machines) so long as the present worth of the payments adds up to $4,646 or more for 8 years of service. The payment schedules are as follows.

Payment schedule (years)	Payment ($)
2	1,723
4	3,000
8	4,646

Thus, unless the government is buying machine B, it is losing money in a very real sense. That is, instead of buying machine A for $2,000, it should buy 2 years of service from the supplier for $1,723; a similar analysis holds for machine C. //

Note that in Example 2.26 the proper discounting rate for evaluating the machines is the market-determined rate, *not* some rate intrinsic to the government.

What if a suitable private supplier had not been convenient in Example 2.26? Would the government then be justified in buying a different machine? For example, one might argue that the government's cost of money is just the interest rate of its bonds, which typically would be lower than a private firm's cost of capital. This might lead the government to choose machine C. Unfortunately, this lower discounting rate includes no compensation for risk. That is, according to the capital asset pricing model of Section 2.3.2, the private firm's discounting rate is higher because the market has determined that there is risk involved in investments of this type. If the government uses the lower discounting rate, it can be said that it is failing to include an important component of cost, namely, the cost of financial risk. Of course, it is not at all clear that the government's risk would be comparable to that of a private firm, but recall that in the capital asset pricing model we are talking only about systematic or nondiversifiable risk. Thus we cannot use the bigness of government as a direct argument that it faces less risk than a relatively smaller firm.

In summary, if there is a private market for some equipment that the government plans to purchase, then the government should use the market-determined discounting rate. If not, then it is not entirely clear what discounting rate would be best, but it seems reasonable that the rate should include a cost of risk.

Of course, governmental decision making is very complex. Final goals and intermediate steps may be linked together inextricably. For example, it may do no good to prove that constructing several small office buildings over a period of years is more economical than constructing a single large one, if the single large office is part of the package that made the whole project politically viable in the first place. For these reasons we can expect governmental decisions, particularly on large expenditures, to be more constrained, independently of economic implications. The constrained optimization approach of Section 2.2.1 may be of value in these situations.

2.6 Length of Time Horizon

How long a period should be used in economic studies? That is, in calculating the present worth of some alternative under consideration, over how long a time interval should revenues and costs be included? We argue that an infinite horizon should be used, at least conceptually.

Example 2.27. Suppose in Example 2.26 a 5-year machine costing $3,500 also had been available, so that in all we had the following choices.

Machine	Cost ($)	Service life (years)	Present worth cost for 8 years ($)
A	2,000	2	5,392
B	3,000	4	4,646
B1	3,500	5	?
C	5,000	8	5,000

The last column is the present worth calculation for 8 years done in Example 2.26. If we naively try to evaluate the 5-year machine on the same basis, we get

$$PW_{B1} = \$3,500\left[1 + e^{-0.15(5)}\right] = \$5,153,$$

which is not only worse than the 4-year machines but also worse than the 8-year machine. The difficulty here is that we have been unfair to the 5-year machine. At the end of the study horizon it still has 2 years of life left for which we have given it no credit. //

We could avoid the difficulty in Example 2.27 by using a 40-year study period, since all of the service lives are factors of 40. But then, what if a $3\frac{1}{3}$-year machine became available? This would lead us to think about an infinite study period, but before we propose that, we look at some other remedies.

One thing that often is done is to calculate an *equivalent annual charge* for each machine. In terms of the revenue requirements model of Section 2.1, this is just the levelized revenue required per unit time to pay for the machine.

Example 2.28. Consider a machine costing K and having a service life T. The equivalent annual charge AC is that constant annuity whose present worth is the cost of the machine:

$$K = AC\left(\frac{1 - e^{-rT}}{r}\right),$$

or

$$AC = K\frac{r}{1 - e^{-rT}} = \$3,000\frac{0.15}{1 - e^{-0.15(4)}} = \$997$$

for machine B. Similarly, for the other machines we get the following.

Machine	Cost ($)	Life (years)	Equivalent annual charge ($)
A	2,000	2	1,157
B	3,000	4	997
B1	3,500	5	995
C	5,000	8	1,073

On this basis, the 5-year machine looks slightly better than the 4-year machine. //

The notion of equivalent annual charge is a very useful one for the simple kind of problem considered in Example 2.27, in which there is a *continuing need* for the service provided by the machine and any machine can be freely chosen *without affecting future choices*. Under these circumstances, the machine with minimal annual charge is clearly the best. What if these conditions are not met?

Example 2.29. (1) What if the machine in the above examples will be needed only for 2 years (assume 0 salvage value at the end)? Clearly, machine A would be best, even though it has the highest equivalent annual charge. (2) What if there were a continuing need for the machines' services, but the physical characteristics of the machines were such that the 5-year machine inevitably would have to be followed by a succession of 2-year machines, whereas the 4-year machines could simply succeed each other ad infinitum? Without even doing the calculations, it is evident that the slight advantage of the 5-year machine over the 4-year machine would be eliminated by the requirement that the much less desirable 2-year machines must be used after the 5-year machine wears out. //

Example 2.29 illustrates that we probably would do well to stay with present worth as the economic measure rather than rely on the derived measure of equivalent annual charge.

Another way to get around the difficulty posed by noncoterminating service life illustrated by Example 2.27 is to use a fixed period such as 8 years, but to adjust for differences in ending conditions under the various alternatives. How this should be done may not always be obvious.

Example 2.30. (1) Suppose in Example 2.27 that we give the 5-year machine credit for a net salvage value of $1,000 at the end of the study? Its present worth cost becomes

$$PW_{B1} = \$5,153 - 1,000e^{-0.15(8)} = \$4,852,$$

which is still more than that of the 4-year machine. Surely, $1,000 is a generous salvage value, since each additional 2 years of service life costs $1,000 for this machine. Why does the 5-year machine not look better than the 4-year machine, as it did by the method of annual charge of Example 2.28? The answer is that we have ignored the fixed-charge portion of the purchase cost. With the 5-year machines, we would not incur *any* additional charges until year 10. (2) Suppose we credit the 5-year machine with the purchase cost of a 2-year machine at the end of the 8-year horizon? Then

$$PW_{B1} = \$5,153 - 2,000e^{-0.15(8)} = \$4,551.$$

Now the 5-year machine comes out ahead of the 4-year machine, but the difference seems to be exaggerated when compared to the method of annual charge of Example 2.28. The discrepancy can be understood if we observe that the calculation in this example is equivalent to assuming in Example 2.27 that we would buy an additional 2-year machine in year 8 under the *A*, *B*, and *C* alternatives. (3) Suppose we credit the 5-year machine with 2 years of annual charges (as calculated in Example 2.28) starting in year 8? Then

$$PW_{B1} = \$5,153 - 995\frac{1-e^{-(0.15)2}}{0.15}e^{-0.15(8)} = \$4,635. \text{ [26]}$$

Now the 5-year machine comes out best, but only by a small margin, as in the method of annual charge. //

Examples 2.27 and 2.30 illustrate that we can get very different results depending upon what we assume will happen *beyond the study horizon!* Since we always are looking beyond the horizon, we naturally are led to using an infinite horizon. That is, at least conceptually, *we should consider the whole, infinite future of consequences associated with each alternative under consideration.* There are cases in which the future consequences beyond some point can be assumed to be identical for each alternative. Then, of course, these consequences will not affect the decision and can be ignored. The natural assumption about the future in some problems is that it will be a repetition of the past (called the *repeated plant* assumption).

Example 2.31. Suppose the machines of Example 2.27 are replaced by like machines at the end of their service lives, ad infinitum. How would their present worth cost compare? For a machine costing *K*, and having service life *T*,

$$PW = \sum_{j=0}^{\infty} Ke^{-rjT} = \frac{K}{1-e^{-rT}}.$$

Thus the infinitely repeated plant present worth and the calculations of equivalent annual charge of Example 2.28 differ only by a factor of *r*. //

In many cases, the *exact* nature of future costs will not be very important—a reasonable guess will suffice. This is a simple consequence of the exponential nature of the factor expressing present worth of a future amount.

Example 2.32. Suppose in Example 2.27 that we assumed the following about the future beyond year 8. No matter what is done up to year 8, from then on we shall be able to obtain the service for $900/year. (Note that this is somewhat optimistic in view of Example 2.28.) The present worths

---

[26] The $995 annual charge is multiplied by the factor for present worth of a 2-year annuity and by the factor for present worth of a future amount at year 8.

for an infinite horizon become

$$PW_A = \$5,392 + 900\left(\frac{1}{0.15}\right)e^{-0.15(8)} = \$7,199,$$

$$PW_B = \$4,646 + 900\left(\frac{1}{0.15}\right)e^{-0.15(8)} = \$6,453,$$

$$PW_{B1} = \$5,153 + 900\left(\frac{1}{0.15}\right)e^{-0.15(10)} = \$6,491,$$

$$PW_C = \$5,000 + 900\left(\frac{1}{0.15}\right)e^{-0.15(8)} = \$6,807.$$

Now the 4-year machine looks slightly better than the 5-year machine. (It does not pay to buy the extra 2 years of service if we can get it for only $900 per year later.) But we would not get drastically different conclusions from this analysis than we would from Examples 2.28 or 2.30. //

In conclusion, *we should consider the consequences of current decisions on the entire infinite future*, at least conceptually. Practically speaking we could, in a particular instance, (1) conclude that all alternatives have sufficiently similar consequences beyond time T so that we can cut off the study at T, (2) assign some reasonable value or cost to differences in ending conditions beyond time T, or (3) assume a repeated plant or a uniform cost per unit time beyond some time T.

2.7 Unbounded Growth and Present Worth

A curious phenomenon crops up when we study certain problems with an exponential growth of demand. *It sometimes appears that the usual discounting rate should be replaced by the growth rate* in present worth calculations. We argue that it is more appropriate to use the usual discounting rate after all.

Example 2.33. Suppose two types of components are available for performing some function. The two are identical except in cost. The only costs associated with the components are the following.

Component	Cost at installation time ($)	Cost 1 year after installation ($)	Present worth ($)
A	2.00	2.00	3.85
B	1.00	3.15	3.91

Here the present worth has been calculated using an 8% discounting rate (e.g., $2.00 + 2.00e^{-0.08} = 3.85$). Is component A the clear choice? Consider the following. What if the need for additional components is expected to grow exponentially at the rate of 16%/year into the indefinite future starting with 100 components at time 0.

Time	0	1	2	3	4	5	6	7	8	9	10	...
additional components used	100	117	138	162	190	222	261	306	360	422	495	...

We can calculate easily the cost at each time depending on which components we buy.

Time	0	1	2	3	4	5	6	7	8	9	10	...
A	$200	434	510	600	704	824	966	1,134	1,332	1,564	1,934	...
B	$100	432	507	597	700	821	950	1,128	1,324	1,556	1,824	...

[For example, at time 2 for component B, $(138)(\$1.00)+(117)(\$3.15)=\$507$]. Using component B costs less *in every period* than using component A. How can component A be the better choice? //

The paradox of Example 2.33 is a special case of a phenomenon that can be studied better in symbolic rather than numerical form. Suppose for one of the components in Example 2.33 that we would have to pay at the rate $c(t)$ for t between 0 and L. Let $z(t)\equiv z(0)e^{gt}$ be the rate at which additional components are required at time t. Using this component, eventually we would be paying at the rate

$$R(t)=\int_0^L c(\tau)z(t-\tau)\,d\tau,$$

or

$$R(t)=z(0)e^{gt}\left[\int_0^L c(\tau)e^{-g\tau}\,d\tau\right],$$

where $c(\tau)$ is the payment for machines purchased τ earlier and $z(t-\tau)$ is the number of machines purchased τ earlier. The factor in brackets is the only one that depends on our choice of component. Thus, we can minimize this rate of expenditure by minimizing the present worth cost of the component, where the *demand growth rate has been substituted for the usual discounting rate*. Although this statement is true, it does *not* say that the present worth cost will be minimized in this way. A crucial missing element is what happens when we first start buying the component. It is easy to check that our earlier expression for $R(t)$ is only valid for $t \geq L$. More generally,

$$R(t) = \begin{cases} \int_0^t c(\tau)z(t-\tau)\,d\tau, & t \leq L \\ \int_0^L c(\tau)z(t-\tau)\,d\tau, & t \geq L, \end{cases}$$

or

$$R(t) = \begin{cases} z(0)e^{gt}\int_0^t c(\tau)e^{-g\tau}\,d\tau, & t \leq L \\ z(0)e^{gt}\int_0^L c(\tau)e^{-g\tau}\,d\tau, & t \geq L. \end{cases}$$

To compute the present worth, we find $\text{PW}^T \equiv \int_0^T R(t)e^{-rt}\,dt$ for some large T (the integral diverges if $g > r$). Integrating the first expression by parts and collecting terms, we obtain

$$\text{PW}^T = z(0)\left\{ \left[\int_0^L c(\tau)e^{-g\tau}\,d\tau\right]\frac{e^{(g-r)T}}{g-r} - \frac{1}{g-r}\int_0^L c(t)e^{-rt}\,dt \right\}.$$

Now if $g < r$, the first term goes to zero as $T \to \infty$, and

$$\text{PW}^\infty = z(0)\frac{1}{r-g}\int_0^L c(t)e^{-rt}\,dt.$$

Thus, in this case the present worth cost is minimized by selecting the component that costs the least *according to the usual present worth criterion*. If $g > r$, the first term dominates the second, and so for large T,

$$\text{PW}^T \approx z(0)\left[\int_0^L c(\tau)e^{-g\tau}\,dz\right]\frac{e^{(g-r)T}}{g-r}.$$

Since our choice of component only affects the term in brackets, it again appears that we should be discounting at the rate g instead of r.

Example 2.34. If we evaluate the components of Example 2.33 at a 16% discounting rate, $\text{PW}_A = 2.00 + 2.00e^{-0.16} = \$3.70$, and $\text{PW}_B = 1.00 + 3.15e^{-0.16} = \$3.68$; thus, component B looks better. //

In a divergent integral such as this one, we should be careful about how we take limits. Suppose that we heed the admonishment of Section 2.6 and look at what happens beyond the horizon T. Specifically, suppose that instead of simply cutting off the whole problem at T (as if the world would end there), we assume that additional demand stops coming in at T, but that we must still pay off obligations incurred up to T. Such a situation may arise, for example, if the component becomes obsolete at T. In that case, the cost per unit time becomes

$$
R(t) = \begin{cases}
\int_0^t c(\tau)z(t-\tau)\,d\tau, & t \le L \\[2mm]
\int_0^L c(\tau)z(t-\tau)\,d\tau, & L \le t \le T \\[2mm]
\int_{t-T}^L c(\tau)z(t-\tau)\,d\tau, & T \le t \le T+L
\end{cases}
$$

(i.e., in the period from T to $T+L$ we just pay for components purchased before T). In calculating the present worth, we get the additional term

$$
\Delta PW = \int_T^{T+L} \int_{t-T}^L c(\tau)z(t-\tau)\,d\tau\,e^{-rt}\,dt,
$$

from which, after we integrate by parts and rearrange, we obtain

$$
\Delta PW = z(0)\left[\frac{-e^{(g-r)T}}{g-r}\int_0^L c(\tau)e^{-g\tau}\,d\tau + \frac{e^{(g-r)T}}{g-r}\int_0^L c(t)e^{-rt}\,dt \right].
$$

We add this to the previously obtained expression for PW^T to obtain

$$
PW^{T'} = z(0)\frac{e^{(g-r)T}-1}{g-r}\left[\int_0^L c(t)e^{-rt}\,dt \right].
$$

If $g<r$, of course we get the same result as before; if $g>r$, however, our conclusion is different. We again have divergence as $T\to\infty$, but now the term in brackets, the only one affected by our choice of component, is the usual present worth.

Example 2.35. In Example 2.33, the leftover obligation is only what we owe for the year immediately following the end of the study.

Time	0	1	2	3	4	5	6	7	8	9	10	11	...
A	—	$200	234	276	324	380	444	522	612	720	844	990	...
B	—	$315	369	435	510	599	699	822	964	1,134	1,329	1,559	...

For example, if we cut off the study at $T=4$ using component B, we would owe $(190)(\$3.15)=\$599$ at $t=5$ for the 190 components we bought at $t=4$. Observe that this leftover time bomb is larger in every case for component B than for component A. If we compute the present worth with the study cut off at T, but including the payment at $T+1$, we get the following.

T	0	1	2	3	4	5	6	7	8	9	10	...
PW_A^T	$385	800	1,252	1,742	2,273	2,845	3,467	4,139	4,869	5,659	6,515	...
PW_B^T	$391	813	1,273	1,771	2,310	2,892	3,523	4,206	4,948	5,750	6,619	...

For example, if we cut off the study at $T=4$ using component B and including the obligation at $t=5$,

$$PW_B^{4'} = \$100 + 432e^{-0.08(1)} + 507e^{-0.08(2)} + 597e^{-0.08(3)}$$
$$+ 700e^{-0.08(4)} + 599e^{-0.08(5)} = \$2,310.$$

And so, component A wins. //

Thus we find that the only instance in which we should abandon the usual present worth criterion is when (1) demand is growing at a rate larger than the discounting rate and (2) *such a growth rate will continue forever.* Example 2.33 shows that this conclusion is not dependent on having to calculate a divergent present worth—the cost using component B was less in *every period.* The weakness of the conclusion is illustrated in Example 2.35. If the growth *ever* stops,[27] the time bomb of accumulated obligations more than offsets any savings in the interim. For practical purposes, we therefore conclude that we should use present worth with the usual discounting rate after all.

2.8 Microscopic/Macroscopic Decision Models

A very useful mental construct in economic decision problems is what we shall call the *microscopic/macroscopic* approach. Actually, this can be viewed as a description of all mathematical modeling. What we mean by the term is that we specify some phenomenon under study in considerable detail (microscopically) and then model the larger world into which it fits in much less detail (macroscopically). This allows us to analyze the phenomenon in question without getting bogged down in an ever expanding, detailed model of the world and at the same time, hopefully, without losing sight of the context in which the phenomenon exists.

The most prevalent instance of the microscopic/macroscopic approach in this chapter is that of the current decision, specified in great detail, versus the total remainder of the investment environment. In a sense, we are saying that *the rest of the investment environment is adequately represented by discounting at rate r.* That is, we need only give the detailed cash flows associated with various alternatives of the decision at hand and also specify a discounting rate. In reality, of course, every investment possibility may be related to every other investment possibility in some very complex, probabilistic manner. In addition to our intuitive feeling that some simple separation is necessary and reasonable, we are encouraged by our mathematical models. The optimization study of Section 2.2.1 suggests that a discounting rate may not be a bad representation of other investment opportunities; and the capital asset pricing model of Section 2.3.2 indicates

---

[27]Or (it can be shown) even if it slows to a rate smaller than the discounting rate.

that correlations between investments may even be adequately accounted for by adjustments of the discounting rate.

In Example 2.32, when we model the future beyond year 8 as costing $900 per year without specifying more detail, we are again applying the microscopic (decisions in the first 8 years) versus macroscopic (decisions beyond year 8) approach. We shall find this device particularly useful.

2.9 Decisions under a Limited Budget

Here we reconsider the mathematical optimization approach to selecting projects that we discussed in Section 2.2.1. There we cast the entire problem as one of maximizing the firm's value subject to constraints on its budget in each period of the study. Here we focus our attention on a short-term constraint. We assume that our discounting rate reflects a realistic long-term cost of money, but that we are restricted from spending all that we would like to in the short term. In the terminology of Section 2.8, we explicitly, or microscopically, model the constraint on spending in the initial period (e.g., the first year), but macroscopically model any possible future limitations by specifying a suitable cost of capital in the form of a discounting rate.

We show that the essentially optimal decisions for this constrained problem can still be made by selecting on a project-by-project basis, provided we charge the correct penalty for each dollar required in the initial, constrained budget period.[28] We explicitly consider the possibility that projects will be available only as discrete choices[29] (e.g., do or do not do something). We show that if there are a large number of projects, and each consumes only a small fraction of the constrained budget, the penalty method of selection will not result in large errors.

We develop the formal mathematical model as follows. We assume that the firm is faced with various projects indexed by $j = 1, \ldots, N$; each project has several alternatives, $i = 1, 2, \ldots, n_j$.

The firm *must choose* exactly one alternative from each project[30] and wishes to do so in such a way as to minimize its total present worth cost of doing business while staying within externally imposed limitations on capital availability. More precisely, the firm wishes to find

$$W = \max_{\{i_j\}} \sum_{j=1}^{N} W^{j,i_j}$$

---

[28] This is a special case of the result on dual multipliers of Section 2.2.1.

[29] By contrast, we assumed in Section 2.2.1 that we could do any fraction of a project.

[30] Note that some projects may have only a "Do" or "Don't do" choice, while others may have a larger array of possibilities. Also, this format can be used to describe projects that are interrelated (e.g., c cannot be done unless either a or b is done) by viewing the combination as a single project with many alternatives (feasible combinations of the individual projects).

subject to

$$\sum_{j=1}^{N} C^{j,i_j} \leq B,$$

where

W^{j,i_j} is the present worth if alternative i_j is selected in project j [31]

C^{j,i_j} is the capital in the initial period if alternative i_j is selected in project j

B is the available capital (budget) in the initial period

$\{i_j\}$ is the set of all feasible alternatives (one for each project).

We can eliminate the constraint by bringing it into the objective function with a Lagrange multiplier:

$$W = \max_{\{i_j\}} \sum_{j=1}^{N} W^{j,i_j} + \lambda \left(B - \sum_{j=1}^{N} C^{j,i_j} \right),$$

or

$$W = \max_{\{i_j\}} \sum_{j=1}^{N} \left(W^{j,i_j} - \lambda C^{j,i_j} \right) + \lambda B,$$

where the second term is a constant that can be dropped from further consideration.

If we further assume that alternatives can be selected independently in the various projects, then the summation and maximization can be interchanged:

$$W = \sum_{j=1}^{N} \max_{i} \left(W^{j,i} - \lambda C^{j,i} \right).$$

That is, *the maximization can be done on a project-by-project basis.* We simply select the alternative that maximizes present worth less a penalty for each dollar of capital required in the budget-limited period. We can think of the Lagrange multiplier as a macroscopic representation of the constraint in our microscopic individual project decision.

The simple form of this model makes it easier to scrutinize than the optimization model of Section 2.2.1. (This is just a special case of the duality result discussed there.) An important question is whether an appropriate multiplier always exists. We proceed with an intuitive argument assisted by pictures. Suppose we plot for a given project the present worth versus capital required in the budget-limited period for every avail-

---

[31]Of course, only the *difference* in W between the alternatives is relevant to the optimization.

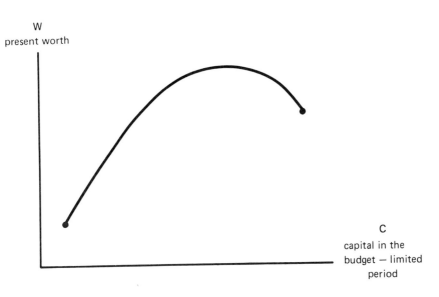

W
present worth

C
capital in the
budget — limited
period

Figure 2.16. Present worth versus capital—the concave continuous case.

able alternative. The best-behaved case is one in which this plot turns out to be a strictly concave curve (i.e., there is actually a continuum of alternatives), as shown in Figure 2.16. If all projects exhibit this kind of behavior, then it can be shown that a unique[32] multiplier exists that determines the optimal solution for each project. That multiplier is the slope of the curve of W versus C at the optimal point.[33] Note that finding the point on W versus C with slope λ is identical to maximizing $W - \lambda C$. Thus, this graphical construction is identical to our mathematical Lagrange multiplier result.

What happens when the curve of W versus C is not concave? In the most interesting case, in fact, it is not actually a curve at all, but a number of discrete points, one for each alternative, as shown in Figure 2.17. In this case, maximizing $W - \lambda C$ corresponds to finding the point (or points) such that when a straight line of slope λ is drawn through it, no feasible points lie above the line. For example, in Figure 2.17 if $\lambda < s_1$, E will be chosen; if $s_1 < \lambda < s_2$, B will be chosen; and if $s_2 < \lambda$, A will be chosen. The points D and F would not be chosen for any value of λ. This is quite appropriate in the case of F, since B has a higher present worth for lower capital. The exclusion of D, however, results in what is called a *duality gap*. To see the

---

[32] Assuming feasibility and assuming that at least one project is not at its upper or lower limits at optimality.

[33] If the slope of some curve is smaller (larger) over its entire range than the multiplier value, then the lowest (highest) feasible value of C is optimal.

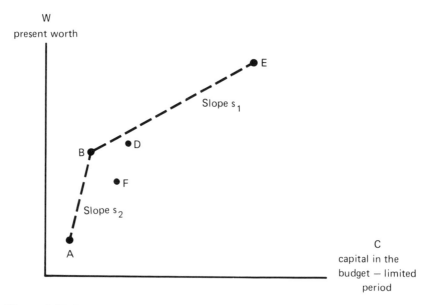

Figure 2.17. Present worth versus capital for a discrete number of project possibilities.

significance of the duality gap, consider the problem of allocating various total amounts of limited-period capital to just two projects—the ones plotted in Figures 2.17 and 2.18. Figure 2.19 shows every combination of alternatives from the two projects (excluding point F). It is straightforward to verify that only the points[34] $A\&a$, $B\&a$, $E\&a$, and $E\&b$ would be chosen as λ is varied over all possible values. Thus, if one of these points has a C value exactly identical to the available budget, we can find the optimal solution by choosing the appropriate λ and maximizing $W-\lambda C$ for each individual project. If, however, the available budget lies between the values of $B\&b$ and $D\&b$, then $B\&b$ will give the best present worth, and therefore no value of λ will find the optimum. The points $D\&a$, $B\&b$, and $D\&b$ are said to fall in a duality gap. The point $A\&b$ is exluded also, but properly so, since it cannot be optimal for any value of the budget. Note that even if the point D were not available in Figure 2.17, the point $B\&b$ would still fall in a duality gap.

The problem of duality gaps turns out to be difficult in general. If we wish to find the exact optimum, we have to employ some combinatorial algorithm (one that tries out various combinations). In the case of a single constraint, we may fruitfully be able to employ a dynamic programming algorithm. Algorithms of both types are discussed later in another context.

---

[34] Points on the upper part of the convex hull of all the points.

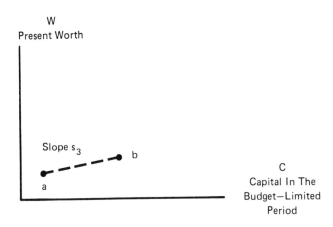

Figure 2.18. Present worth versus capital for a project with two alternatives.

The point of this discussion is that the optimality conditions, as specified via the Lagrange multiplier in this section or the dual variables in Section 2.2.1, are not quite correct when we take nonconcavity (e.g., discrete project alternatives) into account. If, however, the number of projects is large and no individual project consumes a large fraction of the available budget, we can see that the duality gap would be relatively small, and no severe penalty would result from using a dual approach. In many practical problems, the exact values of available budget are not known in advance, or more importantly, are not set without regard to the use of the funds. Thus a solution calling for a somewhat different budget than that nominally specified may be every bit as good as one adhering precisely to the budget.

The value of the Lagrange multiplier approach is that it allows us to decentralize our decision making. We can study each individual project as it comes along, always modeling the impact of a budget limitation by specifying λ. Of course, strictly speaking, we have to solve the central optimization problem to find the appropriate value of λ to use. In practice, we might be able to estimate reasonable values from past experience or from rough models of the firm.

2.10 Summary

We have discussed, from several points of view, *present worth* as a decision criterion. Our intent was twofold; first, to argue that it is quite reasonable to evaluate economic alternatives according to a present worth criterion; and second, to indicate some of the considerations that may go into choosing an appropriate discounting rate.

In Section 2.1, we showed that if we think of investors as lenders of money, we are led naturally to a present worth criterion with the interest

64

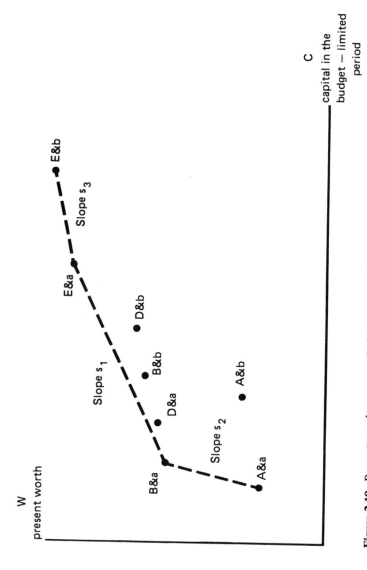

Figure 2.19. Present worth versus capital for the combination of projects shown in Figures 2.17 and 2.18.

rate as the discounting rate. In case there are different classes of investors (e.g., debt and equity) whose interest payments are different and are taxed differently, we are led to a composite discounting rate.

We then argued, in Section 2.2, that we might arrive at a present worth criterion from other viewpoints. In the mathematical optimization approach, shadow prices or dual multipliers were interpretable as interest rates. Also, a set of axioms about how decision makers should behave leads to present worth as the project acceptance criterion.

Important factors in determining the cost of capital, the actual discounting rate to use in cost studies, are *risk* and *price inflation*. In Section 2.3 we discussed the capital asset pricing model, which indicates that the discounting rate increases with increasing systematic risk, or the risk component that is correlated with the stock market. In Section 2.4 we argued that the price inflation rate is roughly an additive component of the cost of capital.

We then discussed various other questions about present worth. In Section 2.5 we argued that one probably should *not* use a different discounting rate for a study just because the decision maker is the government instead of a private concern. We pointed out in Section 2.6 that one should be careful about end effects, economic consequences that will occur beyond the assumed horizon. A good assumption is that, conceptually, the horizon is always infinite, but that a finite-horizon study in which end effects are appropriately modeled may well be justified on practical grounds. We then considered in Section 2.7 a very special case of a study in which the demand for some equipment grows exponentially at a rate larger than the discounting rate. We showed that this equipment should be evaluated using a present worth criterion, but that the equipment growth rate should replace the usual discounting rate. We also showed, however, that this conclusion is valid only if the demand for this same equipment will continue to grow at such a rate *forever*. Otherwise, the usual discounting rate should be used.

In Section 2.8 we philosophized about the fact that any mathematical model will include a detailed (microscopic) description of some aspects of a problem, and a rough (macroscopic) description of others. An example of such a split between microscopic and macroscopic views is our treatment in Section 2.9 of a problem in which the firm's capital budget for the initial period is assumed to be explicitly constrained, but that any possible future constraints are modeled by a single discounting rate.

2.11 Further Reading

The revenue requirements model (Section 2.1) is given a more rigorous and complete presentation in

Peter B. Linhart, Some Analytical Results on Tax Depreciation, *Bell Journal of Economics and Management Science* 1(1), Spring 1970, 82–112.

Linhart also brings up the question of unbounded exponential growth (see Section 2.7).

For a more complete discussion of the "mathematics of money" (Appendix at end of chapter), see

Gerald W. Smith, *Engineering Economy: Analysis of Capital Expenditures*, Ames, Iowa, Iowa State University Press, 1973.

Included in Smith are discussions of alternative investment criteria and income taxes.

H. Martin Weingartner gives a brilliant exposition of the mathematical optimization approach (Section 2.2.1) to project selection in

H. M. Weingartner, *Mathematical Programming and the Analysis of Capital Budgeting Problems*, Chicago, Markham Publishing Co., 1967.

This work, motivated by an earlier, less mathematical, development by

J. H. Lorie, and L. J. Savage, Three Problems in Rationing Capital, *The Journal of Business* 28(4), October 1955, 229–239,

deals extensively with the problems arising from discreteness of project scale (see Section 2.9).

A good, easily readable introduction to risk in the decision-making situation can be found in

Howard Raiffa, *Decision Analysis: Introductory Lectures on Choices Under Uncertainty*, Reading, Mass., Addison-Wesley, 1968.

The theory presented there has served as a foundation for much further work. One of the directions of that work has been to model investor behavior in the market place. For example,

Franco Modigliani, and Gerald A. Pogue, An Introduction to Risk and Return Concept and Evidence, *Financial Analysts Journal* 30(2) March–April 1974, 68–80, and 30(3) May–June 1974, 69–86,

present the capital asset pricing model (Section 2.3.2) developed by Michael C. Jensen, William F. Sharpe, and others. In addition to giving the theoretical concepts, they report on some attempts at statistical validation.

Section 2.2.3 is a summary of

A. C. Williams, and J. I. Nassar, Financial Measurement of Capital Investments, *Management Science* 12(1), July 1966, 851–863.

Our discussion on price inflation is taken from

John Freidenfelds, and Michael Kennedy, Price Inflation and Long-Term Present-Worth Studies, *The Engineering Economist* 24(3), 1979, 143–160,

which owes much to the work of

William P. Yohe, and Denis S. Karnosky, Interest Rates and Price Level Changes, 1952–1969, *Review, Federal Reserve Bank of St. Louis*, December 1969, 18–39,

and to earlier work at the St. Louis Federal Reserve Bank.

Our brief discussion of governmental decision making (Section 2.5) can be supplemented with

J. Hirshleifer, Investment Decision Under Uncertainty: Applications of the State-Preference Approach, *Quarterly Journal of Economics* 80, *May* 1966, 252–277,

and an earlier article by Hirshleifer in the same journal, Volume 79(4), November 1965, 509–536. Quite a different approach was taken by

Stephan A. Marglin, The Social Rate of Discount and the Optimal Rate of Investment, *Quarterly Journal of Economics* 77(1), February 1963, 95–111,

with comments by other authors in the same journal Volume 78(2), May 1964, 336–345, and Volume 78(4), November 1964, 641–644. Here (Section 2.5) we have adopted Hirshleifer's view. Marglin's work seems more related to deciding whether or not the government should invest in some area, and not really what discount rate should be used.

Related to (but not necessarily limited to) governmental decision making is

Stephan A. Marglin, *Approaches to Dynamic Investment Planning*, Amsterdam, North-Holland, 1963 (second printing 1967).

Marglin discusses a dual method of solving project selection problems given tight annual budgetary constraints (see Section 2.2.1). He envisions various agencies optimizing their decisions based on a central planner's shadow prices (dual variables); the agencies, in turn, may readjust the shadow prices to reflect budget scarcity and reinitiate the process.

No study of this general area can be complete without

J. Hirshleifer, *Investment, Interest and Capital*, Englewood Cliffs, NJ, Prentice-Hall, 1970.

Hirshleifer gives a thorough and rigorous analysis of investment decisions from the viewpoint of a classical economist.

Finally, those who feel uncomfortable with mathematical programming, dynamic programming, random variables, statistical independence, and such would do well to study a standard book on introductory operations research such as

Harvey M. Wagner, *Principles of Operations Research*, Englewood Cliffs, NJ, Prentice-Hall, 1969.

Appendix. Mathematics of Present Worth

Here we discuss some computational aspects of present worth. We discuss the distinction between discrete and continuous compounding. We give formulas for the present worth of a constant annuity. Finally, we point out that present worth can be calculated in pieces and then put together to get the total.

2.A.1 Continuous or Discrete Compounding

We have defined the *present worth* of a cash flow, $c(t)$ as

$$PW(c) = \int_0^T c(t) e^{-rt} dt, \tag{2.1}$$

where cash flows are assumed to cease beyond T, and r is the *discounting rate*. Equivalently, we could have used

$$PW(c) = \int_0^T c(t) \left(\frac{1}{1+r'} \right)^t dt, \tag{2.2}$$

where r' is defined so that

$$1 + r' = e^r. \tag{2.3}$$

The choice is really only a matter of aesthetics. If we think of cash flows as deposits and withdrawals from a bank account in which transactions are allowed only at discrete time points, and r' as the interest paid per discrete interval, then a dollar deposited now will grow to $1 + r'$ 1 period hence. Similarly, it will grow to $(1+r')^t$ in t periods. If continuous cash flows are allowed, then it seems natural to think of an interest rate r per arbitrarily small time interval Δt; thus a dollar deposited now will grow to $(1 + r\Delta t)^{t/\Delta t}$ by time t. As Δt gets small, this becomes e^{rt}. Of course, even if cash flows occur only at discrete times, it does no harm to think of them as being compounded continuously at the rate r (rather than r') in the time between periods. It often seems more natural, however, to use r' with discrete time cash flows and to replace the integral in the definition with a sum

$$PW(c) = \sum_{t=0}^T c(t) \left(\frac{1}{1+r'} \right)^t. \tag{2.4}$$

When there is little chance of confusion, we shall drop the notational distinction between discrete and continuous compounding and use the symbol r for both interest rates.

time=0   time=T

Figure 2.20

2.A.2 Present Worth of Annuity

A cash flow that is uniform over some interval is called an *annuity*. In the continuous case, we think of annuities in the following terms:

$$c(t) = \begin{cases} a, & 0 \le t \le T \\ 0, & \text{otherwise.} \end{cases}$$

Symbolically, we represent this as shown in Figure 2.20. Its present worth can be shown from the definition to be

$$PW(c) = a\left(\frac{1-e^{-rT}}{r}\right). \tag{2.5}$$

Similarly, for a discrete flow in which $c(t) = a$ for $t = 1, \ldots, T$, represented in Figure 2.21, the present worth can be shown to be

$$PW(c) = a\left(\frac{1-(1+r')^{-T}}{r'}\right). \tag{2.6}$$

For an annuity that extends over an infinite interval $(T \to \infty)$, the present worth is the amount of the annuity divided by the interest rate.

2.A.3 Some Properties of Present Worth

A property of present worth that follows directly from the definition is that it is an *additive measure* in the following sense. Given two cash flows $c_1(t)$ and $c_2(t)$, the present worth of the total cash flow $c_1(t) + c_2(t)$ is the sum of the present worths of the individual cash flows:

$$PW(c_1 + c_2) = PW(c_1) + PW(c_2). \tag{2.7}$$

Another property helpful in calculating present worth is that the *calculation can be done in stages*. What we mean by this is that the present worth can be calculated relative to some time τ, other than zero, and then that present worth treated as a one-time charge occurring at τ. The idea is best seen from an example.

Example 2.36. Suppose that $c(t)$ is a constant flow of $10 per period over the interval $t = 5, 6, 7$ (Figure 2.22). We can calculate the quantity W, which is the

Figure 2.21

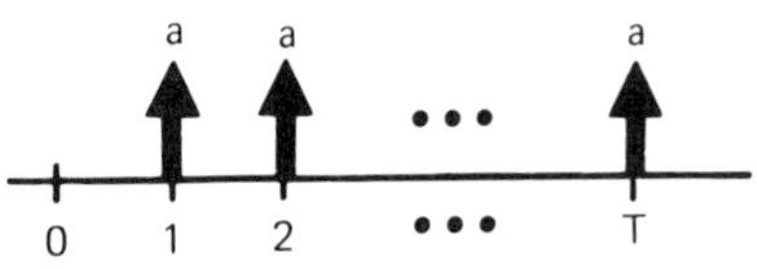

a   a   a

0   1   2   • • •   T

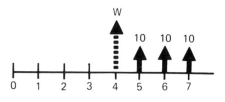

Figure 2.22

present worth of the annuity, as if $t=4$ were the origin, using Equation (2.6) and assuming $r'=0.2$:

$$W = 10\frac{1-(1+0.2)^{-3}}{0.2} = 21.06.$$

Then we treat W as a one-time charge at $t=4$, so that its present worth is

$$PW = 21.06\left(\frac{1}{1+0.2}\right)^{4} = 10.16.$$

This, of course, yields the same solution as

$$PW = 10\left(\frac{1}{1+0.2}\right)^{5} + 10\left(\frac{1}{1+0.2}\right)^{6} + 10\left(\frac{1}{1+0.2}\right)^{7} = 10.16. \; //$$

Mathematically, this property follows from the observation that the present worth can be written

$$PW = \int_{t_1}^{t_2} e^{-rt}c(t)\, dt = e^{-r\tau}\int_{t_1-\tau}^{t_2-\tau} e^{-ru}c(\tau+u)\, du, \tag{2.8}$$

where

$e^{-r\tau}$ is the factor for discounting from time τ to 0, and

$\int_{t_1-\tau}^{t_2-\tau} e^{-ru}c(\tau+u)\, du$ is the present worth with τ treated as the origin.

PART II

SIMPLE MODELS

Chapter 3

The Simplest Model—
Linear Deterministic Demand

We begin our exploration of analytical approaches to capacity expansion in this and the following chapter by studying a very simple model. We assume that the demand for additional units of capacity will grow linearly at rate g over an unbounded horizon, so that starting from time $t=0$, gt additional units will be required at time t in the future. Typically, additional units of capacity are purchased in bulk, either because they only come that way or because it makes economic sense to purchase them that way. In much of our discussion we shall assume that the cost of additional units consists of a fixed cost A plus a linear cost B per unit, so that x additional units cost $A + Bx$. Unless otherwise specified, $A + Bx$ is the present worth cost of providing x units of capacity forever—think of very durable equipment, or of a situation in which a facility, once placed, will always be replaced at the end of its life by a like facility.

This model is meant to capture some important phenomena in capacity expansion problems in the simplest possible setting. It clearly is not meant to be a very accurate reflection of any real-world problems; nevertheless, it may be reasonable to apply the model more or less directly to some situations.

Example 3.1. The demand for additional channels in a satellite communications system is expected to grow at the rate of 1.5 thousand per year. The in-place capital cost of a system with x thousand channels is estimated to be $(16 + 2x)$ thousand dollars. How large a system should we deploy for optimal economic efficiency? //

Example 3.2. A small businessman is starting up a quick-copying service. He expects demand for his service to grow linearly (for lack of any better assumption). He can buy machines of various maximum capacity (copying speed). Most of his investment will be in the purchase of the machines, so he is willing to make that investment decision more or less independently of any other considerations. What capacity machine should he buy? //

Example 3.3. A transmission line connects two points on an electric power grid. The load requirements of that link are projected to grow linearly for a long time to come. There is room for several more lines on the same power poles. When an additional power line is required, what should be its load carrying capacity? //

Example 3.4. Consider the paper shredding machine of Example 2.26. Although that problem is not stated in terms of the model of this chapter, it turns out to be mathematically equivalent if we take the following view. Let $g = 1$ and let the size of the various machines be their service lives. This is an example of the so-called equipment replacement problem, which we shall discuss later (see Example 11.1). //

We show how to solve this model in Section 3.1 with the capacity cost $A + Bx$ and in Section 3.3 with other capacity costs. In Section 3.2 we show that in situations where it is optimal to add capacity frequently over time, our model gives the same result as a well-known formula for inventory lot size. In Section 3.4 we discuss two meanings of economy-of-scale with reference to our simple model. Finally, we give a brief summary in Section 3.5 and indicate some further reading in Section 3.6.

3.1 The Optimal Size

Assuming that we can continue to place additional facilities in the indefinite future at the same cost, it should be pretty clear that we always shall wait until existing facilities are full and then place some facility of size x, called the *relief size*. We wait until the facilities are full simply because it is better to spend later by the present worth criterion. We always use a facility of the same size in this formulation because the costs and the projections of additional demand are identical at every shortage time (more on this point in Chapter 4). Figure 3.1 illustrates the demand and expansion pattern. Thus we wish to find the x that minimizes

$$W = \sum_{n=0}^{\infty} (A + Bx)e^{-r(nx/g)}, \tag{3.1}$$

where the nx/g are the times at which facilities will be placed. With a

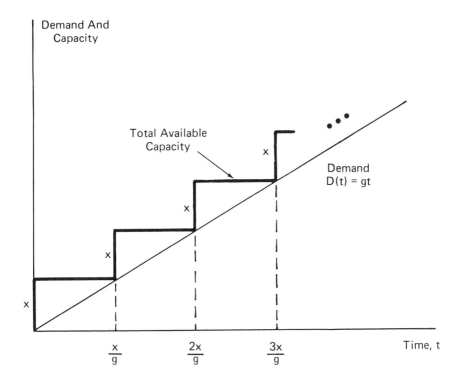

Figure 3.1. Capacity expansions to meet linearly growing demand.

positive discounting rate r, the sum converges to

$$W = \frac{A + Bx}{1 - e^{-r(x/g)}}.$$ (3.2)

It is simple to show that W is a well-behaved convex function for positive x (a sample plot of W versus x is shown in Figure 3.2 for the data given in Example 3.1) and so takes on a unique minimum. Of course, we also can think of the *relief time interval*, or *relief cycle*, $t = x/g$ instead of the relief size, x:

$$W(t) = \frac{A + Bgt}{1 - e^{-rt}}.$$ (3.3)

Figure 3.3 shows the minimizing value of the relief interval versus the ratio of A to B for various values of the growth rate. The curves are made general by plotting rt in place of the relief interval and using g/r in place of the growth rate. To see that this can be done, simply rewrite the equation for W as follows:

$$W/A = \frac{1 + [(g/r)(rt)/(A/B)]}{1 - e^{-rt}}.$$ (3.4)

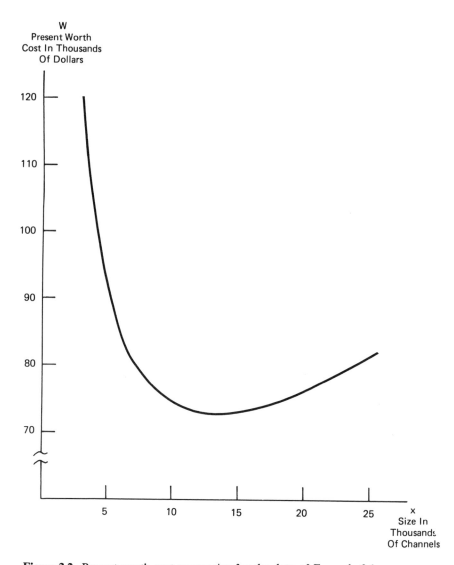

Figure 3.2. Present worth cost versus size for the data of Example 3.1.

Example 3.5. In Example 3.1 we supposed that demand for a satellite communications system was growing at the rate of $g = 1.5$ thousand channels/year; and that additional satellites which can provide x thousand channels cost $A + Bx = 16 + 2x$ thousand dollars. Using a discounting rate of $r = 0.1$, what is the optimal size satellite? To use Figure 3.3, we calculate

$$g/r = 1.5/0.1 = 15,$$
$$A/B = 16/2 = 8.$$

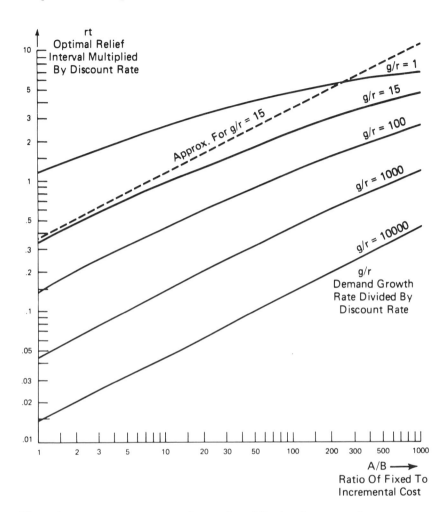

Figure 3.3. Relief interval for various ratios of fixed to incremental cost.

From Figure 3.3, $rt \approx 0.88$, so that the optimal relief cycle is about $t = 0.88/0.1 = 8.8$ years. That is, we should launch a satellite with about $1.5 \times 8.8 = 13.2$ thousand channels every 8.8 years. //

To get a better feel for how the optimal size varies with the parameters, it would be nice to have a direct formula for the x or t that minimizes W. Unfortunately, the best we can do is to get an implicit formula. If we set the derivative of W with respect to t to zero and rearrange terms, we obtain

$$e^{rt} - rt - 1 = Ar/(Bg). \tag{3.5}$$

That is, the t that satisfies this equation is the optimal relief time. While we cannot explicitly solve for t, we can obtain a useful approximation. If rt is small, e^{rt} can be closely approximated by a second-order Taylor series expansion:

$$e^{rt} \approx 1 + rt + \tfrac{1}{2}(rt)^2. \qquad (3.6)$$

Combining these last expressions, we obtain

$$\tfrac{1}{2}(rt)^2 \approx Ar/(Bg),$$

or

$$t \approx \sqrt{2A/(Bgr)} , \qquad (3.7)$$

$$x = gt \approx \sqrt{2Ag/(Br)} .$$

Example 3.6. In the satellite system of Examples 3.1 and 3.5,

$$t \approx \sqrt{\frac{2(16)}{(2)(1.500)(0.1)}} = 10.33 \text{ years,}$$

$$x \approx 15.5 \text{ thousand channels.}$$

Comparing this with Example 3.5, we see that the approximation has not led us *too* far astray. //

The dashed straight line in Figure 3.3 shows the relief time values obtained by the square root formula for $g/r = 15$. While there is considerable error for values of the parameters leading to large relief times, the square root formula is clearly a reasonable representation over much of the range.

3.2 Relation To Inventory Lot Size

Readers having some knowledge of inventory theory undoubtedly have noticed by now the similarity of this capacity expansion model with inventory problems. The square root formulas [Equation (3.7)], in particular, are identical in form with the classical formula for *economic order quantity*. It is interesting to derive that formula and draw the parallel.

Suppose our inventory of some good is depleted at the uniform rate of G items per unit time. Our policy is to order q units (which will last for time $t = q/G$) at a cost of $K + Dq$ whenever we run out. Note that the larger we make q, the less frequently we shall incur fixed cost K. The desirability of larger inventories is limited, however, by the fact that we must also pay a holding cost H per unit time per item in inventory. Our total cost over one inventory cycle is

$$C = K + Dq + \int_0^t H(q - G\tau)\, d\tau, \qquad (3.8)$$

where

$K + Dq$ is the cost of ordering q items,

$\int_0^t$ the integral is taken over the inventory cycle, and

$(q - G\tau)$ is the inventory held at time τ.

Carrying out the integration and substituting $t = q/G$,

$$C = K + Dq + H\left[q^2/(2G) \right]. \tag{3.9}$$

The average cost per unit time, c, is this divided by the inventory reordering interval $t = q/G$, which can be written in the intuitively appealing form

$$c = G\left(\frac{K + Dq}{q} \right) + H\left(\frac{q}{2} \right), \tag{3.10}$$

where

G is the rate at which items are used

$(K + Dq)/q$ is the average cost per item

H is the holding cost per unit of inventory

$q/2$ is the average amount of inventory.

The *optimal lot size* q is generally taken to be the size that minimizes the average cost per unit time. Although this is not the usual present worth optimization criterion discussed in Chapter 2, we shall show that it leads to the same decisions for typical inventory problems.

The two terms of (3.10) show that the average cost per item decreases with larger lot sizes (first term), but that this is counterbalanced by an increasing inventory holding cost (second term). See Figure 3.4.

It is easily verified that c [Equation (3.10)] is a convex function over positive q, so that its minimum can be found by setting the derivative to 0. This yields the standard formula for inventory lot size:

$$q = \sqrt{2KG/H} . \tag{3.11}$$

Comparing Equation (3.7) for the capacity expansion problem with (3.11) for the inventory problem, we see that the fixed charges A and K, respectively, play identical roles in the two problems. Similarly, the demand growth rate g can be identified with the inventory depletion rate G. To make the identification complete, we suppose that the inventory holding cost H is an interest charge for money tied up in inventory, where the value per unit of inventory is taken to be the marginal ordering cost D. That is, $H = Dr$.

Thus, we can interpret the capacity expansion problem in terms of the inventory analogue, and vice versa. For example, Figure 3.4 can be taken as an explanation of the capacity expansion problem. (The data is identical to that for Example 3.6.) That is, the average cost per unit time of adding

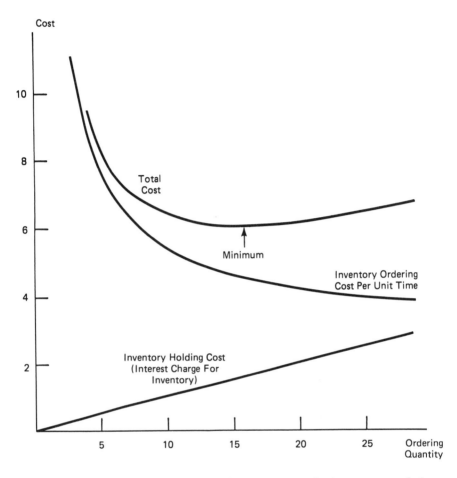

Figure 3.4. Inventory ordering and holding cost per unit time versus ordering quantity (lot size).

capacity decreases with size, while the interest charges for excess capacity increase with size; the optimum is a balance between these competing forces.

Finally, we reconsider the optimization criterion (3.10), the average cost per unit time, used for the inventory problem. We argued in Chapter 2 that present worth is the appropriate criterion [i.e., Equation (3.2) for the capacity expansion version of this problem]. The identification of the two square root formulas (3.7) and (3.11) shows that the average cost per unit time can be taken as a surrogate for present worth cost, provided the relief interval (inventory reordering interval) is small. In inventory problems, the optimal reordering interval might typically be a few days to a few months, making the criterion of average cost per unit time a very good approximation. On the other hand, in capacity expansion problems optimal expansion intervals are typically several years, making the approximation less good. Therefore, we shall view this inventory analogue as a model that provides insight into the capacity expansion problem rather than as a computational aid.

3.3 Other Capacity Cost Functions

So far, we have used a fixed plus linear cost $A + Bx$ for x units of additional capacity. Suppose that we wished to consider a general capacity cost $C(x)$ instead. The present worth cost would then be

$$W = \frac{C(x)}{1 - e^{-r(x/g)}} \tag{3.12}$$

instead of Equation (3.2). Of course, for an arbitrary C function, W may not be convex. In that case, we would have to find the minimum by trying out many values of x—we could not simply use calculus, for instance.

Example 3.7. Suppose, for the problem of Example 3.1, in which the demand for communication channels was projected to be growing at 1.5 thousand channels/year, that satellites were available only in capacities of 2.4, 10, and 25 thousand channels. Since intermediate sizes are not available $C(x)$ is *not* a convex function. Thus we must choose the size that minimizes (3.12):

x	$C(x)$ ($)1000	Relief time (years)	W
2.4	20.8	1.60	140.7
10	36.0	6.67	74.0
25	66.0	16.67	81.4

The 10 thousand-channel system wins. How much would the cost of the 25 thousand-channel system have to come down to make it the best choice? The 25 thousand-channel system would be preferable if its cost $C(25)$ were low enough that it beat the 10 thousand-channel system in present worth:

$$\frac{C(25)}{1 - e^{-0.1(25/1.5)}} < \frac{36.0}{1 - e^{-0.1(10/1.5)}},$$

or

$$C(25) < (1.67)(\$36) = \$60 \text{ thousand.}$$

That is, the larger system would be attractive in this case only if its cost were no more than 1.67 times that of the smaller system. //

In addition to the form $A + Bx$, another commonly used model of capacity cost (which we shall call the *exponential* cost model) is

$$C(x) = Kx^\alpha \quad \text{with} \quad 0 < \alpha < 1.$$

Then

$$W = \frac{Kx^\alpha}{1 - e^{-r(x/g)}}, \tag{3.13}$$

or in terms of the relief interval $t = x/g$,

$$W = \frac{Kg^\alpha t^\alpha}{1 - e^{-rt}}. \tag{3.14}$$

We can reduce the number of parameters [as in deriving Equation (3.4)] by looking at W/K, rt, and g/r:

$$W/K = \frac{(g/r)^\alpha (rt)^\alpha}{1 - e^{-rt}}. \tag{3.15}$$

We immediately note that the optimal relief interval is *independent of the growth rate* g. Of course, the relief size is directly proportional to growth, and the present worth cost is proportional to g^α.

We can find a necessary and sufficient condition for the optimal relief interval by setting the derivative of (3.15) to 0, which yields

$$\frac{e^{rt} - 1}{rt} = \frac{1}{\alpha}. \tag{3.16}$$

Figure 3.5 shows the optimal value of rt versus α. Using the same Taylor series approximation for e^{rt} as before [Equation (3.6)], the optimal relief interval is approximately

$$t \approx \left(\frac{2}{r}\right)\left(\frac{1}{\alpha} - 1\right). \tag{3.17}$$

Example 3.8. Suppose, as in Example 3.1, that demand grows at $g = 1.5$ thousand channels/year, but that the cost of satellite capacity is given by $C(x) = 9x^{0.6}$, where x is thousands of channels and C is thousands of dollars. From Figure 3.5, $rt = 0.95$, so that $t = 9.5$ years (using $r = 0.1$); thus the optimal size is $x = (1.5)(9.5) = 14.25$ thousand channels. In this example we have arrived at a solution very similar to that obtained in Example 3.5 ($t = 8.8$; $x = 13.2$). This is not surprising since the capacity costs used in the two examples are nearly identical in the range of about 10 to 20 thousand channels (see Figure 3.6). //

3.4 Economy of Scale

What we usually mean by economy of scale is that cost per unit decreases as we purchase more units. This phenomenon is clearly exhibited in the two capacity expansion cost models discussed in Sections 3.1 and 3.3. In

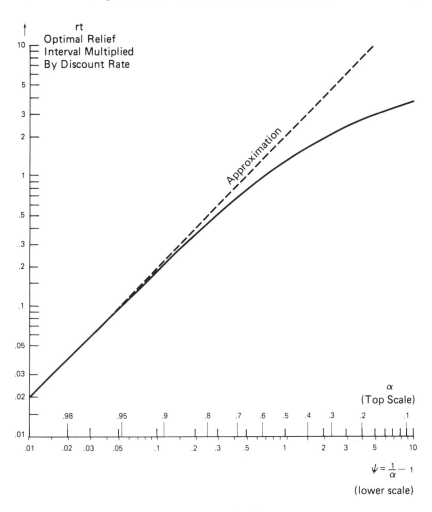

Figure 3.5. Relief interval versus economy-of-scale parameter.

the case of capacity cost given by $A + Bx$, a larger ratio A/B indicates more economy of scale, while in the case of capacity cost represented by Kx^α a smaller value of $\alpha > 0$ indicates more economy of scale.

Since either the linear or exponential capacity cost is probably an approximation of some more general $C(x)$ function, it is interesting to see how the two might relate. Suppose we fit the models at some point x_0 as follows. Select A and B so that

$$A + Bx_0 = C(x_0),$$
$$B = C'(x_0), \tag{3.18}$$

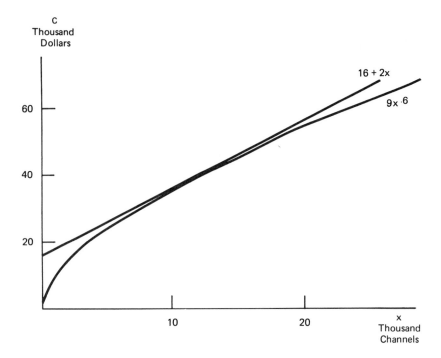

Figure 3.6. Two models of capacity cost.

and select K and α so that

$$Kx_0^\alpha = C(x_0),$$
$$K\alpha x_0^{\alpha-1} = C'(x_0), \tag{3.19}$$

where the prime denotes derivative. It is easy to see that

$$A = C(x_0) - x_0 C'(x_0),$$
$$B = C'(x_0), \tag{3.20}$$

while

$$\alpha = x_0 C'(x_0)/C(x_0)$$
$$K = C(x_0)/x_0^\alpha. \tag{3.21}$$

Alternatively, we could have equated the left-hand sides of (3.18) and (3.19) and after some manipulation obtained

$$\frac{A/B}{x_0} = \left(\frac{1}{\alpha} - 1\right) \equiv \psi. \tag{3.22}$$

This demonstrates the relation between the ratio A/B and α expressions of economy-of-scale. The parameter ψ defined by this equation is sometimes called, instead of α, the *economy-of-scale parameter*.

Example 3.9. In the satellite problem of Example 3.8, we used an exponential capacity cost function with $\alpha = 0.6$. The corresponding ratio A/B would be found from

$$\frac{A/B}{x_0} = \frac{1}{0.6} - 1 = 0.667,$$

where x_0 is measured in thousands of channels. If we make the cost curves coincide at 12 thousand channels (see Figure 3.6), we get $A/B = 8$, the scale economy factor used in Example 3.5. //

So far, we have talked about economy-of-scale as it applies to a single capacity expansion. A related, and perhaps more important, issue is the extent to which economies of scale can be realized in practice. That is, the mere availability of systems that are larger and have lower unit costs will not inevitably yield lower cost solutions.

Example 3.10. In Example 3.7, we considered the communication satellite capacity expansion problem with demand growing at $g = 1.5$ thousand channels/year and with three available sizes. The solution was to use 10 thousand-channel systems for a total present worth cost of $74.0 thousand. What if a 50 thousand-channel system became available at $90 thousand? Note that this is well below the $A + Bx = 16 + 2(50) = \$116$ thousand of Example 3.1. Even so, we clearly would not buy the 50 thousand-channel system for the 1.5 thousand-channel-per-year growth rate of Example 3.7, since its present worth cost must be something more than $90 thousand; and the 10 thousand-channel system is available at a present worth cost of $74 thousand. Thus, even though the 50 thousand-channel system costs only half as much per channel as the 10 thousand-channel system, it would not yield an achievable economy of scale if the demand growth rate of Example 3.7 is typical. //

Given the economies of scale we have been discussing, what kind of advantage is there to bigness? For example, how much more cheaply might some good or service be provided if a larger geographical area were to be served? In our simple model, this would correspond to a higher demand growth rate g. To examine this question, we introduce an *equivalent cost per unit time per customer in service c*, which is sometimes called the *equated cost* and is defined by

$$\int_0^\infty cgte^{-rt}\,dt = \frac{C(x)}{1 - e^{-(rx/g)}}, \tag{3.23}$$

where gt is the number of customers in service at time t, x is the size of each capacity expansion, and $C(x)$ is its present worth cost. Thus

$$c = \frac{r^2 C(x)}{g\left[1 - e^{-(rx/g)}\right]}. \tag{3.24}$$

Intuitively, c is the minimal annual rental fee that we could charge per unit of capacity and still pay for the equipment.

Example 3.11. In Example 1, we considered the satellite capacity expansion problem in which the growth rate was $g = 1.5$ thousand channels/year and capacity expansion cost $C(x) = 16 + 2x$ thousand dollars for x thousand channels of capacity. Suppose x were limited to the single size $x = 10$ (e.g., only the 10 thousand-channel system were available in Example 3.7). What cost per unit time per channel in use would result if this system were used for the demand growth rate of Example 3.7? What would be the cost

Figure 3.7. Equated cost per channel versus demand growth rate.

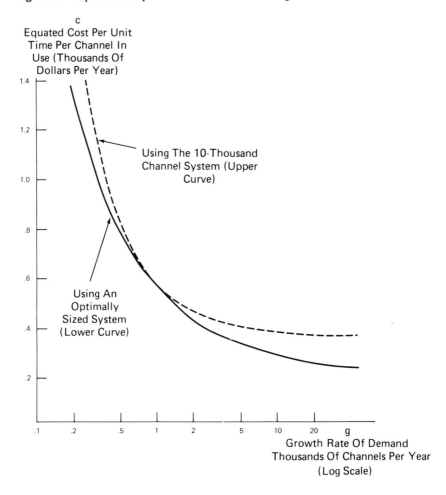

with other growth rates?

$$c = \frac{(0.1)^2 36}{g\{1 - e^{-[(0.1)10/g]}\}} = 0.49 \quad \text{for } g = 1.5.$$

The upper curve of Figure 3.7 plots c versus g. Note that as $g \to \infty$, $c \approx rC(x)/x$, which is independent of g. //

Example 3.11 demonstrates that we may have a significant economy-of-scale effect even without what we usually think of as economy of scale in the equipment cost—only one size was available. The economy of scale results, in this example, from a more rapid utilization of spare capacity when the demand growth rate is higher. The advantage of a more rapid utilization is a consequence of having to *pay for capital*, as expressed by the use of a positive discounting rate.

A further economy of scale is possible if we assume that the capacity size can be optimized for each growth rate g. For illustration, suppose that $C(x)$ is the fixed plus linear cost model of Equation (3.3) and that the size x will be optimized for each growth rate g. Then we can rewrite (3.3) for the optimal relief interval t^* by substituting (3.5) and rearranging:

$$W = \left(A + Bgt^* + \frac{Bg}{r} \right),$$

or

$$c = rB\left(1 + \frac{rA}{gB} + rt^* \right). \tag{3.25}$$

In this convenient form we can see, for instance, that c will decrease with g and that $c \to rB$ as $g \to \infty$.

Example 3.12. How will the upper curve of Figure 3.7, calculated in Example 3.11, shift if we use the optimal size at each growth rate? It is straightforward to calculate c either from (3.24) or (3.25) using the optimal relief interval as found from Figure 3.2. The bottom curve of Figure 3.7 shows the result. Note that the curves coincide at about $g = 1$. This is because the 10 thousand-channel system assumed for the upper curve is optimal for that growth rate. //

In summary, we have discussed two related, but distinct, economy-of-scale effects. One is the observation that it usually costs less to buy more units of capacity at a time. The magnitude of this effect is often expressed as the ratio A/B of fixed cost to incremental cost or as a scale parameter α, where doubling the size only multiplies the cost by 2^α.

We also observed that the equivalent cost per unit of capacity in service is lower if we serve a larger constituency (larger growth rate g). Of course, this does not necessarily mean that bigger is better. As we serve a larger geographical area, for example, transportation costs may increase and more than offset any gains in capacity costs. We shall touch upon this kind of question later, when we briefly discuss location models in Section 11.3.

As one might expect, these are not the only economy-of-scale effects that may be observed in capacity expansion problems. For example, Section 7.3 discusses the reduction in uncertainty that may result from serving larger aggregates of demand. Other effects are discussed in the references given in Section 3.6.

3.5 Summary and Discussion

The simplest capacity expansion model is one in which demand for additional capacity is projected to grow linearly over an infinite future. Capacity must be added over time to serve that demand. Any capacity added is assumed to last forever; or equivalently, the cost of capacity is assumed to include replacement by like equipment at the end of its life. These simplifying assumptions make it possible to analyze the problem easily and thoroughly. We showed, for example, that the capacity expansion problem is very similar to an inventory problem. We also discussed economies-of-scale, pointing out two distinct effects: first, that equipment tends to cost less per unit in larger batches; and second, that it tends to cost less per customer to serve larger aggregations of customers even if equipment is only available in one size.

In future chapters we shall relax some of the simplifying assumptions made here. The resulting problems become more difficult, but qualitatively retain much of the character of this simplest capacity expansion problem.

3.6 Further Reading

A classic and highly readable source on capacity expansion problems is

A. S. Manne, ed., *Investments for Capacity Expansion*: *Size*, *Location and Time-Phasing*, London, Allen and Unwin, 1967.

Manne gives applications in manufacturing. Application of some of the same methods to satellite communications may be found in

M. S. Snow, *International Commercial Satellite Communications*, New York, Praeger, 1976.

That the economy-of-scale issue is much more complex than we have indicated is amply illustrated by several articles in

IEEE Transactions on *Systems, Man and Cybernetics* 5(1), January 1975.

Chapter 4

Some Solution Methods—
Sensitivity Studies
and a Look Ahead
to More Complex Models

Here we introduce some solution methods that will serve as our *basic approaches* to solving capacity expansion problems. The model of Chapter 3 is simple enough that it really does not call for more sophisticated methods, but we present our solution methods in terms of that model nevertheless. The reader, hopefully, will find it easier to follow the explanation of these methods applied to a simple, familiar problem, although he may not immediately appreciate their relevance. The immediate benefits of this chapter will be to gain further insight into the simple capacity expansion problem, and particularly, to see some sensitivity results.

Section 4.1, the *backward dynamic programming* formulation, is an approach we shall use again and again in more complex settings. The *forward dynamic programming* approach of Section 4.2 gives us additional insights into the time horizon, and as we shall see in Chapter 5, gives us a unique capability for some problems with a very high demand growth rate. In Section 4.3 we present an *integer programming* formulation that turns out to be solvable by ordinary *linear programming* methods. Finally, in Section 4.4 we discuss two schemes for finding approximate solutions when demand is nonlinear. These formulations produce optimal solutions for the linear demand case.

4.1 Backward Dynamic Programming

We started Section 3.1 by arguing that we would use always the same size capacity expansion, and therefore we wished to minimize the sum given by Equation (3.1). Instead of assuming identical capacity expansions at the outset, suppose that we had looked for a sequence of sizes: x_0, to be placed at time $t_0 = 0$; x_1, to be placed at $t_1 = x_0/g; \ldots; x_n$, to be placed at $t_n = \sum_{i=0}^{n-1}(x_i/g); \ldots$. Then, in place of Equation (3.1) we would have

$$W = C(x_0) + \sum_{n=1}^{\infty} C(x_n)e^{-(r/g)\sum_{i=0}^{n-1} x_i}, \tag{4.1}$$

which can also be written

$$W = C(x_0) + \left[C(x_1) + \sum_{n=2}^{\infty} C(x_n)e^{-(r/g)\sum_{i=1}^{n-1} x_i} \right] e^{-(r/g)x_0}, \tag{4.2}$$

where we are using the more general capacity cost $C(x)$ in place of $A + Bx$. The reason for writing the sum in the alternative form (4.2) is that the term in brackets is independent of x_0. Designating that term as W_F, *the cost of the future*,

$$W = C(x_0) + W_F e^{-(r/g)x_0}. \tag{4.3}$$

Equation (4.3) is in the usual backward dynamic programming form. It is backward in the sense that if we can solve the future problem, that of determining optimal $x_1, x_2, \ldots$, and its associated present worth cost W_F, then the determination of the optimal x_0 is a straightforward, 1-dimensional minimization. It is dynamic programming in that it is a recursive formulation. That is, the W_F optimization problem is identical in form to the W problem; in fact, for the case shown here it is mathematically equivalent.

Intuitively, Equation (4.3) says that we must pay for a capacity expansion now; and depending on the size we install, we shall be faced with another capacity expansion problem at $t = x_0/g$. Thus, for example, it pays to install more capacity now (larger x_0) if the marginal cost of the additional capacity is more than offset by the savings due to deferring the future expenditures W_F. Figure 4.1 plots W versus x_0 for various values of W_F using the data of Example 3.1. Note that for a fixed W_F, the W versus x_0 curve is more shallow than the curve of W versus x of Figure 3.1, shown as a dashed curve here.

4.1.1 Computational Notes

The purpose of casting this problem in the dynamic programming format (4.3) is to assist in optimizing the capacity expansions. If the cost of future expansions W_F were known, whether or not that cost is associated with an optimal expansion schedule, the optimal initial expansion corresponding to that future cost could be found by a simple minimization over a single variable,

$$W_{opt} = \min_{x} \left[C(x) + W_F e^{-r(x/g)} \right]. \tag{4.4}$$

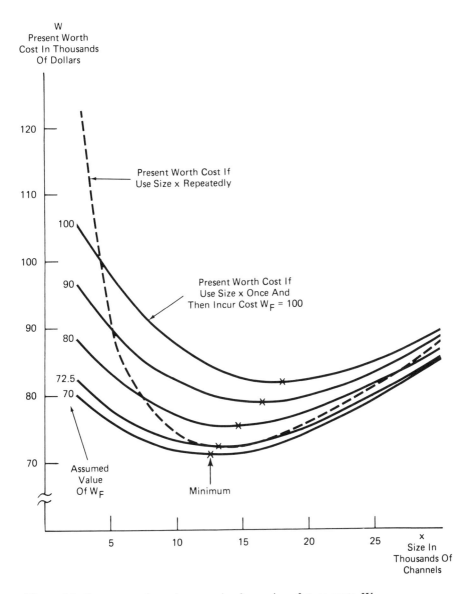

Figure 4.1. Present worth cost versus size for various future costs W_F.

For example, if $C(x) = A + Bx$, then we can get an explicit expression for the minimizing x by setting the derivative of the right-hand side to 0:

$$x_{opt} = \frac{g}{r} \ln \frac{rW_F}{Bg}. \qquad (4.5)$$

This is the optimal value among *positive* x. Sometimes it may make sense to also consider $x=0$, that is, to avoid $C(x)$ altogether and incur W_F right away. That possibility must be evaluated in addition to (4.5). Other times it may be more appropriate to set a lower limit on the x_{opt} to be considered.

In the more general case, we are trying to optimize the entire expansion sequence, and so we would be interested in using the *optimal* cost of the future W_F in the right-hand side; but, of course we do not know its value at the outset. Fortunately, it turns out that we can use (4.4) iteratively, starting with some initial guess at W_F, using W_{opt} as an improved estimate of W_F for the next iteration, and so on. The appendix at the end of the chapter shows why this iterative procedure should converge to the optimal solution; the following example illustrates this.

Example 4.1. Suppose $C(x) = 16 + 2x$, $g = 1.5$, and $r = 0.1$ as in the satellite problem of Example 3.1. Let us start out with $W_F = 1,000$ and apply (4.4) successively to obtain a new estimate of W_F. Table 4.1 shows several iterations of this process. Eventually, the estimates of x and W stop changing, for all practical purposes, and we have the optimal solution (same as we found in Example 3.5). //

Note that because the W and W_F problems are identical in form, the sizes of all expansions in the optimal schedule will be identical.

Example 4.1 is sometimes called the *value iteration* method to distinguish it from that of the following related procedure, which is called a *policy iteration* method. Suppose that whenever we obtain an improved estimate of the capacity size [Equation (4.5)], we assume that that size will be used for all subsequent capacity expansions. The resulting present worth cost would be given by Equation (3.2), repeated here:

$$W = \frac{A + Bx}{1 - e^{-r(x/g)}}. \qquad (4.6)$$

Table 4.1. Iterations for the Backward Dynamic Programming Solution—Value Iteration (Example 4.1)

Iteration	W_F	x_{opt} [Eq. (4.5)]	W [Eq. (4.4)]
1	1,000	52.6	151.2
2	151.2	24.3	94.5
3	94.5	17.2	80.4
4	80.4	14.8	75.6
5	75.6	13.9	73.7
6	73.7	13.5	73.0
7	73.0	13.3	72.7
8	72.7	13.3	72.5
9	72.5	13.2	72.5
10	72.5	13.2	72.5

Table 4.2. Iterations for the Backward Dynamic Programming Solution—Policy Iteration (Example 4.2)

Iteration	W_F	x_{opt} [Eq. (4.5)]	W [Eq. (4.6)]
1	1,000	52.6	124.9
2	124.9	21.4	77.4
3	77.4	14.2	72.6
4	72.6	13.2	72.5
5	72.5	13.2	72.5
6	72.5	13.2	72.5

We then use Equation (4.6) to estimate W_F instead of (4.4) in the iterations.

Example 4.2. Table 4.2 repeats the calculations of Example 4.1, only using Equation (4.6) to determine the new estimate of W_F in place of (4.4). We again obtain the same solution, but in less iterations.[1] //

Intuitively, the rapid convergence found in Example 4.2 results from the relative insensitivity of the present worth cost to the capacity size (see Figure 4.1) and from the fact that a substantial part of the total present worth cost is due to the cost of the initial decision.

This formulation of the capacity expansion problem in terms of the cost of the future is a handy approach. The next two sections make use of it, and later in Section 10.2 it provides an easy solution for a special case of a very hard capacity expansion problem.

4.1.2 Changes in the Future Costs

Another use of the backward dynamic programming equation, (4.3), is to do some sensitivity analysis. How much is the current decision affected by assumptions about future decisions? We can vary W_F in Equation (4.3) to model the effects of using suboptimal decisions or incurring different capacity expansion costs for future decisions. This may be a way to account for the effects of anticipated technological change, for instance.

An immediate observation is that the effect on W of changes in W_F will be proportional to the present worth factor, $e^{-(r/g)x_0}$. Thus, of course, the longer the initial relief interval x_0/g, the less will present worth cost W depend on future costs W_F. This effect is nicely illustrated as follows.

---

[1]It can be shown that near the optimal solution, quadratic convergence is obtained with this form of the algorithm, whereas only linear convergence is obtained with the form used in Example 4.1.

Suppose that the cost of all future expansions is W_F and that the cost of the initial expansion is $C(x) = A + Bx$, so that the optimal solution is x_{opt}, as given by (4.5), and the total present worth cost is W_{opt}, as given by (4.4). Now, if the future expansions actually end up costing $W_F' = (1 + \varepsilon)W_F$, the actual present worth cost will be

$$
\begin{aligned}
W' &= C(x_{opt}) + (1 + \varepsilon)W_F e^{-r(x_{opt}/g)} \\
&= C(x_{opt}) + W_F e^{-r(x_{opt}/g)} + \varepsilon W_F e^{-r(x_{opt}/g)} \\
&= W_{opt} + \varepsilon W_F e^{-r(x_{opt}/g)} \\
&= W_{opt} + \frac{Bg}{r}\varepsilon,
\end{aligned}
\tag{4.7}
$$

where the third equality is from (4.4) and the last equality from (4.5).

Example 4.3. In the satellite capacity expansion problem of Example 4.1, we had a growth rate of $g = 1.5$, a capacity cost of $C(x) = 16 + 2x$, and a discounting rate of $r = 0.1$. The solution was $x_{opt} = 13.2$, with $W_F = W_{opt} = 72.5$. If the cost of future expansions changes by the fraction ε, the total present worth cost will be [Equation (4.7)]

$$
W' = 72.5 + \frac{2(1.5)}{0.1}\varepsilon = 72.5 + 30\varepsilon,
$$

as shown in the second column of Table 4.3. It is also interesting to look at the relative change in total present worth cost

$$
\frac{W' - 72.5}{72.5} = 0.41\varepsilon.
$$

Thus, there will be only 41% as much change in total cost as there was in future costs. //

Table 4.3. Sensitivity to Changes in the Cost of Future Expansions

$\varepsilon = \dfrac{W_F' - W_F}{W_F}$	W' [Eq. (4.6)]	$\ln(1+\varepsilon)$	x'_{opt} [Eq. (4.7)]	W'' [Eq. (4.8)]
−0.5	57.5	−0.693	2.8	51.7
−0.2	66.5	−0.223	9.9	65.8
−0.1	69.5	−0.105	11.6	69.3
0	72.5	0	13.2	72.5
0.1	75.5	0.095	14.6	75.4
0.2	78.5	0.182	15.9	78.0
0.5	87.5	0.405	19.3	84.7
1	102.5	0.693	23.6	93.3

A more interesting situation is one in which we are allowed to optimize the initial decision *anticipating* the modified future cost. Suppose again that W_F is the cost of all future expansions; x_{opt}, the optimal expansion size given by (4.5); and W_{opt}, the total present worth cost given by (4.4). As before, let future costs be modified to be $W_F' = (1+\varepsilon)W_F$; but now suppose that this is learned *before* the initial expansion has been undertaken. Then we should recalculate the optimal expansion from (4.5):

$$x_{opt}' = \frac{g}{r} \ln \frac{r(1+\varepsilon)W_F}{Bg}$$

$$= \frac{g}{r} \ln \frac{rW_F}{Bg} + \frac{g}{r} \ln(1+\varepsilon)$$

$$= x_{opt} + \frac{g}{r} \ln(1+\varepsilon). \tag{4.8}$$

Substituting into (4.4) and going through simplifications similar to those leading to (4.7), the total present worth cost turns out to be

$$W'' = W_{opt} + \frac{Bg}{r} \ln(1+\varepsilon). \tag{4.9}$$

For small ε, this will be nearly identical to (4.7); for larger ε, it will be noticeably smaller.

Example 4.4. The last two columns of Table 4.3 illustrate how the optimal size and total present worth cost change with future cost for the data given in the previous example. For instance, a 50% increase in future costs ($\varepsilon = 0.5$) changes the optimal size from $x = 13.2$ to $x' = 19.3$, and the total cost from $W = 72.5$ to $W'' = 84.7$. If the size has to remain at $x = 13.2$, the total cost is $W' = 87.5$. //

In this kind of sensitivity study, we typically find the following:

1. If the future cost W_F is calculated on the basis of some reasonable capacity expansions, it will not be too far different from the optimum (e.g., see Figure 3.1).
2. The optimal initial size assuming a different future cost varies only moderately for moderate changes in the future cost (fourth column of Table 4.3).
3. The optimal total present worth cost changes even more moderately with changes in the future cost, particularly when the initial capacity decision is modified to anticipate the changed future cost (second and fifth columns of Table 4.3).

4.1.3 Sizing under a Limited Budget

The backward dynamic programming formulation is also convenient for studying the effect on sizing of a short-term budget constraint as discussed in Section 2.9.

In Section 2.9, we argued that an overall budget constraint on expenditures in the near term could be reasonably represented by the use of a Lagrange multiplier λ. There, we found that instead of just maximizing the objective function alone, we should maximize the objective function less λ times the initial budget required. In our sizing problem we get

$$\max_x \left[-W(x) - \lambda C(x) \right],$$

or

$$\min_x \left[W(x) + \lambda C(x) \right], \tag{4.10}$$

where $W(x)$ is the total present worth cost given by (4.3) with x the size of the initial expansion. Substituting (4.3) for $W(x)$, we have

$$\min_x \left[(1+\lambda)C(x) + W_F e^{-(r/g)x} \right], \tag{4.11}$$

which is equivalent to

$$(1+\lambda)\min_x \left[C(x) + \frac{W_F}{1+\lambda} e^{-(r/g)x} \right]. \tag{4.12}$$

Therefore, the effect of a budget limitation is identical to a decrease in W_F, which we have already studied in Section 4.1.2. There we developed explicit formulas for the case of $C(x) = A + Bx$. The optimal size in that case is given by Equation (4.8) with $1+\varepsilon = 1/(1+\lambda)$:

$$x = x_* - \frac{g}{r}\ln(1+\lambda), \tag{4.13}$$

where x_* is the optimum without a budget constraint ($\lambda = 0$). The optimal size decreases, of course, with increasing λ. The present worth cost using the reduced size is

$$W = A + B\left[x_* - \frac{g}{r}\ln(1+\lambda) \right] + W_F e^{-(r/g)[x_* - (g/r)\ln(1+\lambda)]},$$

which after some manipulation becomes

$$W = W_* + \frac{Bg}{r}\left[\lambda - \ln(1+\lambda) \right], \tag{4.14}$$

where W_* is the present worth cost using the unconstrained optimal size x_*.

It is interesting to note that for small λ, the two expressions become

$$x \approx x_* - \frac{g}{r}\lambda, \tag{4.15}$$

$$W \approx W_* + \frac{Bg}{r}\frac{\lambda^2}{2}. \tag{4.16}$$

The change in size is proportioned to λ, while the present worth cost penalty is only proportional to λ^2—another manifestation of the shallowness of the objective function.

Example 4.5. Telephone transmission cables in the Mom & Pop Telephone Company cost $1.5 + 0.005x$ dollar per foot for a capacity of x customers. The M&P engineers figure that their relief projects for this year are about equally divided (1,000 feet of cable each) among cables that serve demand growth rates of 20 customers/year, 100 customers/year, and 200 customers/year. Due to hard times, M&P would like to reduce its ideal capacity expansion budget for this year by 10%. What value of the multiplier λ should they use in their individual sizing decisions? How will the cuts be apportioned? What will the penalty be?

We first find the optimal sizes and present worth cost either using the curves of Section 3.1 or one of the iterative algorithms of Section 4.1.1. Using $r = 0.1$ and $A/B = 1.5/0.005 = 300$, Table 4.4a shows the optimal size and cost for growth rates of $g = 20$, 100, and 200 pairs per year. Now as we try increasing values of λ, using Equation (4.13) for x, we obtain reduced sizes and, hence, reduced budgets, as shown in Table 4.4b. Of course the resulting present worth cost [Equation (4.14)] increases with λ. From Table 4.4b, we see the following: with $\lambda = 0.07$ the total current cost would be $13.22/14.30 = 0.924$, or about 92% of the ideal budget; with $\lambda = 0.10$ it would be $12.78/14.30 = 0.893$, or about 89% of the ideal budget. On this basis we decide to use $\lambda = 0.10$ (although $\lambda = 0.09$ would probably get us

Table 4.4a. Optimal Sizes and Costs Without a Budget Constraint

g	x_*	$A + Bx_*$	W_*
20	269	2.85	3.85
100	686	4.93	9.93
200	1,004	6.52	16.52
Total	—	14.30	30.30

Table 4.4b. Optimal Sizes and Cost With Various Budget Constraints (Various λ)

	$\lambda = 0.04$			$\lambda = 0.07$			$\lambda = 0.10$		
g	x (4.13)	$A + Bx$	W (4.14)	x (4.13)	$A + Bx$	W (4.14)	x (4.13)	$A + Bx$	W (4.14)
20	261	2.81	3.85	255	2.78	3.85	250	2.75	3.85
100	647	4.74	9.93	618	4.59	9.94	591	4.46	9.75
200	926	6.13	16.53	869	5.85	16.55	813	5.66	16.57
Total	—	13.68	30.31	—	13.22	30.34	—	12.78	30.37

closer to the goal of a 10% budget reduction). Note that this cut affects the high-growth jobs much more than the low-growth jobs, both in terms of size reductions and in terms of expenditure reductions. The present worth cost penalty would be about $30.37 - 30.30 = \$0.07$ for the 3 feet of cable considered, or $70 total. Compared to the $30,300 total present worth cost, this is quite trivial; but of course the revenue requirements model of Chapter 2 tells us that the $70 penalty should be viewed as the equivalent of a one-time additional expense, and so may be significant. That is, the customers of M&P will have to be charged the equivalent of $70 more this year as a result of M&P's unwillingness or inability to invest the ideal amount in new plant. //

4.2 Forward Dynamic Programming

Instead of thinking about the present worth cost of providing capacity from some time onward [W_F in Equation (4.3)], suppose that we think of the cost of providing capacity up to some time t. Let $w(t)$ be the cost of optimally providing capacity to last until time t. Then, in place of (4.3) we can write

$$w(T) = \min_{0 \le t < T} \left\{ w(t) + C[x(t, T)] e^{-rt} \right\}, \qquad (4.17)$$

where $C[x(t, T)]$ is the amount of capacity needed to serve additional demand arising from time t to T. In the linear demand case currently under consideration, $x(t, T) = g(T - t)$, but this formulation is not limited to linear demand. In words, the minimum cost $w(T)$ of adding capacity to serve the demand up to time T can be obtained by considering an optimal scheme $w(t)$ for various shorter intervals $t < T$, plus buying enough capacity at t to last until T. Note that if we build up the $w(T)$ function starting with $T = 0$ and $w(0) = 0$, $w(t)$ in the right-hand side will always be a known quantity. This process is the classical *forward dynamic programming* technique. Of course, for this optimization process to be practical, we must limit the search to discrete rather than continuous t.[2]

Comparing the forward and backward dynamic programming formulations of this and the previous section, we note that here w is an explicit function of time, while W is not. When we consider nonlinear demand functions in Chapter 5, we shall see that this advantage of the backward formulation is strictly dependent on the assumptions of a uniform future that we have made for our simplest model. That is, in a more general case W and W_F in Equation (4.3) would depend also on time. The following example illustrating the application of (4.17) shows how

---

[2] Interesting technical questions arise with respect to strict optimality in the discretized problem—see the discussion by Manne and Veinott in A. S. Manne's book cited at the end of Chapter 3.

much more computational effort is involved when we must consider time explicitly.

Example 4.6. Let us again solve the satellite problem: $r=0.1$, $g=1.5$, $C(x)=16+2x$, or in the notation of (4.17), $C[x(t,T)]=16+2g(T-t)=16+3(T-t)$. Only now we limit the possibility of capacity expansion to 4-year intervals. We thus preclude the 8.8-year relief interval obtained earlier, and will settle for a choice among 4 years, 8 years, 12 years, etc. Starting with $w(0)=0$, we get $w(4)=C[x(0,4)]=16+3(4)=28$. To calculate $w(8)$, we construct Table 4.5a, each row leading to a computation of the right-hand side of (4.17) for some allowed t. Thus $w(8)=40$ with $t=0$, which means that if we only had to serve 8 years of demand, we would do it with a single capacity expansion of 8 years. Similarly, Table 4.5b shows the calculations for $w(12)$, and Table 4.5c for $w(16)$. Table 4.5c says that we should do the first 8 years of capacity expansion according to the solution developed for $T=8$, that is, the 8-year relief interval found in Table 4.5a, followed by a $16-8=8$-year relief interval. If we were to

Table 4.5a. Forward Dynamic Programming Solution for an 8-Year Horizon (Example 4.6): $T=8^a$

t	$w(t)$	$C[x(t,8)]$	Ce^{-rt}	$w+Ce^{-rt}$
0	0	40	40	40 minimum
4	28	28	18.8	46.8

[a] Thus $w(8)=40$ with the optimal $t=0$.

Table 4.5b. Forward Dynamic Programming with 12-Year Horizon (Example 4.6): Next Iteration, $T=12^a$

t	$w(t)$	$C[x(t,12)]$	Ce^{-rt}	$w+Ce^{-rt}$
0	0	52	52	52 minimum
4	28	40	26.8	54.8
8	40	28	12.6	52.6

[a] Thus $w(12)=52$ with the optimal $t=0$.

Table 4.5c. Forward Dynamic Programming with 16-Year Horizon (Example 4.6): Next Iteration, $T=16^a$

t	$w(t)$	$C[x(t,16)]$	Ce^{-rt}	$w+Ce^{-rt}$
0	0	64	64	64
4	28	52	34.9	62.9
8	40	40	18.0	58.0 minimum
12	52	28	8.4	60.4

[a] Thus $w(16)=58.0$ with the optimal $t=8$.

continue this process for increasing T, we would obtain the solutions shown in Table 4.6. As T gets large, the solution sequence appears to be approaching 8-year expansion intervals. //

The example illustrates two important general points with respect to the forward dynamic programming algorithm. (1) When the horizon T coincides with a time at which it is optimal to relieve in the infinite-horizon problem, the optimal capacity expansions will be identical to the first expansions in the infinite-horizon problem (e.g., $T=8$, 16, and 32). (2) As the horizon T gets large, the early decisions converge to the corresponding optimal infinite-horizon solutions. For instance, in Table 4.6 the size of the first capacity expansion is identical to that for the infinite-horizon problem whenever T is larger than 16. In fact, it turns out that we get ever improving bounds on the optimal infinite-horizon solutions as we solve problems with larger and larger T.

These points show up more clearly in a more refined analysis. Figure 4.2 displays the optimal initial relief interval t_1 as we increase T, while Figure 4.3 plots the resulting present worth cost $w(T)$ (the dark curves in both figures). These curves could have been generated using a very small discretization interval in place of the 4-year interval in Example 4.6. Actually, they were generated using recursion relations developed in Appendix 2 to Chapter 5. Note that whenever T is a multiple of the infinite-horizon solution $t_* = 8.8$ years, the optimal initial relief interval is $t_1 = t_*$. Also, variations of the optimal initial relief interval are bounded between their extreme values at the last "jump." For example, in Figure 4.2 the initial expansion interval t_1 increases linearly with the horizon time, T until it jumps from $t_1 = 12.2$ to $t_1 = 7.2$ at $T = 12.2$; then it rises smoothly (nearly linearly) again until it jumps from $t_1 = 9.9$ to $t_1 = 8.3$ at $T = 21.5$;

Table 4.6. Solution for Various Horizon Values

Horizon T	Present worth cost $w(T)$	Sequence of optimal capacity expansion intervals
0	0	0
4	28	4
8	40	8
12	52	12
16	58.0	8,8
20	63.4	8,12
24	66.0	8,8,8
28	68.5	8,8,12
32	69.7	8,8,8,8
36	70.8	8,8,8,12
⋮	⋮	⋮
∞	72.6	8,8,8,8,...

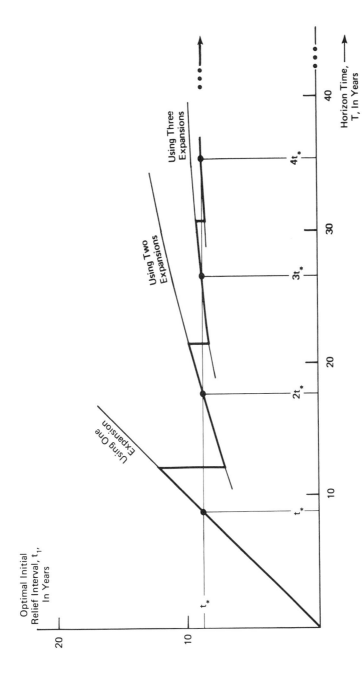

Figure 4.2. Optimal initial relief interval t_1 versus horizon time T.

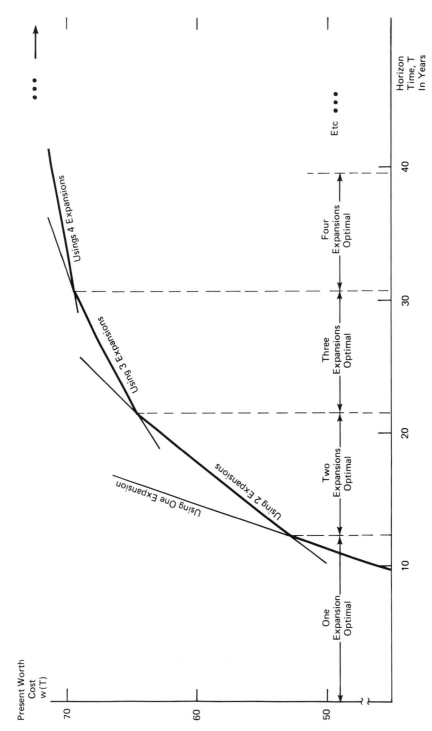

Figure 4.3. Optimal present worth cost versus horizon time.

and so on. Note that the optimal initial expansion interval for T larger than 12.2 lies between the extremes $7.2 < t < 12.2$; for $T > 21.5$ it lies between the extremes $8.3 < t < 9.9$; and so on. Thus, for example, if we were solving this problem by forward dynamic programming for larger and larger horizon times, we would obtain these improving bounds on the optimal solution periodically.

In fact, we shall show in Appendix 1 to Chapter 5 that these bounds on the initial expansion interval are much more powerful than one might expect, providing a very interesting sensitivity observation. It turns out that if the demand grows linearly up to the time of one of these jumps (e.g., to $T = 21.5$ in Figure 4.2), the extreme values of the initial expansion interval at that time (e.g., $8.3 < t_1 < 9.9$ in Figure 4.2) are bounds on the optimal initial expansion interval *regardless of the future demand beyond that time*. Thus, for example, if demand is linear, as assumed in Example 4.6, up to $T = 21.5$ years and is completely *unknown* beyond that, we can still say with confidence that the optimal initial relief interval is between 8.3 and 9.9 years! Since we are really most interested in the initial expansion, and since the present worth cost is relatively shallow, this observation should relieve considerably our anxiety about having to forecast demand over an *infinite* horizon.

Furthermore, this observation indicates that if it is convenient, we *can* reasonably use a finite horizon in our solution methods, provided the horizon is sufficiently distant. Philosophically, we still think in terms of an infinite horizon; but pragmatically, events in the far future have little influence on the current decision and may be ignored.

4.3 A Mathematical Programming Formulation

Here we discuss a formulation of the capacity expansion problem which is interesting because it is very different from our solution approaches up to this point. It is a bit cumbersome for the immediate problem at hand, but it does introduce another way of looking at capacity expansion problems which may be useful in other contexts. For example, Section 11.1.3 suggests an approach like this one for the much more difficult problem in which replacement of worn-out capacity is to be undertaken in conjunction with expansions.

In this formulation, we consider capacity expansions to serve a finite number of successive time periods $k = 1$ through N starting at times $t_1, t_2, \ldots, t_N$. We define decision variables Z_{ij} that are allowed to take on values of 0 or 1, where a value of 1 indicates that a capacity expansion is to take place at time t_i of sufficient size to serve all additional demand arriving from the ith through the jth periods. We let C_{ij} designate the present worth cost of such an expansion, that is,

$$C_{ij} = C\big(x(t_i, t_{j+1})\big)e^{-rt_i}, \tag{4.18}$$

where $x(t_i, t_{j+1})$ is the capacity required to serve the additional demand arising during periods i through j. As in the forward dynamic programming formulation, demand need not be linear in this formulation.

Our capacity expansion problem can be expressed in terms of these decision variables and cost coefficients as follows:

$$W = \min_{Z_{ij}=0 \text{ or } 1} \sum_{i=1}^{N} \sum_{j=1}^{N} C_{ij} Z_{ij}, \tag{4.19}$$

subject to the requirement that each period's additional demand be met by at least one expansion

$$\sum_{i=1}^{k} \sum_{j=k}^{N} Z_{ij} \geq 1 \quad \text{for } k=1, \ldots, N. \tag{4.20}$$

From our knowledge of capacity expansion problems, we know that in the usual case (increasing demand, increasing capacity cost) it will not pay to expand capacity until spare goes to 0, and so we may as well take the inequalities (4.20) to be equalities.

Example 4.7. Consider, again, the data of Example 4.6: $r=0.1$, $g=1.5$, $C(x)=16+2x$, and expansions allowed only at 4-year intervals. We therefore let $t_1=0$, $t_2=4$, $t_3=8$, $t_4=12$, $t_5=16$. Thus, for instance, $Z_{24}=1$ designates the addition of capacity at $t=4$ (in the second period) to last until $t=16$ (i.e., through the fourth period). The corresponding cost is

$$C_{24} = \left[16 + 2(1.5)(16-4) \right] e^{-0.1(4)} = 34.9.$$

Undertaking this expansion would satisfy additional demand arising in periods 2, 3, and 4, that is, would satisfy (4.20) for $k=2$, 3, and 4. Table 4.7 shows the coefficients of (4.19) and (4.20) for this example. The first row displays C_{ij} corresponding to the Z_{ij} listed at the bottom, while the next five rows show the nonzero coefficients of (4.20). This table has been constructed under the assumption that expansions lasting more than 12 years are not available. //

Table 4.7 illustrates a potential difficulty with this formulation. If we wish to consider a large number of periods (fine granularity or long

Table 4.7. Mathematical Programming Formulation (Example 4.7)

$W=$	28	40	52	18.8	26.9	34.9	12.6	18.0	23.4	8.4	12.0	15.7	5.7	8.1	10.5	
t_1:	1	1	1													$=1$
t_2:		1	1	1	1	1										$=1$
t_3:			1		1	1	1	1	1							$=1$
t_4:						1		1	1	1	1	1				$=1$
t_5:									1		1	1	1	1	1	$=1$
	Z_{11}	Z_{12}	Z_{13}	Z_{22}	Z_{23}	Z_{24}	Z_{33}	Z_{34}	Z_{35}	Z_{44}	Z_{45}	Z_{46}	Z_{55}	Z_{56}	Z_{57}	

horizon), we need a large number of variables and equations. This, at first glance, is particularly disturbing since we require the Z_{ij} to be *integers*. Integer programming problems are typically *much* more difficult to solve than continuous ones. Fortunately, it turns out that the structure of this formulation is such that ordinary (continuous variable) linear programming techniques will yield the desired integer solution (see Veinott and Wagner, cited in Section 4.6).

Example 4.8. Actually, solving the linear program of Example 4.7 (Table 4.7) would take us too far afield, but Table 4.8 shows the final tableau that would be obtained by standard linear programming pivoting methods. The system of equations shown in Table 4.7 has been solved in Table 4.8 for the variables shown at left in terms of the variables listed along the bottom. The first row is the objective function $w = 63.4 + 3.5 Z_{11} + 0.6 Z_{13} + \cdots$, the second is $Z_{12} = 1 - Z_{11} - Z_{13}$, and so on. Letting all of the variables listed at the bottom be 0 produces the so-called basic solution $w = 63.4$, $Z_{12} = 1$, $Z_{35} = 1$, the rest 0. Starting from this basic solution, it would not be advantageous to increase any of the nonbasic variables from 0 since that would only tend to increase w (for example, w would increase by 1.4 per unit of increase in Z_{24}). This, it turns out, is the test that proves that the current basic solution is optimal. It is easy to check that this solution is the same one obtained in Example 4.6. //

In later chapters we shall find the previous dynamic programming approaches more useful for our purposes than this mathematical programming approach. Nevertheless, it is always good to have another tool at our disposal.

4.4 Approximation Algorithms

4.4.1 Equated Cost

In Section 3.4 we introduced a concept we called the *equivalent cost per unit time per customer in service*. That cost, c, was defined as the constant

Table 4.8. Optimal solution of Problem Shown in Table 4.7 (Example 4.8)

$W = 63.5$	3.5	0.6	3.3	1.4	1.2	1.8	3.7	0.3	2.7	5.1
$Z_{12} = 1$	-1	-1								
$Z_{23} = 0$	1		-1	-1						
$Z_{34} = 0$						-1		1	1	1
$Z_{35} = 1$	-1	-1	1	1	-1	1		-1	-1	-1
$Z_{45} = 0$	1	1	-1	-1	1	-1	-1			
	Z_{11}	Z_{13}	Z_{22}	Z_{24}	Z_{33}	Z_{44}	Z_{46}	Z_{55}	Z_{56}	Z_{57}

charge per unit time per unit capacity that would just pay for all required capacity expansions [Equation (3.23)]:

$$\int_0^\infty cD(t)e^{-rt}dt = W, \tag{4.21}$$

where

$D(t)$ is the total demand (number of customers) at time t

W is the present worth cost of the capacity expansions.

Of course, c is thus directly proportional to present worth cost and may be used interchangeably with it.

In this chapter we wish to consider a slightly different equivalent cost concept, sometimes called the *equated cost* ε. Intuitively, the equated cost is the rental we would have to charge customers using the system installed *at one capacity expansion* to just pay for that expansion. It is defined by

$$\int_0^T \varepsilon D(t)e^{-rt}dt + \int_T^\infty \varepsilon D(T)e^{-rt}dt \equiv C[D(T)], \tag{4.22}$$

where

T is the relief time interval

$D(t)$ is the demand function, assumed nondecreasing, with $D(0)=0$

$C(\cdot)$ is the cost of a single capacity expansion

ε is the equated cost (a function of T).

The first term is the present worth of rental received while the system is filling up, and the second is the present worth of rental received thereafter. Solving for ε gives

$$\varepsilon = \frac{C[D(T)]}{\int_0^T D(t)e^{-rt}dt + \int_T^\infty D(T)e^{-rt}dt}; \tag{4.23}$$

in case $D(t)$ is differentiable, the denominator can be simplified, yielding

$$\varepsilon = \frac{C[D(T)]}{(1/r)\int_0^T g(t)e^{-rt}dt}, \tag{4.24}$$

where $g(t)$ is the derivative of $D(t)$.

If each new capacity expansion had to pay for itself, then our objective would be to minimize the equated cost. For example, if a separate corporate entity were established each time an additional facility were built and each entity were allowed to charge its customers at different rates, minimizing the equated cost would minimize revenue requirements for the one system. Since we are not making that assumption here, we shall think of ε as an approximation [defined by (4.21)] to c and thus to the present worth.

When demand is linear, $g(t) = g$, a constant for all t, and (4.24) becomes

$$\varepsilon = \frac{C(gT)}{(1/r)g\left[(1-e^{-rt})/r\right]} = c. \tag{4.25}$$

That is, in the linear demand case, minimizing equated cost is *identical* to minimizing present worth cost. In the general case, however, the two will be different. We shall find in Section 10.3 that the equated cost formulation can be a useful approximation, since the computation of $\varepsilon(T)$ only requires demand information up to time T.

4.4.2 Project Sequencing

In Section 11.2 we shall study briefly a problem known as project sequencing—Given a set of n capacity expansion projects, in what order should they be done? Here we present an approximation based on a simple observation for that problem. Consider two potential projects: one is of size x_1, relief interval t_1; and the other is of size x_2, relief interval t_2. If we are going to do both capacity expansions sequentially, which should we do first? The answer is simply to do i before j if

$$C(x_i) + C(x_j)e^{-rt_i} < C(x_j) + C(x_i)e^{-rt_j}, \tag{4.26}$$

or, after rearranging,

$$\frac{rC(x_i)}{1-e^{-rt_i}} < \frac{rC(x_j)}{1-e^{-rt_j}}. \tag{4.27}$$

This prompts us to define the *annual cost* $AC(i)$ of project i, as

$$AC(i) = \frac{rC(x_i)}{1-e^{-rt_i}}. \tag{4.28}$$

It is easy to check that $AC(i)$ has been defined in such a way that its present worth over the expansion interval is precisely the expansion cost:

$$\int_0^{t_i} AC(i)e^{-rt}\,dt = C(x_i). \tag{4.29}$$

Inequality (4.27) suggests that we simply select the project with the lowest annual cost, $AC(i)$. When there are only two projects to select, of course, this will yield the optimal solution. It turns out, as discussed in Section 11.2, that it also yields the optimal sequence for any number of projects when demand is linear. Otherwise, this selection rule might be used as an approximation to the optimum.

The same approximation is applicable to the usual capacity expansion problem in which facilities may be replicated. Select the expansion interval

T that minimizes

$$\mathrm{AC}(T) = \frac{rC\left[D(T)\right]}{1 - e^{-rT}}. \tag{4.30}$$

As before, $\mathrm{AC}(T)$ is the constant continuous annuity whose present worth over the interval 0 to T is just enough to pay for the expansion $C[D(T)]$. Note that this is similar in concept to the equated cost approximation of the previous section [Equation (4.23)]. There we found the expansion interval that minimizes the equivalent uniform rental *per customer in service*; here we find the expansion interval that minimizes the equivalent constant charge *per unit time* over the expansion interval.

As in the case of the equated cost approximation, it is easy to see that if demand is linear, minimizing annual cost is equivalent to minimizing present worth [compare Equations (3.12) and (4.30), for example]. Thus, the approximation yields the exact solution if demand is linear.

In Section 11.2, we use the annual cost approximation for project sequencing problems. There we also introduce higher-order generalizations of this approximation that are increasingly closer to the optimum, but require more computation to solve.

4.5 Summary

Here we have delved more deeply into capacity expansion computations. Although all of our sample calculations were on the linear demand case, the formulations of Sections 4.2, 4.3, and 4.4 are applicable to nonlinear demand as well.

There are many ways of looking at this problem, each yielding its own insights. The backward dynamic programming formulation of Section 4.1 accentuates the interpretation of slack capacity as an investment made now to postpone expansions that will have to be made later. The forward dynamic programming approach emphasizes that initial capacity expansion decisions tend to be insensitive to assumed demand very far into the future. The mathematical programming discussion of Section 4.3 indicates that since this version of the capacity expansion problem can be solved by ordinary *linear programming* methods (as opposed to integer programming methods for the formulation in Section 11.1), it is not a computationally difficult problem. Finally, the equated cost and annual cost approximations of Section 4.4 suggest that *myopic* approaches that only look at the next expansion might yield good decisions if demand is nearly linear.

In later chapters, we shall find the most use for the dynamic programming outlooks.

4.6 Further Reading

In addition to Wagner (introductory operations research), cited in Chapter 2, and Manne (capacity expansion), cited in Chapter 3, we recommend

N. Valcoff, Optimal Size of Telephone Transmission Systems, *Proc. IFAC Symp.*, June 1968, 26–35,

for a discussion of the backward dynamic programming approach, and

F. W. Sinden, The Replacement and Expansion of Durable Equipment, *The Journal of the Society for Industrial and Applied Mathematics* 8(3), September 1960, 466–480,

for forward dynamic programming.

The mathematical programming formulation is from

Arthur F. Veinott, Jr., and Harvey M. Wagner, Optimal Capacity Scheduling I and II, *Operations Research* 10(4), 1962, 518–546.

Appendix. Convergence of Backward Dynamic Program

The object is to find the optimal solution of

$$W = \min_{x_{min} \le x \le x_{max}} \left[C(x) + W_F e^{-rx/g} \right], \tag{4.31}$$

where W_F is the minimum of a problem that is mathematically identical to this one. We assume that the size is bounded to lie within an interval of positive numbers x_{min} and x_{max} to avoid unnecessary mathematical complications. Let W_* denote the minimum W, which by definition is also the minimum W_F. Clearly we must have

$$W_* = \min_x \left[C(x) + W_* e^{-rx/g} \right], \tag{4.32}$$

where the minimization will always be taken over the same positive interval.

Suppose now that we start with $W_F = W_* + \Delta$ for some positive Δ. Then

$$W = \min_x \left[C(x) + W_* e^{-rx/g} + \Delta e^{-rx/g} \right]. \tag{4.33}$$

Since the third term in the brackets is positive and the first two terms are bounded below by W_* [according to Equation (4.32)],

$$W > W_*. \tag{4.34}$$

Also, (4.33) can be written

$$W = \min_x \left[C(x) + W_* e^{-rx/g} - \Delta(1 - e^{-rx/g}) \right] + \Delta. \tag{4.35}$$

The third term in the brackets is again positive, and so necessarily will reduce the minimum to less than that achieved in (4.32). Thus

$$W < W_* + \Delta. \tag{4.36}$$

Combining (4.34) and (4.36), we see that the W will be closer to the optimal W_* than was W_F.

A similar argument can be made for negative Δ. Thus the backward dynamic programming solution approach will converge to the optimal solution.

PART III

MORE COMPLEX MODELS

Chapter 5

Nonlinear Demand

We still retain the assumption that demand is deterministic and known to us at the outset, but in place of the very restrictive assumption that it is linear over all time, we consider what happens when we introduce various nonlinearities.

At this point it is probably worthwhile to ponder a bit about where the demand function comes from in the first place. We must remember always that it is a *forecasted* quantity; and in the nature of many capacity expansion problems, this may involve forecasts far into the future. Thus, in practical situations we are much more likely to run into best-guess demand functions specified by something like a growth rate than detailed year-by-year demand estimates. There are, nevertheless, many practical problems in which nonlinearities in the demand are an essential feature. In Chapter 6, for example, we shall study a problem in which two types of capacity are to be added. It turns out that even though demand is assumed to be linear, the interaction of the two capacity types effectively produces a nonlinear demand. In other cases, demand may be relatively well known, and highly nonlinear, over the next few years; or a known major shift in demand may be upcoming due to changes in an import law to take effect at some definite date in the future. Furthermore, even if we wish to use a simple best-guess demand function, why should we not use, for example, an exponential rather than a linear function?

In this chapter we show that capacity expansion problems with general nonlinear but deterministic demand can be handled readily by either backward or forward dynamic programming (Sections 5.2 and 5.3). Also, some special cases can be solved much more easily. In Section 5.1, we show that if demand is linear with only a jump in the beginning, the solution involves a minor modification of the linear growth solution. In Section 5.4 we show that if capacity cost is a power function Kx^α and demand is exponential, the solution is no more difficult than for linear demand with a nonlinear capacity cost.

Throughout the chapter we lean heavily on viewpoints developed in our discussion of the linear demand case.

5.1 Linear Demand with an Initial Jump

Suppose demand is projected to be linear, but we allow a jump in demand at the beginning, as illustrated in Figure 5.1. A positive value of D_0 might correspond to pent-up demand, while a negative value could reflect an early expansion forced by external factors such as coordination with some other construction project. That is, in Figure 5.1A the expansion at 0 actually should have taken place D_0/g time units earlier, while in Figure 5.1B the expansion is assumed to be undertaken at time 0, although within the context of the model it really is not needed until $-D_0/g$ time units later.

The simplest solution is to use the *cost of the future* formulation of Section 4.1. Since demand is linear following the initial expansion, all future expansions can be calculated using the standard methods of Section 3.1 or 4.1, for example. Let W_F be the present worth cost of those expansions as measured from the time of the next expansion after the one at time 0. Then the optimal initial expansion x satisfies

$$W = \min_{\substack{x \geq 0 \\ x \geq D_0}} \left[C(x) + W_F e^{-r(x-D_0)/g} \right], \qquad (5.1)$$

which can also be written

$$W = \min_{\substack{y \geq -D_0 \\ y \geq 0}} \left[C(y+D_0) + W_F e^{-ry/g} \right], \qquad (5.2)$$

with $x = y + D_0$. That is, y is the spare capacity immediately following the capacity addition and the jump in demand at time 0.

In the case of a fixed plus linear capacity cost, $C(x) = A + Bx$, this further reduces to

$$W = \min_{\substack{y \geq -D_0 \\ y \geq 0}} \left(A + By + W_F e^{-ry/g} \right) + BD_0. \qquad (5.3)$$

If we ignore the constraint $y \geq -D_0$ in the minimization, then the optimal y is just the optimal capacity size for the linear demand problem [e.g., see Equation (4.5)]:

$$y = x_* \equiv \frac{g}{r} \ln \frac{rW_F}{Bg}. \qquad (5.4)$$

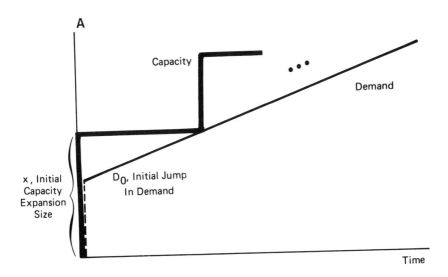

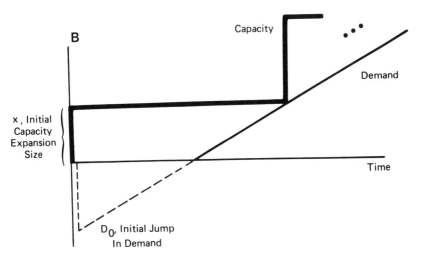

Figure 5.1. Linear demand with an initial jump: A. positive jump; B. negative jump.

Thus the optimal initial capacity size x is

$$x = x_* + D_0. \tag{5.5}$$

That is, *the optimal size is just what the size would have been without the jump plus sufficient capacity to satisfy the jump* D_0. Of course, if D_0 is negative (Figure 5.1b), Equation (5.5) may yield a negative amount of capacity (recall that we ignored the constraint on y). In that case it is not economical to install capacity at time 0 even if the only cost of that capacity is the incremental or B cost.

Example 5.1. (Same data as Example 3.8) Suppose that $C(x) = 9x^{0.6}$ thousand dollars, for x thousand channels and $r = 0.1/\text{year}$. In addition, assume that 8 thousand channels will be used up immediately ($D_0 = 8$). We found in Example 3.8 that the optimal size for the linear growth problem with a growth rate of $g = 1.5$ thousand channels/year is $x_* = 14.25$ thousand channels. If we were working with a fixed plus linear capacity cost, the solution for this problem would be

$$x = x_* + D_0 = 14.25 + 8 = 22.25.$$

As it is, we must use the more general equation, (5.1). We first find the present worth cost for the linear growth problem [Equation (3.12)]:

$$W_F = \frac{9x_*^{0.6}}{1 - e^{-0.1x_*/1.5}} = 72.26.$$

Table 5.1 shows the present worth cost for several values of x as calculated by Equation (5.1). The solution is about 26 thousand channels. This is somewhat greater than the 22.25 thousand channels we would have obtained with a fixed plus linear capacity cost function. The increased size reflects the greater economy-of-scale exhibited by the power function capacity cost at large capacities (see Section 3.4). //

5.2 Backward Dynamic Programming for Nonlinear Demand

Suppose we let the cumulative demand $D(t)$ be any nonlinear function over time interval $t = 0$ to T. It is not restrictive to assume that $D(t)$ is nondecreasing, since capacity, once installed, is assumed to last forever;[1] and we do not consider removal of capacity. Beyond T, we assume that

Table 5.1. Optimal Capacity Expansion With Initial Jump In Demand (Example 5.1)

x	$C(x)$	W (5.1)	
22	57.50	85.92	
25	62.09	85.35	
26	63.57	85.33	minimum
27	65.02	85.38	

---

[1] Or to be replaced by like capacity at the end of its life.

demand is linear: $D(t) = D(T) + g(t - T)$. The model of Section 5.1 thus can be viewed as a special case of this one.

We can write the dynamic programming formula

$$W(t) = \min_{\tau \geq t} \left[C[x(t, \tau)] + W(\tau) e^{-r(\tau - t)} \right], \tag{5.6}$$

where

$W(t)$ is the present worth cost of serving all additional demand starting at time t with no spare capacity

$x(t, \tau) \equiv D(\tau) - D(t)$ is the additional capacity required to serve the demand arriving between t and τ.

Since we have assumed linear demand beyond $t = T$, we can use $W(t) = W_F$ for $t \geq T$. It is interesting to note that if the demand is entirely linear,

$$x(t, \tau) = g(\tau - t),$$
$$W(\tau) = W_F,$$

and so we can write (5.6) as

$$W(t) = \min_{x \geq 0} \left[C(x) + W_F e^{-rx/g} \right].$$

That is, the optimal expansion size is independent of t, and we get the same formulation as in Section 4.1.

In general, the most straightforward way to solve this dynamic program is to consider discrete relief times, so that $W(t)$ is defined only for $t = t_1, t_2, \ldots, t_n$. Then we can calculate the values of $W(t_i)$ successively, starting with the largest t_i. Note that in this way the values of $W(\tau)$ required for the right-hand side always will be known. For each value of t, the τ or corresponding size x that minimizes the right-hand side tells us what the optimal expansion would be if we were to run out of spare capacity at that time. Thus, if we save these optimal values of τ or x for each t, we can easily construct the optimal expansion sequence once we have calculated W for the smallest t_i.

Example 5.2. Suppose we are trying to satisfy the demand shown in Figure 5.2, in which growth is linear at $g = 1.5$ after $t = 10$. Let facilities cost $C(x) = 9x^{0.6}$, and use $r = 0.1$ (as in Example 5.1). For purposes of computation, limit the possible expansion sizes to multiples of 3; thus, we are restricting expansion times to $t = 0$, 1, 6, 6.5, 7, 10, and so forth. Since growth is linear after $t = 10$, we assume $W(t) = 72.26$ for $t \geq 10$ (as calculated in Example 5.1).

Starting with the largest required t in the nonlinear region, $t = 7$, we try various values of τ in the dynamic program [Equation (5.6)]. Table 5.2a shows the calculations. Thus, if an expansion were required at $t = 7$, we would use $x = 12$, and the total cost from then on would be $W(7) = 69.35$.

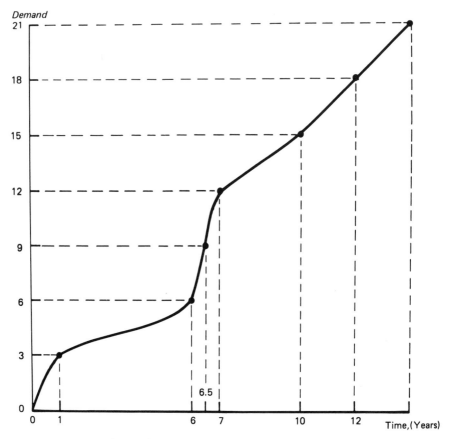

Figure 5.2. A nonlinear demand function (Example 5.2).

This is all we need from Table 5.2a. (For example, if we were electronic computers, we would not need to use up storage locations to keep the rest.)

Next we repeat the calculation for $t=6.5$ in Table 5.2b using $W(7)=69.35$ found in Table 5.2a. The optimum is $x=15$ with $W(6.5)=73.65$. Similarly, we successively calculate $W(6)$, $W(1)$, and $W(0)$ in Tables 5.2c, 5.2d, and 5.2e. Finally, we trace back through the tables to find the optimal solution. From Table 5.2e, at $t=0$ we would install a system of size $x=6$ that will last until $\tau=6$. Thus we next go to Table 5.2c and find that at $t=6$ we would install $x=18$ that would last until $\tau=16$. This has taken us into the linear growth region; and so any expansions beyond this point would be calculated as in Chapter 3, for example. //

We note that in generating the Tables 5.2a–5.2e, we have truncated the calculation at the point where the objective function (last column) started

Table 5.2. Iterations of the Backward Dynamic Program (Example 5.2)

τ	$x(t,\tau)$	$C(x)$	$W(\tau)$	$C+We^{-r(\tau-t)}$	
		a. $t=7^a$			
10	3	17.40	72.26	70.93	
12	6	26.37		70.20	
14	9	33.63		69.52	
16	12	39.97		69.35	minimum
18	15	45.70		69.75	
		b. $t=6.5^b$			
7	3	17.40	69.35	83.37	
10	6	26.37	72.26	77.29	
12	9	33.63		75.32	
14	12	39.97		74.10	
16	15	45.70		73.65	minimum
18	18	50.98		73.86	
		c. $t=6^c$			
6.5	3	17.40	73.65	87.46	
7	6	26.37	69.35	89.12	
10	9	33.63	72.26	82.07	
12	12	39.97		79.63	
14	15	45.70		78.17	
16	18	50.98		77.56	minimum
18	21	55.92		77.68	
		d. $t=1^d$			
6	3	17.40	77.56	74.86	minimum
6.5	6	26.37	73.65	78.27	
7	9	33.63	69.35	80.12	
10	12	39.97	72.26	75.85	
12	15	45.70		75.08	
14	18	50.98		75.03	
16	21	55.92		75.61	
		e. $t=0^e$			
1	3	17.40	74.86	85.14	
6	6	26.37	77.56	68.94	minimum
6.5	9	33.63	73.65	72.08	
7	12	39.97	69.35	74.41	
10	15	45.70	72.26	72.28	
12	18	50.98		72.74	

[a]Result: $W(7)=69.35$; optimal $x=12$.

[b]Result: $W(6.5)=73.65$, optimal $x=15$.

[c]Result: $W(6)=77.56$, optimal $x=18$.

[d]Result: $W(1)=74.86$, optimal $x=3$.

[e]Result: $W(0)=68.94$, optimal $x=6$.

to increase after τ was in the linear growth region. This is justified in the usual case where the right-hand side of Equation (5.6) takes on a unique minimum with $W(\tau)$ fixed at W_F (e.g., see Figure 4.1). In the case of a capacity cost $A + Bx$ we could avoid extending these tables into the linear growth region at all. That is, if at any time t it were optimal to install capacity to last into the linear growth region, we could find the optimal size and cost very quickly using the observations of Section 5.1. Example 5.3 illustrates this.

Example 5.3. (See Table 5.2c and Figure 5.2 referring to Example 5.2) In this example, we wish to consider only the optimal capacity expansion at $t = 6$ in Figure 5.2. That is, assuming we first run out of spare capacity at $t = 6$, what size would we install? Precisely that problem is solved in Table 5.2c. Here we note that if we projected the linear demand curve back to $t = 6$, we would find an initial jump of 3 at the begining. This is illustrated in Figure 5.3. Thus, if the optimal expansion at $t = 6$ extends into the linear growth region at all, we would expect it to be the size obtained for the linear growth problem plus the initial jump as given by Equation (5.5). In our case, $x \approx 14.25 + 3 = 17.25$ (approximately equal because our capacity cost is not actually of the form $A + Bx$). Since we only allow capacity increments of 3, we use $x \approx 18$ instead. This analysis tells us that once we consider a capacity addition sufficiently large to last into the linear region, the *only* one we have to consider is $x = 18$. That is, we can restrict our attention to the rows in Table 5.2c corresponding to $\tau = 6.5, 7, 10$, and 16. //

5.3 Forward Dynamic Programming for Nonlinear Demand

The forward dynamic programming formulation of Section 4.2 is, as we have already mentioned there, directly applicable to the case of nonlinear demand. In the forward dynamic programming formulation, we let $w(t)$ be the cost of optimally providing capacity up to time t, and we write the recursion (4.17) as

$$w(T) = \min_{0 \le t \le T} \left\{ w(t) + C[\, x(t, T)\,] e^{-rt} \right\}, \tag{5.7}$$

where $x(t, T)$ is the capacity required to serve demand arising from t to T, just as in Equation (5.6). The direct application of Equation (5.7) already has been illustrated in Section 4.2. The reader is invited to work Example 5.2 in like fashion.

We devote the rest of this discussion to more technical, but very interesting, aspects of the forward dynamic programming formulation. In Section 4.2, we alluded to obtaining bounds on the magnitude of the initial capacity expansion for the infinite-horizon problem from solutions of finite-horizon problems. Here we show that such bounds can be obtained

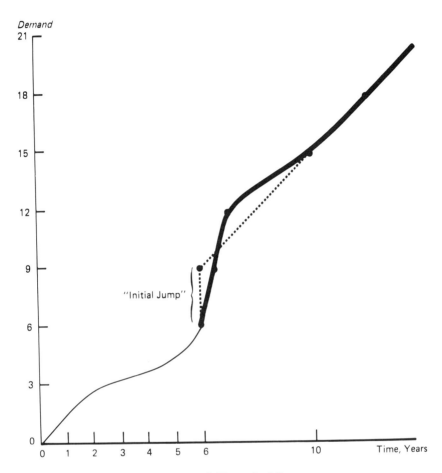

Figure 5.3. Effective jump in demand (Example 5.3).

more generally. We also show that these bounds can be used to solve a problem whose present worth of capacity cost is infinite.

For this analysis we view the forward dynamic programming problem somewhat differently. We still consider solving capacity expansion problems over finite time intervals 0 to T, but now consider solutions using various numbers n of capacity expansions. That is, for each time interval we find the least costly solution using $n = 1, 2, 3, \ldots$ expansions during the interval. For any T, the optimal solution is the one corresponding to the n that minimizes present worth cost. In Figure 4.3, for example, the present worth cost using $n = 1$ expansion, $n = 2$ expansions, and $n = 3$ expansions have been plotted versus T. Over the initial interval in that figure it is least costly to use 1 expansion, over the next interval to use 2 expansions, and so forth. Figure 4.2 plots the corresponding size of the first expansion versus

T. The jumps in that curve occur at points at which it becomes optimal to use 2 expansions instead of 1, 3 instead of 2, and so forth. We have already indicated in Chapter 4 that these jumps define upper and lower bounds on the size of the initial relief interval for the infinite-horizon problem. Appendix 1 to this chapter shows that this conclusion holds for *any* nondecreasing, future demand when capacity cost is of the form $A + Bx$. Computationally, this gives us a stopping rule for the forward dynamic programming algorithm—that is, stop when the upper and lower bounds are sufficiently close together. Perhaps more significantly, the bounds may be a very useful indicator of the sensitivity of our solution to assumptions about future demand (see Section 4.2).

Both of these points are powerfully illustrated by the following example. In this example, demand is assumed to grow exponentially at a rate sufficiently large that the present worth cost of supplying that demand is infinite! In our standard formulation, the problem is not even solvable because we cannot minimize something that is infinite. Instead, we find the optimal size of the initial expansion over larger and larger horizons T and show that the bounds soon get sufficiently close together that we declare the problem solved.

Example 5.4. Consider a capacity expansion problem with the following data: $r = 0.1$ (discounting rate); $C(x) = 16 + 2x$ (capacity cost); and $D(t) = 2(e^{0.2t} - 1)$ (demand function). With demand growing this rapidly, the reader may wish to check that the present worth of expansions over an infinite horizon is unbounded (because $e^{0.2t}e^{-0.1t}$ increases with t). Suppose we find the optimal capacity expansions for various horizons T. We could do this by discretizing the time line and applying the forward dynamic programming algorithm [Equation (5.7)]. Since $D(t)$ is an analytically described function, we can get some help from calculus. Appendix 2 shows that we can set to 0 the derivatives of $w(T)$ with respect to intermediate expansion times. This gives recursive equations that can be solved readily for the optimal expansion times given the horizon T and the number of expansions to be used over that horizon. Figure 5.4 plots the optimal initial relief interval versus the horizon time. It is clear that the optimum converges to about $t_1^* = 8.3$ years. Furthermore, even if the demand is assumed to be *completely unknown* beyond 15 years into the future, for example, the jump at $T = 15$ tells us that the optimal initial expansion will still be between about $t_1 = 7.7$ and 9.3 years (see Figure 5.4). //

This example raises some doubt about our basic formulation of the capacity expansion problem. That is, in Chapter 2 we argued that it was reasonable to minimize the present worth of costs over an infinite horizon. Yet, here we have a seemingly reasonable solution to a problem whose present worth cost is unbounded. The example shows that we can get

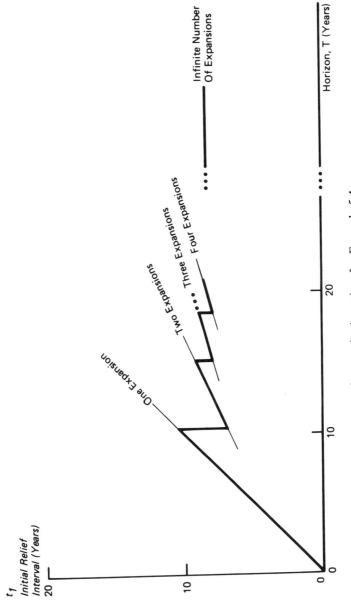

Figure 5.4. Optimal initial relief interval versus horizon time for Example 5.4.

around the problem in at least some cases by simply solving problems over a longer and longer horizon; although the present worth cost increases without bound, the optimal size of the initial capacity expansion converges nicely. However, does this not raise doubts about using the present worth over an infinite horizon as an objective function in the first place? For example, in Chapter 2 our revenue requirements model interprets the present worth cost as the present worth of revenues required to compensate investors adequately. What does it mean for this present worth to be infinite? In this example, it simply means that the revenues to support the project must grow at the same exponential rate as the demand. A little more careful analysis would show that if we only considered revenue streams growing at the same exponential rate as the demand, then the investment decisions obtained in Example 5.4 could be supported by the smallest such revenue stream.

At this point, we could go back and try to carefully redefine our objective function to encompass the difficulty raised by this example. Such an exercise probably would not be worthwhile in our context. In capacity expansion problems the assumption of growth continuing to infinity in a finite world is made more for mathematical convenience than to reflect reality. Note that this is true even for such nonphysical quantities as prices, if the inflation model of Section 2.4 is roughly correct. Thus it is probably inadvisable to handle problems arising from such assumptions by changing our basic philosophy. Example 5.4, for instance, indicates that early decisions are not much affected by assumed demand far in the future. This suggests that we might modify the assumed demand function to make the present worth cost finite without changing the early decisions. Figure 5.4 indicates that we would have obtained very nearly the optimal initial decision in Example 5.4 if we had assumed no further growth in demand after, say, 30 years.

5.4 Special Cases—Exponential Demand That Looks Linear

Here we consider two interesting special cases of nonlinear demand—one with unbounded exponential growth, the other with saturating exponential growth. In both cases, capacity cost is assumed to be a power function $C(x) = Kx^\alpha$. It turns out that the solution of these problems is equivalent to that of certain problems with linear demand. As in the case of linear demand, the optimal relief intervals are constant over time; only here, of course, the optimal expansion *sizes* vary with time.

5.4.1 Unbounded Exponential Growth

Suppose the cumulative demand at time t is

$$D(t) = Q(e^{gt} - 1), \qquad (5.8)$$

where Q and g are positive numbers. Let $H(t)$ be the cost of installing sufficient capacity at time 0 to last until t:

$$H(t) \equiv K[D(t) - D(0)]^{\alpha},$$

or

$$H(t) = KQ^{\alpha}(e^{gt} - 1)^{\alpha}. \tag{5.9}$$

The cost at time τ of adding capacity to last until time t is

$$K[D(t) - D(\tau)]^{\alpha} = KQ^{\alpha}[e^{gt} - e^{g\tau}]^{\alpha}$$

$$= KQ^{\alpha}e^{\alpha g\tau}[e^{g(t-\tau)} - 1]^{\alpha}$$

$$= e^{\alpha g\tau}H(t-\tau). \tag{5.10}$$

In words, this says that the cost of providing capacity for the time interval τ to t is the cost of providing capacity for the same interval starting at time 0 multiplied by the growth factor $e^{\alpha g\tau}$.

Suppose capacity is added at times $t_0, t_1, t_2, \ldots$, where $t_0 = 0$ and the other t_i are to be determined. The total present worth cost will be

$$W = \sum_{i=0}^{\infty} e^{-rt_i} e^{\alpha g t_i} H(t_{i+1} - t_i),$$

or

$$W = \sum_{i=0}^{\infty} e^{-\nu t_i} H(t_{i+1} - t_i), \tag{5.11}$$

where

$$\nu \equiv r - \alpha g. \tag{5.12}$$

But now, if ν is positive, Equation (5.11) is precisely the same form as Equation (4.1) in the linear demand case with ν replacing r and $H(t_{i+1} - t_i)$ replacing $C[x(t_i, t_{i+1})]$. Thus, by the same argument as in Section 4.1, the optimal relief interval is constant over time, and is the value of τ that minimizes

$$W = \frac{H(\tau)}{1 - e^{-\nu\tau}}. \tag{5.13}$$

Example 5.5. Suppose that the discounting rate is $r = 0.1$, the cost of x units of additional capacity is $C(x) = 9x^{0.6}$, and demand is projected to be

$$D(t) = 15(e^{0.08t} - 1).$$

Then the effective discounting rate is

$$\nu = r - \alpha g = 0.1 - (0.6)(0.08) = 0.052,$$

and the cost of serving customers arriving from time 0 to t is

$$H(t) = 9(15)^{0.6}(e^{0.08t} - 1)^{0.6} = 45.7(e^{0.08t} - 1)^{0.6}.$$

Thus, the optimal relief interval minimizes

$$\frac{45.7(e^{0.08\tau}-1)^{0.6}}{1-e^{-0.052\tau}},$$

which is plotted in Figure 5.5. From Figure 5.5 we see that the optimal relief interval is $\tau \approx 8$ years, which corresponds to $x = 15(e^{(0.08)8} - 1) = 13.5$ for the capacity of the initial system. Of course, the optimal size of subsequent systems will be larger since with exponential growth, more demand will arrive in subsequent 8-year intervals. //

The discussion so far has assumed that the parameter ν [Equation (5.12)] is positive. If the growth rate is large or the economies of scale are not very pronounced (i.e., large α), it is possible that ν will be 0 or negative. In that case, the sum in Equation (5.11) will diverge. That is, the present worth cost will be infinite as it was in Example 5.4. Using the notion of optimality that we developed in Example 5.4, we show in Appendix 3 to this chapter that the optimal relief interval is the τ that minimizes

$$h = \frac{\nu H(\tau)}{1 - e^{-\nu\tau}}, \tag{5.14}$$

Figure 5.5. Present worth cost versus relief interval in Example 5.5.

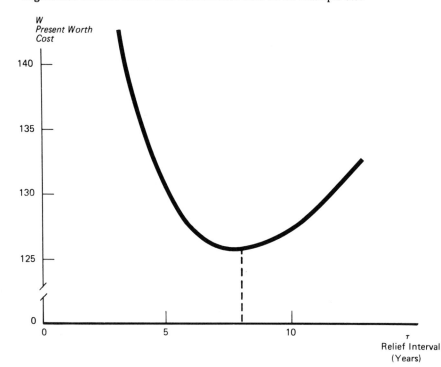

which reduces to

$$h = \frac{H(\tau)}{\tau} \qquad (5.15)$$

if $\nu = 0$ and, of course, gives the same result as (5.13) when $\nu > 0$.

Example 5.6. Consider the following variant of Example 5.4. Let $r = 0.1$, $D(t) = 2(e^{0.2t} - 1)$ as in Example 5.4; but suppose $C(x) = 9x^{0.6}$ instead of the form $A + Bx$ assumed there. Then we can apply the special formulas developed here. We calculate $\nu = r - \alpha g = 0.1 - (0.6)(0.2) = -0.02$; and since this is negative, use (5.14):

$$h = \frac{(-0.02)9(2)^{0.6}(e^{0.2\tau} - 1)^{0.6}}{1 - e^{0.02\tau}},$$

or

$$h = \frac{0.27(e^{0.2\tau} - 1)^{0.6}}{e^{0.02\tau} - 1}.$$

Trying several values of τ, we find that the optimum is at about $\tau = 6.4$ years. We note that this solution is considerably different from the value of $\tau = 8.3$ found for the initial expansion in Example 5.4. Since the capacity cost function used here is one we have used previously as an approximation to the capacity cost function of Example 5.4, we might have expected better agreement. Part of the difference in results can be explained by looking at Figure 3.4. This shows that the two capacity cost functions, $16 + 2x$ and $9x^{0.6}$, are nearly identical around $x = 12$. In our current problems, the sizes corresponding to $\tau = 6.4$ and 8.3 are 5.19 and 8.52, respectively. If we had chosen K and α so that the two capacity cost curves coincide for smaller values of x, the results of Example 5.4 and this one would have been more similar. Of course, we cannot expect perfect agreement since the two problems *are*, in fact, different; but we may decide that the agreement is sufficient for many practical situations. This would allow us to use the much simpler optimization procedure illustrated here for problems with exponentially growing demand even when the capacity cost is not of the form Kx^{α}. //

5.4.2 Saturating Exponential Growth

Suppose the cumulative demand at time t is

$$D(t) = D_{\infty}(1 - e^{-gt}), \qquad (5.16)$$

where g is a positive number and D_{∞} is a positive number that represents the ultimate, or saturation, level of demand. As before, let $H(t)$ be the cost of installing sufficient capacity at time 0 to last until t:

$$H(t) = K[D(t) - D(0)]^{\alpha},$$

or

$$H(t) = KD_{\infty}^{\alpha}(1 - e^{-gt})^{\alpha}. \tag{5.17}$$

It is straightforward to show that the following property, analogous to (5.10), holds:

$$K[D(t) - D(\tau)]^{\alpha} = e^{-\alpha g\tau}H(t - \tau); \tag{5.18}$$

therefore, as in (5.11), the total present worth cost is

$$W = \sum_{i=0}^{\infty} e^{-\nu t_i}H(t_{i+1} - t_k), \tag{5.19}$$

where $\nu \equiv r + \alpha g$ (note that it was $r - \alpha g$ before). We again conclude that the optimal relief interval is constant over time and is the value of τ that minimizes (5.13), but with the new definitions of H and ν. Of course, successive relief sizes will now decrease rather than increase.

Example 5.7. Consider a problem similar to Example 5.5 with discounting rate $r = 0.1$ and capacity cost $C(x) = 9x^{0.6}$, but now with the saturating demand $D(t) = 15(1 - e^{-0.08t})$. Then the effective discounting rate is

$$\nu = r + \alpha g = 0.1 + (0.6)(0.08) = 0.148,$$

and the cost of serving customers arriving between 0 and t is

$$H(t) = 9(15)^{0.6}(1 - e^{-0.08t})^{0.6} = 45.7(1 - e^{-0.08t})^{0.6}.$$

Thus, the optimal relief interval minimizes

$$W = \frac{45.7(1 - e^{-0.08\tau})^{0.6}}{1 - e^{-0.148\tau}}.$$

Trying a few values indicates that the minimum occurs at about $\tau = 12.3$, which corresponds to $x = 15(1 - e^{-0.08(12.3)}) = 9.4$ for the initial system. We note that this is a longer relief interval, but a smaller size than the corresponding $\tau = 8$ and $x = 13.5$ in Example 5.5, just as we might have anticipated by looking at the two demand functions. //

We could go on to analogous results for the case $\nu < 0$, but these are not as interesting, since they would require a negative discounting rate r, which is unlikely in view of the discussion in Chapter 2.

5.4.3 Generalizations

The power function capacity cost and exponential growth cases we have considered in the previous two sections as well as the linear growth model of Chapters 3 and 4 are all examples in which a property such as (5.10) holds. This property makes it possible for us to obtain (5.11) and conclude that the optimal relief interval is constant and satisfies (5.13) or (5.14).

We note here that the property given by (5.10) is essentially all that is required to obtain these results. That is, if that property holds, then the problem looks like one with linear growth.

5.5 Discussion

In Chapters 3 and 4 we had assumed that demand for additional capacity would grow linearly into the indefinite future. Here we discussed what happens when we make various other assumptions about the demand function. Our results ranged from minor modifications of the linear growth calculations to allow jumps in demand at $t = 0$; to dynamic programming formulations for general nonlinear demand; to special cases of exponential demand that look linear.

A new phenomenon that does not come up when demand is linear is that present worth cost may be infinite. We showed that it is possible to solve some of these problems by considering solutions over increasingly large, but finite, horizons. These solutions further emphasize our observations of Chapter 4 that initial decisions tend to be little affected by assumptions about the distant future. This insensitivity is fortunate, indeed, in view of our typically monumental ignorance of the future.

5.6 Further Reading

The forward dynamic programming approach of Section 5.3 and Appendix 2 to this chapter is adapted from Sinden's paper, cited in Chapter 4. The treatment of exponential demand in Section 5.4 and Appendix 3 to this chapter is from

R. L. Smith, General Horizon Results for the Deterministic Capacity Problem, *Proc. International Conference on Communications, Vol. II*, 1976, 32-15–32-20.

Smith also discusses, in great detail, solving the finite-horizon expansion problem.

Appendix 1. Bounds on the Initial Relief Interval

Here we extend our observations about the sawtooth shape of the optimal size of the first expansion as shown in Figure 4.2 by allowing demand to be a nondecreasing function. To avoid technical difficulties, we assume that solutions of all optimizations are unique. This restriction can be lifted without major changes in the results. As in the text, we let $D(t)$ designate demand at time t; we let $0, t_1^*, t_2^*, t_3^*, \ldots$ be the relief times of the optimal infinite-horizon problem; and we let $t_1^n(T)$ be the optimal initial relief interval when demand up to time T is to be served with n capacity expansions.

Observation 1

$t_1^n(T)$ *is nondecreasing in T for fixed n.* This is clearly true for $n=1$. We shall demonstrate that it is also true for $n=2$ and leave the rest as a challenge to the interested reader. Figure 5.6 pictures what we are trying to establish. That is, suppose that t_1 is the optimal initial relief interval over the horizon T (the solid line stair step). Then, can it be that for some larger horizon T', $t_1' < t_1$ will be the size of the optimal initial relief (the dashed line stair step)? To show that this cannot happen, we generate a better solution for the T' horizon problem starting with the optimal one for the T horizon problem. From the optimality of the T horizon problem (see Figure 5.6 for symbols),

$$A + BD_1 + [A + B(D_2 - D_1)]e^{-rt_1} \le A + BD_1' + [A + B(D_2 - D_1')]e^{-rt_1'}. \quad (5.20)$$

Since $t_1' < t_1$,

$$B(D_2' - D_2)e^{-rt_1} \le B(D_2' - D_2)e^{-rt_1'}. \quad (5.21)$$

Adding these inequalities,

$$A + BD_1 + [A + B(D_2' - D_1)]e^{-rt_1} \le A + BD_1' + [A + B(D_2' - D_1')]e^{-rt_1'}. \quad (5.22)$$

Figure 5.6. Can optimal initial expansion size decrease with increasing horizon?

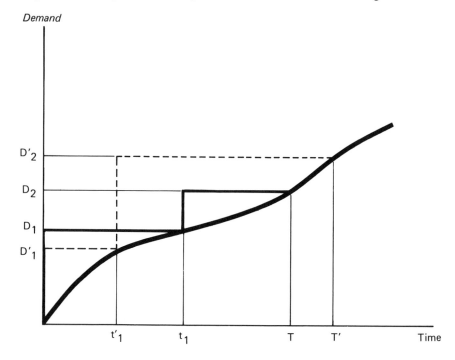

That is, it is better to use t_1 for the initial relief interval. This does not say that t_1 is still optimal for the T' horizon problem, only that t_1' cannot be optimal if $t_1' < t_1$, which establishes Observation 1.

Observation 2

$t_1^m(T) \le t_1^n(T)$ *whenever* $m \ge n$, *for any* T.   We do the case $m = 3$, $n = 2$ and leave the rest to the reader. Suppose that the optimal 2-expansions solution over the horizon T is given by expansions at times 0 and t_1 and that an optimal 3-expansions solution over T is given by expansions at 0, t_1', and t_2'. Now consider the 2-expansions problem over the shorter horizon t_2'. The optimal solution of this problem must have expansions at times 0 and t_1' (otherwise we could improve upon the 3-expansions problem over T). By observation 1, $t_1' < t_1$ since t_1' is the optimal initial expansion in a shorter-horizon problem, which establishes Observation 2.

Observation 3

The number of expansions in the optimal solution over T years is nondecreasing with T.   As before, we demonstrate only for a special case. Suppose expansions at times 0 and t_1 are optimal for the T horizon problem (i.e., it is optimal to use 2 expansions). Then for any $T' > T$, we can easily generate a solution that is better than the single expansion for the T' horizon problem as follows:

$$A + BD_1 + [A + B(D_2 - D_1)]e^{-rt_1} \le A + BD_2 \qquad (5.23)$$

by optimality of expansions at 0 and t_1, where $D_1 = D(t_1), D_2 = D(T)$. Now, letting $D_3 = D(T')$,

$$B(D_3 - D_2)e^{-rt_1} \le B(D_3 - D_2); \qquad (5.24)$$

therefore, adding the inequalities gives

$$A + BD_1 + [A + B(D_3 - D_1)]e^{-rt_1} \le A + BD_3. \qquad (5.25)$$

That is, it is better to add the extra capacity at t_1 than at time 0. Thus, the single expansion cannot be optimal, which establishes Observation 3.

Observation 4

Whenever $T = t_n^*$, *a relief time for the infinite-horizon problem, the optimal finite-horizon solution is identical to the infinite-horizon solution.*   If not, substitute the finite-horizon solution for the first n expansions of the infinite-horizon solution and vice versa. It is interesting to note that this observation holds for a general capacity cost function.

Putting all of these observations together, we conclude that the size of the initial expansion must have, basically, the characteristics of Figure 4.2. That is, for small horizon times T, a single expansion will be optimal. As T increases, 2 expansions will become optimal (unless a single expansion is optimal for $T = \infty$). At this point there will be a downward jump in the size of the initial expansion. The highest value, immediately before the jump, is an upper bound on the optimal size of the initial expansion; and the lowest value, immediately after the jump, is a lower bound on the optimal size of the initial expansion. Recall that these bounds hold for *any* nondecreasing future demand. As T increases further, the size of the initial expansion increases, passing through its infinite-horizon optimum. (Of course, at this point we don't know what that optimum is.) Eventually, it becomes better to use 3, rather than 2 expansions, and the size of the initial expansion takes another downward jump. Its extreme values at the jump define new bounds on the infinite-horizon optimum that are at least as good as the previous ones; and so on.

Since we have been using an unspecified (but nondecreasing) demand function, the bounds established by this process at any given horizon time apply for *any* future demand function beyond the horizon time.

Appendix 2. Recursive Equations for the Finite-Horizon Problem

Suppose we expand capacity at times designated $0, t_1, \ldots, t_{n-1}$. The present worth cost is

$$w = \sum_{i=1}^{n} \left\{ A + B[D(t_i) - D(t_{i-1})] \right\} e^{-rt_{i-1}}. \tag{5.26}$$

Setting $0 = dw/dt_i$ and rearranging terms gives

$$D(t_{i+1}) = D(t_i) + D'(t_i) \frac{e^{r(t_i - t_{i-1})} - 1}{r} - \frac{A}{B}, \tag{5.27}$$

where D' is the derivative and the equation holds for $i = 1, \ldots, n-1$ when we define $t_0 = 0$ and $t_n = T$, the horizon time.

With $D(t) = Q(e^{gt} - 1)$ as in Example 5.4, we can solve for t_{i+1}:

$$t_{i+1} = \frac{1}{g} \ln \left\{ e^{gt_i} \left[1 + \frac{g}{r} (e^{r(t_i - t_{i-1})} - 1) \right] - \frac{A}{BQ} \right\}. \tag{5.28}$$

Although in principle we could solve (5.27) or (5.28) backward, starting with $t_n = T$, it is easier to start with t_1 and iterate n times to get t_n. Then t_1 is the optimal initial relief interval for the horizon $T = t_n$. Each of the curves labeled 1 expansion, 2 expansions, 3 expansions, and so forth, on Figure 5.4 can be generated readily in this fashion. The points at which the curve jumps from 1 expansion being optimal to 2 being optimal, and so forth, can be found readily by substituting the sequences of t_i generated by (5.28) into (5.26).

Note that Figure 4.2 can be generated this way using $D(t) = gt$ in (5.27).

Appendix 3. Optimal Relief Interval When $\nu \leq 0$

Given relief times $0 = t_0, t_1, \ldots$, Equation (5.11) is the present worth cost

$$W = \sum_{i=0}^{\infty} e^{-\nu t_i} H(t_{i+1} - t_i). \tag{5.29}$$

Here we think of $H(t_{i+1} - t_i)$ as a cost incurred at time t_i that is to be discounted to time 0 at the rate ν. Equivalently, we may think of paying an amount h_{i+1} per unit time over the interval t_i to t_{i+1}, where h_{i+1} is defined by

$$\int_{t_i}^{t_{i+1}} h_{i+1} e^{-\nu t}\, dt = e^{-\nu t_i} H(t_{i+1} - t_i), \tag{5.30}$$

or

$$h_{i+1} \equiv \frac{\nu H(t_{i+1} - t_i)}{1 - e^{-\nu(t_{i+1} - t_i)}}. \tag{5.31}$$

Then (5.29) becomes

$$W = \sum_{i=0}^{\infty} \int_{t_i}^{t_{i+1}} h_{i+1} e^{-\nu t}\, dt, \tag{5.32}$$

or if we define

$$h(t) \equiv h_{i+1} \quad \text{whenever} \quad t_i < t \leq t_{i+1},$$

$$W = \int_0^{\infty} h(t) e^{-\nu t}\, dt. \tag{5.33}$$

In case $\nu < 0$, W is infinite, and so we are interested in

$$W_T \equiv \int_0^T h(t) e^{-\nu t}\, dt \tag{5.34}$$

as T gets large. Now it should be intuitively clear that W_T will be minimized for all sufficiently large horizon times if successive relief intervals $t_{i+1} - t_i$ are chosen so as to minimize (5.31). Figure 5.7 illustrates this. Since the lower $h(t)$ function is never above the upper one, it will yield a lower value of W in (5.34).

Figure 5.7. Equivalent cost per unit time (Appendix 3).

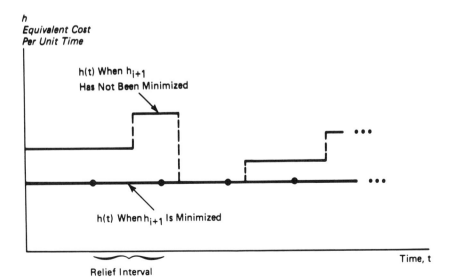

Chapter 6

The Interaction of Two Different Capacity Types

Up to now we have assumed that there is only one type of capacity subject to expansion. Here we study a situation in which two different types of demands and capacities interact.

Example 6.1. A deluxe machine that produces close-tolerance plastic bushings for the aircraft industry can also be used to make knobs for radio and TV sets. Since tolerances are less critical in the latter application, a less expensive standard machine could do the job. In the face of rising demand for both products, and economies-of-scale in the cost of the machines, the manufacturer plans to add enough capacity to serve demand anticipated well into the future. But what *type* of machine should he add, and what size? Clearly, this problem can be solved, in general, only by looking at *both* of the capacity types simultaneously. //

There are many instances of interactions of this kind, different ones requiring different modeling assumptions. We shall focus on a particular problem, abstracted from a telephone application to be discussed in Chapter 10. But our solution methods, especially the approximations of Section 6.3, should have a more general applicability.

This chapter should be viewed as illustrating how much more difficult the simple capacity expansion problem can become if we need to keep track of more than one capacity type. With the assumptions we make here (Section 6.1), it turns out that a relatively favorable dynamic programming formulation is still possible (Section 6.2). The main point, however, is that we can learn a great deal about this problem from our knowledge of the problem we have studied thus far in which there is a single capacity type. That is, we can develop very good approximate solutions (Section 6.3) with significantly less computational effort than the dynamic program. Furthermore, we can tell quickly (Section 6.4) when the expansion problem in which there are two capacity types, considered here, degenerates into the simple single capacity type problem.

6.1 Statement of the Problem

We suppose that there are two *types* of demand. A *standard*, generally less expensive, type of capacity can serve only the standard demand, while a *deluxe* capacity can serve both the standard and deluxe demand. We make the same general assumptions as in the simple single capacity type problem we have studied so far (e.g., durable capacity and no restrictions on the number of expansions). In addition, we assume that

1. Demand in each of the two types grows linearly (deterministically) over time.
2. Capacity can be added in any positive size (continuum of sizes).
3. There is no difference in the cost of *using* the two types (only of buying them in the first place).
4. The cost of rearranging demand from one facility type to the other is negligible.

These assumptions correspond reasonably well to some real-world applications and make the problem mathematically tractable, although certainly not as simple as the single capacity type problem.

We start our analysis with a discussion of what constitutes a shortage of capacity. Let $D_1(t)=D_1(0)+g_1t$ be the demand that can be served only by the deluxe facility; $D_2(t)=D_2(0)+g_2t$ be the demand for the standard facility; and X_1, X_2 be the available capacities of the two types. Under our assumptions, an expansion will next be required either when we run out of deluxe capacity, defined by

$$D_1(0)+g_1t=X_1, \tag{6.1}$$

or when we run out of combined capacity

$$D_1(0)+g_1t+D_2(0)+g_2t=X_1+X_2. \tag{6.2}$$

This prompts us to think of spare capacity as a 2-dimensional quantity, the spare in deluxe capacity

$$s_1(t)=X_1-D_1(0)-g_1t\equiv s_1(0)-g_1t \tag{6.3}$$

and the spare in combined capacity

$$s_{12}(t)\equiv X_1+X_2-D_1(0)-D_2(0)-(g_1+g_2)t$$
$$\equiv s_{12}(0)-(g_1+g_2)t. \tag{6.4}$$

Thus, starting with initial spare capacities of $s_1(0)$ and $s_{12}(0)$, the next shortage of facilities will be at

$$t = \min\left[\frac{s_1(0)}{g_1}, \frac{s_{12}(0)}{g_1 + g_2}\right]. \tag{6.5}$$

The addition of deluxe capacity (of size x_1, say) adds to both the deluxe and combined spare, while the addition of standard capacity (of size x_2, say) only adds to the combined spare. Thus, if we start with $s_1(0)$ and $s_{12}(0)$ spare at time 0 and add capacities of size x_1 and x_2, the resulting spare will be

$$s_1' = s_1(0) + x_1,$$

$$s_{12}' = s_{12}(0) + x_1 + x_2. \tag{6.6}$$

Clearly, we would only want to add one type of capacity at any given time. (The other can always be postponed for a savings in present worth.) Furthermore, if the shortage is in deluxe capacity [the first term in Equation (6.6) is smaller], we *must* add deluxe capacity; while for a combined shortage we could add either.

6.2 Dynamic Programming Solution

We are now in a position to write a dynamic programming formulation of this problem:

$$W(s_1, s_{12}) = \min_{x_1, x_2} \left\{ C_1(x_1) + C_2(x_2) \right.$$

$$\left. + W[s_1(x_1, x_2), s_{12}(x_1, x_2)] e^{-r\tau(x_1, x_2)} \right\}, \tag{6.7}$$

where

$W(s_1, s_{12})$ is the present worth cost of optimally satisfying all future demand starting with spare levels of s_1 and s_{12}

$x_1, x_2, C_1(x_1)$, and $C_2(x_2)$ are the sizes and costs of capacity expansions in the two types

$\tau(x_1, x_2)$ is the time of the next shortage starting with s_1 and s_{12} spare plus expansions of size x_1 and x_2:

$$\tau(x_1, x_2) \equiv \min\left(\frac{s_1 + x_1}{g_1}, \frac{s_{12} + x_1 + x_2}{g_1 + g_2}\right) \tag{6.8}$$

$s_1(x_1, x_2)$ and $s_{12}(x_1, x_2)$ are the levels of spare in deluxe and combined capacity at the time of next shortage, starting with s_1, s_{12}, spare capacity and adding x_1, x_2:

$$s_1(x_1, x_2) \equiv s_1 + x_1 - g_1\tau(x_1, x_2),$$

$$s_{12}(x_1, x_2) \equiv s_{12} + x_1 + x_2 - (g_1 + g_2)\tau(x_1, x_2). \tag{6.9}$$

Since we are interested in capacity expansions only when there is a shortage, we can restrict our attention to combinations of spare levels, s_1, s_{12} in which *at least one of them is* 0. Note that one of the quantities given by (6.9) *will* always be 0. Thus the state space of the dynamic program (6.7) is really only 1-dimensional—a very important computational consideration. Moreover, the minimization over x_1 and x_2, as has already been indicated, is also 1-dimensional. (It never pays to expand both at once.)

Example 6.2. Consider the expansion problem involving two types of capacity whose parameters are given in Table 6.1. For a discounting rate of $r = 0.07$, what is the optimal expansion policy starting with no spare of either capacity type? Solution via the dynamic program (6.7) is a relatively straightforward computer exercise. Figure 6.1 plots the resulting present worth cost versus spare. Toward the right of the origin, combined spare s_{12} increases from 0 with deluxe spare s_1 held at 0. Toward the left from the origin, s_1 increases from 0 while s_{12} stays at 0. Figure 6.2 shows the corresponding optimal expansion size and type for each spare level. Note that standard expansions (x_2 scale at the left) are optimal on the left side (for $s_1 > 140$) and deluxe expansions (x_1 scale at the right) are optimal on the right side.

The optimal policy may be found from the data plotted in Figure 6.2 and Equations (6.8), (6.9). Starting with $s_1 = s_{12} = 0$, the optimal expansion is about $x_1 = 693$ (see Figure 6.2). From (6.8), the time of the next shortage is

$$\tau = \min\left(\frac{0+693}{40}, \frac{0+693+0}{160} \right) = 4.33 \text{ years.}$$

At that time, the spare capacities will be [Equation (6.9)]

$$s_1 = 0 + 693 - (40)(4.33) = 520,$$

$$s_{12} = 0.$$

Referring to Figure 6.2 again, the optimal expansion is then of standard type, $x_2 = 1,045$. Again, finding the time interval until the next shortage

Table 6.1. Data on the Two Capacity Types for Example 6.2

Type i	Demand growth g_i	Capacity cost $C_i(x) = A_i + B_i x$
1 (deluxe)	40	$1 + 0.005x$
2 (standard)	120	$1 + 0.003x$

138

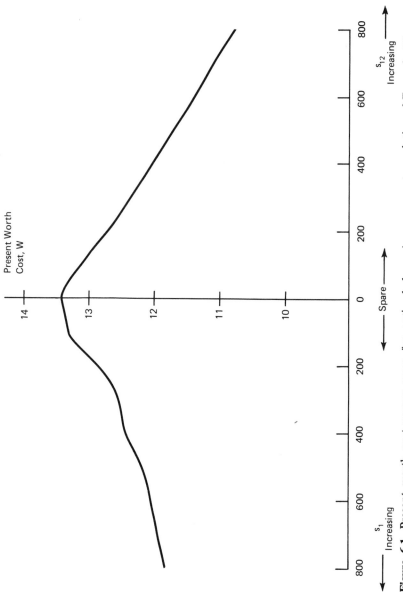

Figure 6.1. Present worth cost versus spare for optimal dynamic programming solution of Example 6.2.

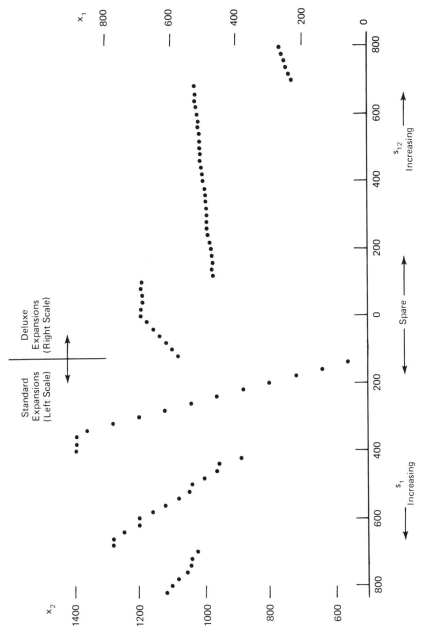

Figure 6.2. Optimal expansion size versus spare at the time of expansion for Example 6.2.

Table 6.2. Solution of Capacity Expansion Problem with Two Capacity Types (Example 6.2)

Time	Spare		Expansion	
(years)	s_1	s_{12}	x_1	x_2
0	0	0	690	
4.3	520	0		1,045
10.9	260	0		1,040
17.3	0	0	690	
21.6	520	0		1,045
32.5	260	0		1,040
			$\vdots$	

(6.8) and the spare capacities at that shortage (6.9) gives

$$\tau = \min\left(\frac{520+0}{40}, \frac{0+0+1045}{160} \right) = 6.53 \text{ years,}$$

$$s_1 = 520 + 0 - (40)(6.53) = 258.5,$$

$$s_{12} = 0.$$

Since we have discretized the spare levels in steps of 20, we use the optimal size corresponding to $s_1 = 260$, $s_{12} = 0$, which is $x_2 = 1,040$ (see Figure 6.2.) Repeating the next shortage calculation gives

$$\tau = \min\left(\frac{258.5+0}{40}, \frac{0+0+1,040}{160} \right) = 6.46 \text{ years,}$$

$$s_1 = 0,$$

$$s_{12} = 0 + 1,040 - (160)(6.46) = 6.0 \approx 0.$$

Since both spare capacity types are 0 (for practical purposes), the same sequence of expansions would repeat. The solution is summarized in Table 6.2. The total present worth cost is read off from Figure 6.1 at 0 spare: $W(0,0) = 13.43$. //

Although the solution obtained in Example 6.2 was characterized as a straightforward computer exercise, it is not completely trivial. Judgment must be exercised, for instance, in choosing a discretization granularity for the spare levels and the capacity expansion sizes. Note that the present worth cost curve in Figure 6.1 is bumpy. It decreases with spare, but not in a convex fashion. We could not, expect, therefore, the dynamic programming minimization (6.7) to be unimodal in x_1 or x_2—in general, the program must try all values over some reasonable range. Similarly, there is no way a priori to limit the range of spare levels over which the optimization should be done. It turns out that in the usual case, a standard expansion will be optimal for sufficiently large levels of deluxe spare, s_1 (see Section 6.4). Thus, for a sufficiently large (but unknown at the outset) range of spare levels, the spare at the next shortage following the current expansion will lie within the same range. That is, the dynamic program over this finite interval will find the optimal solution.

Finally, a straightforward dynamic programming application leaves us wondering whether a solution such as the one shown in Figure 6.2 is just a scattering of points liable to change in some arbitrary fashion with changes in the data, or whether there is some simple underlying order. For instance, should we *expect* solutions that eventually return to a spare level of $s_1 = s_{12} = 0$? This appeared to be happening in Example 6.2, but with discretization errors one can never be certain. The approximate solutions explored in the following section help to answer these questions.

6.3 Approximate Solutions

It is not immediately obvious why the solution curves shown in Figure 6.1 and 6.2 should have the shape that they do. It turns out, however, that most of the points on the curves can be explained by some relatively simple observations that serve not only to enhance our understanding of this problem, but provide extremely good approximate solutions.

6.3.1 Formulation for Approximate Solution

For this formulation, we rewrite Equations (6.3), (6.4), which define a shortage

$$s_1(t) = s_1(0) + X_1(t) - g_1 t,$$
$$s_{12}(t) = s_{12}(0) + X_1(t) + X_2(t) - (g_1 + g_2)t, \qquad (6.10)$$

where $X_1(t)$, $X_2(t)$ are the total deluxe and standard capacities, respectively, added between time 0 and t. Our expansion problem requires that these spare levels be nonnegative. The nonnegativity conditions can be expressed as

$$X_1(t) \geq -s_1(0) + g_1 t,$$
$$X_2(t) \geq -s_{12}(0) + (g_1 + g_2)t - X_1(t). \qquad (6.11)$$

Thus, if the sequence of deluxe expansions $X_1(t)$ were known, then the right-hand side of the second inequality could be treated as an effective demand for standard capacity (see Figure 6.3).

The expansion sequence for standard capacity $X_2(t)$, shown in Figure 6.3, is unlikely to be an optimal sequence. An optimal sequence is likely to take advantage of the jumps in the demand function occasioned by the addition of deluxe capacity. For example, if the initial expansion size x_2^1 is cut in half, it still will be enough to get past the jump corresponding to the

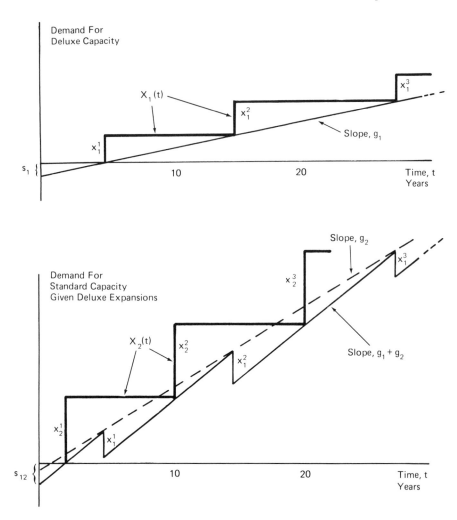

Figure 6.3. Expansion of two capacity types.

installation of x_1^1, advancing the next expansion by 3 years (only 35% of the original interval). Then if x_2^2 is increased slightly, it will be enough to get past the next jump corresponding to x_1^2, and so on. Figure 6.4 shows such a policy. Note that for the policy shown in Figure 6.4, the spare for *both* $s_1(t)$ and $s_{12}(t)$ goes to 0 at 5, 15, and 27.5 years.

We shall refer to expansion policies in which the total spares of both types periodically go to 0 as *coordinated* policies. If we restrict our attention to coordinated policies, it may be possible to reduce significantly the amount of searching that must be done, since the optimal expansion policy

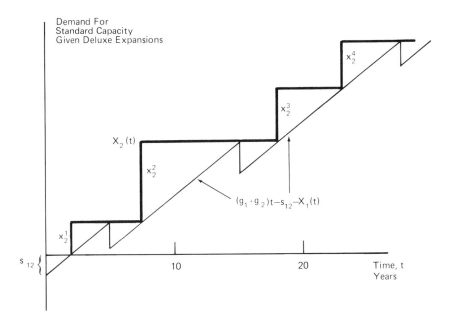

Figure 6.4. A coordinated standard expansion sequence for the demand of Figure 6.3.

can be taken to be identical between any two times at which total spare is 0.

6.3.2 Zero Levels of Spare

Here we illustrate the idea of coordinated policies on the two-types expansion problem of Example 6.2. Consider first a coordinated expansion policy of the form illustrated in Figure 6.5. That is, a deluxe expansion of size x_1 lasts until time t_{12}, at which time a standard expansion of size x_2 is undertaken that lasts until 0 total spare is once more achieved at time t_1. Observe that the choice of the initial deluxe expansion x_1 determines the entire policy t_1, t_{12}, x_2:

$$t_1 = x_1/g_1,$$

$$t_{12} = x_1/(g_1 + g_2),$$ \hfill (6.12)

$$x_2 = (g_1 + g_2)(t_1 - t_{12}) = \frac{g_2}{g_1} x_1.$$

The present worth cost can be written as

$$W = C_1(x_1) + W_2(x_2)e^{-rt_{12}} + We^{-rt_1},$$ \hfill (6.13)

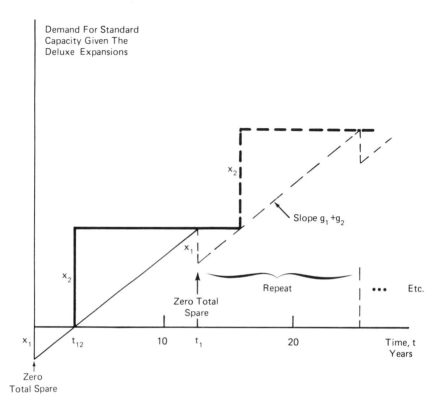

Figure 6.5. A coordinated expansion sequence starting with 0 total spare.

where

C_1 is the cost of the deluxe capacity x_1

W_2 is the cost of the standard expansion x_2, referenced to time t_{12}:

$$W_2(x_2) = C_2(x_2) = C_2\left(\frac{g_2}{g_1}x_1\right), \qquad (6.14)$$

with C_2 the cost of standard capacity.

Solving for W in (6.13) and expressing variables in terms of x_1 gives

$$W = \frac{C_1(x_1) + W_2\left(\dfrac{g_2}{g_1}x_1\right)e^{-rx_1/(g_1+g_2)}}{1 - e^{-rx_1/g_1}}. \qquad (6.15)$$

Example 6.3. For the growth and cost data used in Example 6.2 (see Table 6.1), the present worth cost is [Equations (6.14), (6.15)]

$$W_2(x_2) = 1 + \frac{120}{40}x_1 = 1 + 3x_1,$$

$$W = \frac{1 + 0.005x_1 + (1 + 3x_1)e^{-0.07x_1/(120+40)}}{1 - e^{-0.07x_1/40}}.$$

The curve marked $n=1$ in Figure 6.6 plots W versus x_1. The minimum occurs at a solution of about $x_1 = 470$ with a present worth cost of 13.57.

Figure 6.6. Present worth cost versus initial expansion size for some coordinated policies.

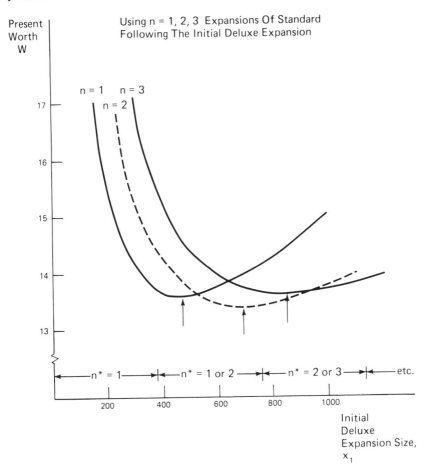

The corresponding standard expansion is given by (6.12):

$$x_2 = \frac{120}{40} 470 = 1{,}410.$$

Thus, the solution using the type of coordinated policy illustrated in Figure 6.5 is to install $x_1 = 470$ and, later, $x_2 = 1{,}410$. //

Note that the solution obtained in this example differs from that of Example 6.2 (see Table 6.2), although the present worth costs are not very different.

We next consider a variation of the simple coordinated policy illustrated in Figure 6.5. That is, instead of the single standard expansion x_2, we allow that expansion to be undertaken in two or more steps.

Given the initial deluxe expansion x_1, we can view the subproblem of determining the optimal schedule of standard expansions until the following deluxe expansion as a finite-horizon problem (discussed in Section 4.2). Referring to Figure 6.5, the finite-horizon problem is to supply standard capacity for demand growing at the rate $g_1 + g_2$ over the time interval t_{12} to t_1. If we had a solution to this finite-horizon problem, we could use it to replace Equation (6.14) for $W_2(x_2)$ and calculate the present worth using Equation (6.15) as before. Since a complete analysis of the finite-horizon problem is rather involved, we choose, instead, to approximate $W_2(x_2)$ by considering equal-sized expansions. The present worth cost $W_2(x_2, n)$ of supplying a total capacity of x_2 in n equal steps is given and discussed in the appendix [Equation (6.28)] and is illustrated by the following example.

Example 6.4. The calculations shown in Example 6.3 can be viewed as a special case in which the standard expansion is done in a single step [i.e., with $n = 1$ in Equations (6.27) and (6.28)]. For the same data, Figure 6.6 shows the analogous results for $n = 2$ and $n = 3$. The overall minimum is achieved at $x_1 = 693$ for $n = 2$. The sizes of the corresponding standard expansions are (6.27)

$$x_2^2 = \frac{1}{2}\left(\frac{120}{40} 693 \right) = 1{,}039.5,$$

and the present worth cost [using Equation (6.28) for W_2 in Equation (6.15)] turns out to be 13.43. //

Comparing the approximate solution obtained here with the "exact" solution obtained in Example 6.2, we note that the present worth cost and the initial expansion size turned out identical to within the accuracy shown. This is reassuring since the initial expansion is generally of the most immediate concern. The next two expansions (standard capacity) turned out slightly different, but it is not clear which are more nearly optimal. Recall that in Example 6.2 since we had calculated the optimal solution only for spare capacity increments of 20, we still had to approximate to get the optimal sizes. In fact, in that example, when we ended up with spare capacity $s_1 = 0$, $s_{12} = 6.0$, we declared it to be approximately 0. In view of the analysis of this section, it is highly unlikely that it would be truly optimal to add enough standard capacity to end up with a nonzero s_{12} at that point.

In Example 6.4, we simply tried several values of n to find the optimal number of standard expansions. The Appendix at the end of the chapter shows that for the usual capacity cost functions it is never necessary to try more than *two* values of n if we know the optimal solution to the infinite-horizon, single capacity type problem with expansion cost $C_2(x)$ and growth rate $g_1 + g_2$. Example 6.8 illustrates this using the same data as in Example 6.4.

So far, we have limited our attention to coordinated policies of the form illustrated in Figure 6.5, that is, a deluxe expansion x_1 followed later by standard expansions totaling x_2. There are, of course, many other coordinated policies that potentially could come into play.

For example, Figure 6.7 shows a viable policy for a situation in which standard capacity displays much more economy-of-scale than, and is

Figure 6.7. A coordinated expansion policy that might hold if standard capacity displays strong economies-of-scale and is relatively inexpensive.

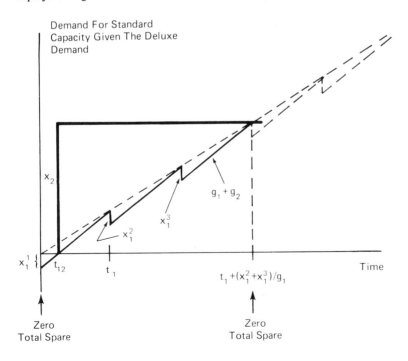

relatively inexpensive compared to, deluxe capacity. In such a situation the
deluxe expansions $(x_1^1, x_1^2, x_1^3, \ldots)$ basically would be determined by deluxe
demand alone; and standard expansions (x_2) would tend to be sized to
last until some deluxe expansion point. Note that Figure 6.7 can be viewed
as a generalization of Figure 6.5 in which larger x_2 values are allowed.

Another example is indicated in Figure 6.8. There, a policy is shown that
might be good if standard capacity is more expensive than in the previous
case, but is still less expensive than deluxe capacity on a sufficiently large
scale. Deluxe capacity (x_1^1, x_1^2) is used initially for both types of demand.
Then at some point a large standard expansion (x_2) becomes viable. Such
a situation is more likely if the demand growth rate for standard capacity
g_2 is small relative to that for deluxe capacity g_1. Note that Figure 6.8 can
be viewed as a special case of Figure 6.5 in which the initial deluxe
expansion x_1 is allowed to proceed in stages rather than in a single step.

Figure 6.8. A coordinated expansion policy that might hold if standard capacity
displays strong economies-of-scale and is relatively expensive.

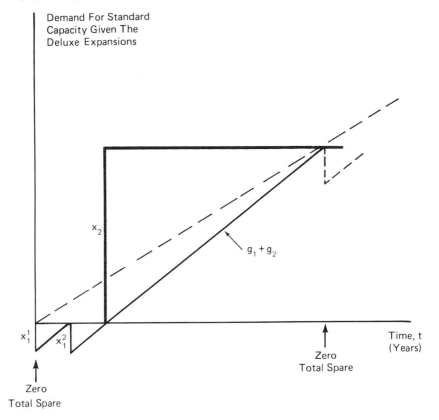

It turns out that coordinated policies of the forms illustrated by Figure 6.5 (a deluxe expansion followed by one or more standard expansions leading to 0 total spare), Figure 6.7 (deluxe, standard, one or more deluxe), and Figure 6.8 (deluxe expansions to satisfy both demands followed by standard expansion) provide very good approximations to the optimal policy over a wide range of parameter values.

6.3.3 Nonzero Levels of Spare

In the previous section we showed that it might be possible to obtain easily very good approximate solutions to our two-types capacity expansion problem. There we assumed a zero initial spare level for both capacity types. Here we show that the same idea of using coordinated policies can be employed fruitfully for determining near-optimal expansion sizes when spare is nonzero as well. This allows us to generate approximate solutions for direct comparison with the dynamic programming solutions obtained in Sections 6.2 (Figures 6.1 and 6.2).

Consider first a situation in which there is sufficient spare in deluxe capacity $[s_1(0) > 0]$, but there is a shortage in combined capacity $[s_{12}(0) = 0.]$ If $s_1(0)$ is large enough, typically it will be optimal to install standard capacity (more on this point in Section 6.4). In such a situation, the next deluxe expansion will have to be undertaken when[1] [see Equations (6.11)]

$$t_1 = \frac{s_1(0)}{g_1} ;$$

the resulting demand for standard capacity in the interim will be [the second of Equations (6.11)]

$$X_2(t) \geq (g_1 + g_2)t.$$

Figure 6.9 illustrates this. Note that there is a downward jump in the demand at t_1, the time of the next deluxe expansion. As we have already discussed in the previous section, the optimal standard expansion schedule is likely to be the solution of the finite-horizon problem with growth rate $g_1 + g_2$ over time interval 0 to t_1. Instead of finding the exact solution of this finite-horizon problem, we again note that a policy of using equal-sized expansions probably will be nearly optimal. At time t_1, there is again no spare of either type; therefore, the cost from that time onward, call it W_0, is known from the calculations of Section 6.3.2. The total present worth

---

[1]It may be optimal to do the deluxe expansion sooner than t_1, that is, to place deluxe capacity even though there is deluxe spare. This possibility is discussed later.

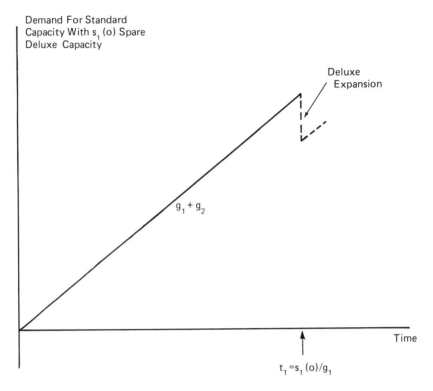

Figure 6.9. Demand for standard capacity when $s_1(0)$ spare deluxe capacity remains at the time of shortage.

cost using n equal standard expansions can be written

$$W = W_2(x_2, n) + W_0 e^{-rt_1}, \qquad (6.16)$$

where

$$t_1 = s_1(0)/g_1,$$

$$x_2 = (g_1 + g_2)t_1,$$

and W_2 is the present worth cost of adding x_2 standard capacity in n equal steps [given by Equations (6.27) and (6.28)].

Example 6.5. In Example 6.4 we found that the present worth cost of providing capacity for the problem of Example 6.2 was $W_0 = 13.43$ starting with no spare of either type. What would be the optimal expansion size and cost if we had spare deluxe capacity of $s_1 = 200$ and 0 combined spare (i.e., the 200 units of deluxe capacity are currently serving standard demand)? The time until the next deluxe expansion is

$$t_1 = \frac{200}{40} = 5 \text{ years.}$$

Over this period a total of

$$x_2 = (120 + 40)(5) = 800$$

units of standard capacity will have to be provided. Since this is less than the infinite-horizon optimal size $x_2^{**} = 1{,}133$, as calculated in Example 6.8, it is optimal to use a single expansion; thus,

$$W_2(800, 1) = C_2(800) = 1 + (0.003)(800) = 3.40,$$

and from (6.16) the total present worth cost is

$$W = 3.40 + 13.43e^{-(0.07)5} = 12.86.$$

Checking Figures 6.1 and 6.2, we find this solution indistinguishable from the solution obtained by dynamic programming. //

The results of similar calculations for various initial levels of $s_1(0)$ are plotted in the left half of Figures 6.10 and 6.11. The minimum of the curves in Figure 6.10 is nearly identical with the dynamic programming solution shown in Figure 6.1. There is a slightly greater discrepancy in the optimal sizes shown in Figure 6.11 (the optimal sizes of Figure 6.2 are also shown for comparison.) Over much of the range, the agreement is extremely good. The most notable failure is for small values of s_1 (see curve a in Figure 6.10, below $s_1 = 140$). In this range, it turns out optimal to *overdesign*—that is, to install deluxe capacity despite the existing deluxe spare. Better approximations for this region will be discussed shortly.

A slight anomaly is also evident at about $s_1 = 360{-}400$. Over this range, the approximation calls for a single standard expansion to cover the entire interval from time 0 to t_1 shown in Figure 6.9. The optimal solution turns out to use a smaller, single, standard expansion and to install the next deluxe expansion when that exhausts, prior to t_1 (i.e., to overdesign the *following* expansion). Our approximation would have to allow a considerably more complex coordinated strategy to capture this phenomenon. We note that only a small cost penalty appears to result from using the rougher approximation and do not pursue the matter further here.

We consider next the case in which an initial deluxe expansion is needed. These include, of course, the cases in which deluxe spare is 0 $[s_1(0) = 0, s_{12}(0) > 0]$, but also include cases with only a "small" deluxe spare $[s_1(0)$ small, $s_{12}(0) = 0]$, as discussed above. Coordinated policies for these cases are developed very much as in the case of 0 spare already studied in Section 6.3.2, only with slight modifications to account for the initial spare.

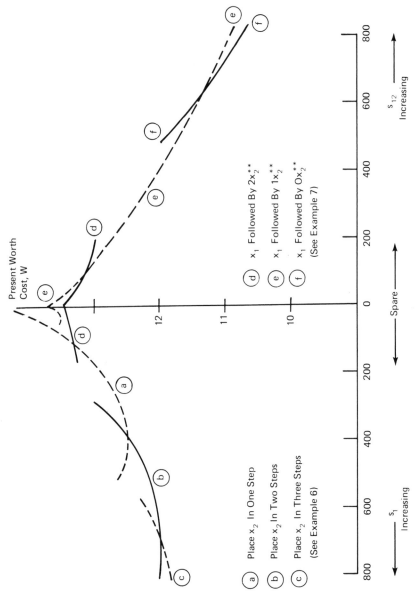

Figure 6.10. Present worth cost for approximate solutions.

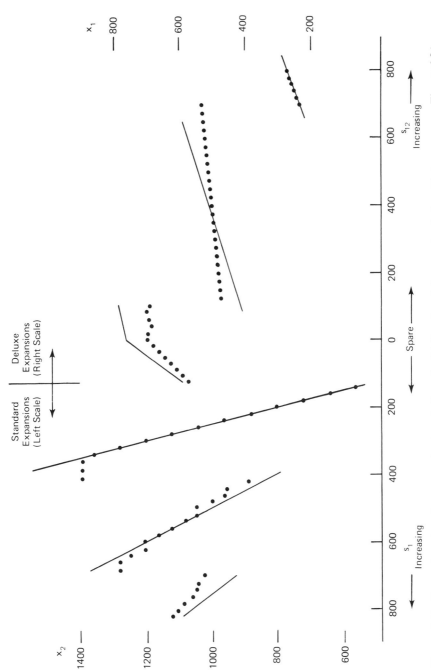

Figure 6.11. Expansion sizes for approximate solutions (solid lines) and for exact solution (dots—same as Figure 6.2.)

For the kind of situation shown in Figure 6.5, Equations (6.12) are replaced by

$$t_1 = \frac{s_1(0) + x_1}{g_1},$$

$$t_{12} = \frac{s_{12}(0) + x_1}{g_1 + g_2}, \qquad (6.17)$$

$$x_2 = (g_1 + g_2)(t_1 - t_{12}),$$

where t_{12} is the time of the next standard expansion, t_1 is the time of the following deluxe expansion, and x_2 is the total standard capacity that must be added between these standard expansions. The present worth cost, Equation (6.13), becomes

$$W = C_1(x_1) + W_2(x_2)e^{-rt_{12}} + W_0 e^{-rt_1}, \qquad (6.18)$$

where C_1 is the cost of deluxe capacity. W_2 is the cost of one or more standard expansions to provide a total of x_2 capacity [Equations (6.14) or (6.28)] and W_0 is the present worth cost of providing all future capacity starting with 0 total spare (assumed known from Section 6.3.2).

At this point it is straightforward to optimize the initial deluxe expansion x_1 and the corresponding standard expansions covering x_2 by a direct search as illustrated in Section 6.3.2 (e.g., see Examples 6.3, 6.4, and 6.8). It also may be useful to consider a further approximation that limits the search to certain promising sizes, as illustrated in the following example.

Example 6.6. In view of the discussion following Example 6.8, we should expect to obtain reasonably low costs if expansion sizes are chosen so that x_2, the total standard capacity required, is an integral number of the optimal sizes x_2^{**}. Recall that x_2^{**} is the optimal expansion for an auxiliary infinite-horizon problem in which only standard capacity is added to serve demand growing at the combined growth rate $g_1 + g_2$. In Example 6.8 it is indicated that $x_2^{**} = 1{,}133$ for the problem at hand. We can solve Equations (6.17) easily for x_1 in terms of x_2:

$$x_1 = \frac{g_1}{g_2}\left[x_2 + s_{12}(0) - \left(1 + \frac{g_2}{g_1}\right)s_1(0) \right]. \qquad (6.19)$$

We now examine the special case in which $s_1(0) = s_{12}(0) = 0$. Then

$$x_1 = \frac{40}{120}\left[n(1133) \right] = 378n,$$

for $n = 1, 2, \ldots$, will result in x_2 being precisely n times the optimal size x_2^{**}. The corresponding present worth cost for each n is obtained from (6.18). For this special case, however, essentially the same results can be obtained from Figure 6.6. The points $x_1 = 378$, 756, and 1,134 are shown there as the break points between the regions of x_1, where $n^* = 1$, $n^* = 1$ or 2, and $n^* = 2$

or 3. Note that each of these falls relatively near the minimum of its corresponding cost curve. The lowest cost is achieved for $n=2$, yielding $x_1 = 756$ and a present worth cost of 13.44. This compares favorably with the "exact" solution of $x_1 = 693$, $W = 13.43$ obtained earlier. //

Similar calculations can be carried out for various values of $s_1(0)$ and $s_{12}(0)$. The results are plotted in the right half of Figures 6.10 and 6.11. Once again, agreement with the dynamic programming solution is nearly perfect for this example. Of course, one should not infer that such good approximate solutions are always this easy to obtain. In general, we would expect to have to try a greater variety of promising solutions. For instance, it may be reasonable under some circumstances to try solutions whose initial deluxe expansion x_1 is near the optimum for the deluxe problem alone.

In conclusion, we have demonstrated that for the example studied earlier by dynamic programming, it is relatively easy to obtain approximate solutions that are very nearly optimal. Furthermore, Figure 6.10 goes further toward explaining the solutions (e.g., the bumps in W versus spare) than the corresponding Figure 6.1. This demonstration should *not* be viewed as an exhaustive description of how to obtain approximate solutions for these problems, but rather an illustration of how to proceed with such a task.

6.4 Solutions in an Extreme Case

So far, we have assumed that it will be optimal to use both types of capacity. The problem formulation dictates, of course, that deluxe expansions will be required as long as there is any growth in deluxe demand. However, depending on the costs and demand growth rates, it may not pay *ever* to use standard expansions. We show here that it will be optimal to use exclusively deluxe expansions if it is less expensive in total present worth cost to supply all demand $g_1 + g_2$ with deluxe capacity than it would be to supply all demand $g_1 + g_2$ with standard capacity (even though standard capacity cannot actually be used for deluxe demand). If this condition is not met, it will be optimal to use standard capacity for some expansions. The following development also shows that the present worth costs of supplying all demand $g_1 + g_2$ with deluxe and standard capacity provide upper and lower bounds, respectively, on the cost of the optimal solution.

Assume that there is initially no spare capacity of either type. It is easy to get an *upper bound* on total present worth cost by assuming that all capacity will be provided by deluxe facilities, since this is a feasible solution to the problem. The cost will be

$$W_1^{**} \equiv \min_x \frac{C_1(x)}{1 - e^{-r[x/(g_1+g_2)]}}, \qquad (6.20)$$

where $C_1(x)$ is the cost of deluxe capacity. This is just a simple one-type expansion problem analyzed in Chapters 3 and 4. It is also easy to get a *lower bound* on total present worth cost as follows. Suppose either capacity type could be used interchangeably to serve either type of demand. The cost would be

$$W_{12}^{**} \equiv \min_{x} \frac{C_{12}(x)}{1 - e^{-r[x/(g_1 + g_2)]}}, \qquad (6.21)$$

where

$$C_{12}(x) \equiv \min[C_1(x), C_2(x)]. \qquad (6.22)$$

That is, for any contemplated expansion size x, we would always use the less expensive capacity type. The minimization in (6.21) is equivalent to

$$W_{12}^{**} = \min(W_1^{**}, W_2^{**}), \qquad (6.23)$$

where W_2^{**} is the minimum present worth cost if we used standard capacity to satisfy all demand:

$$W_2^{**} = \min_{x} \frac{C_2(x)}{1 - e^{-r[x/(g_1 + g_2)]}}. \qquad (6.24)$$

Thus, we observe that if

$$W_1^{**} \leq W_2^{**}, \qquad (6.25)$$

then W_1^{**} is both an upper and a lower bound on the present worth cost, and thus (6.20) provides the optimal solution.

To recapitulate, if it is less expensive to provide capacity for all of the growth $(g_1 + g_2)$ with deluxe facilities (6.20) than with standard facilities (6.24), then it is optimal to use exclusively deluxe facilities [optimal size given by (6.20)]. If inequality (6.25) is not satisfied, then the two costs provide upper and lower bounds on the optimal cost W_{opt}:

$$W_2^{**} \leq W_{\text{opt}} \leq W_1^{**}. \qquad (6.26)$$

Example 6.7. Consider a two-type expansion problem in which the cost of each capacity type is given by an exponential function as studied in Section 3.3: $C_1(x) = K_1 x^{\alpha_1}$, $C_2(x) = K_2 x^{\alpha_2}$. If $K_2 < K_1$ and $\alpha_2 < \alpha_1$, then standard capacity is less expensive for any size expansion, and so it will pay to use standard capacity at some point [inequality (6.25) does not hold]. A more interesting case is one in which $K_2 > K_1$, but $\alpha_2 < \alpha_1$; that is, standard capacity is less expensive *in sufficiently large quantities only*. In this case, for very low growth rates, it will pay to use exclusively deluxe capacity [inequality (6.25) will hold].

Consider the parameter values $K_1 = 1$, $\alpha_1 = 0.77$ and $K_2 = 3$, $\alpha_2 = 0.58$. Recall from Section 3.3 that the optimal expansion interval for a one-type expansion problem with this form of capacity cost function depends only

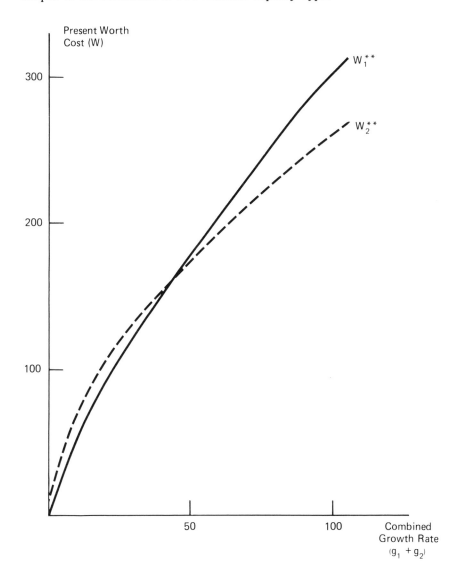

Figure 6.12. Present worth cost versus combined growth for deluxe (W_1^{**}) and standard (W_2^{**}) expansion costs.

on α. Using discounting rate $r = 0.1$, we obtain $t_1^{**} = 5$, $t_2^{**} = 10$ years, respectively, from Figure 6.3 of Section 3.3. The optimal sizes for the combined growth problem are $x_i^{**} = (g_1 + g_2)t_i^{**}$, and the present worth costs are

$$W_i^{**} = \frac{K_i\left[(g_1 + g_2)t_i^{**}\right]^{\alpha_i}}{1 - e^{-rt_i^{**}}}.$$

For the problem at hand,

$$W_1^{**} = \frac{(1)(5)^{0.77}}{1 - e^{-0.1(5)}} (g_1 + g_2)^{0.77} = 8.78(g_1 + g_2)^{0.77},$$

$$W_2^{**} = \frac{(3)(10)^{0.58}}{1 - e^{-0.1(10)}} (g_1 + g_2)^{0.58} = 18.04(g_1 + g_2)^{0.58}.$$

These costs versus the combined growth rate $(g_1 + g_2)$, are plotted in Figure 6.12. Note that below about $g_1 + g_2 = 45$, $W_1^{**} < W_2^{**}$, and so it would be best to use only deluxe facilities. Above that growth rate, the optimal solution would use a mix of the two, and the optimal cost would lie between the two curves. //

In case both types of capacity are to be used, the following further observation can be made: A standard expansion will be optimal for all sufficiently large levels of deluxe spare $s_1(0)$ at the time of expansion. To see this, note that the effective demand (see Section 6.3.2) for standard capacity is linear at a growth rate of $g_1 + g_2$ over a time horizon proportional to $s_1(0)$ (see Figure 6.9). Thus, as $s_1(0)$ gets large, the solution gets arbitrarily close to that given by (6.24). That is, as deluxe spare increases, eventually it becomes optimal to install standard capacity. Thus, it is optimal to use exclusively deluxe capacity if and only if inequality (6.25) holds.

This observation can be used to justify rigorously limiting the state space in the dynamic programming algorithm of Section 6.2, as was done in Example 6.2. Of course it does not indicate a priori just how large a state space will be necessary to ensure an optimal solution.

6.5 Conclusions

The capacity expansion problem becomes much more difficult when we need to keep track of different types of capacities interacting with one another. In this chapter we have dealt extensively with one such problem. We showed that our ability to solve the single capacity type problem could be used to great advantage. First, we developed detailed approximations (Section 6.3) that turned out to provide very good solutions for the sample problem studied, with much less computational effort than even the straightforward, 1-dimensional state space, dynamic programming solution (Section 6.2). In addition, we showed (Section 6.4) that solving two single capacity type problems would tell us when it would be optimal to use exclusively deluxe capacity to serve all demand and would provide quick upper and lower bounds on the optimal present worth cost.

The success of the approach in Section 6.3 in this problem suggests that it might be worth trying in other circumstances with different assumptions. In particular, one might be able to develop reasonable approximate solutions by looking at the effective demand for one type of capacity as a single capacity type problem based on some educated assumptions about expansions of the other capacity type(s).

6.6 Further Reading

Capacity expansion problems with more than one type of capacity have been around for some time. In the book edited by A. S. Manne (cited in Section 3.5), several chapters were devoted to problems with multiple producing areas. Goods produced in one area were assumed to be transportable to other areas, at a cost.

The dynamic programming formulation of Section 6.2 is essentially identical to that of

D. Erlenkotter, A Dynamic Programming Approach to Capacity Expansion with Specialization, *Management Science* 21(3), 1974, 360–362.

The coordinated policies of Section 6.3 are similar to the constant cycle approach found in A. S. Manne's book and the alternating policy approximation in

Lynn O. Wilson, and Andrew J. Kalotay, Alternating Policies for Non-Rearrangeable Networks, *INFOR* 14(3), October 1976, 193–211.

The analysis of Section 6.4 calculating bounds and finding conditions under which only one type of capacity would be used is also reminiscent of the approach taken by Wilson and Kalotay (and Kalotay in two earlier papers).

A different approach to problems of this kind is taken by

C. O. Fong, and M. R. Rao, Capacity Expansion with Two Producing Regions and Concave Costs, *Management Science* 22(3), November 1975, 331–339;

Hanan Luss, A Capacity Expansion Model for Two Facilities, *Naval Logistics Research Quarterly* 26(2), 1979, 291–303; A Network Flow Approach for Capacity Expansion Problems with Two Facility Types, *NLRQ* 27(4), 1980.

These authors allow nonlinear demand and develop extremal properties of the solution that are useful in computation.

Appendix. Approximate Solutions for a Finite-Horizon Problem

In Section 6.3, we need to solve a finite-horizon problem for demand growing at the rate $g_1 + g_2$ between times t_{12} and t_1 (see Figure 6.5). Here we develop and discuss the formulas for an approximate solution in which expansions of equal size are used. The size of each expansion will be

$$x_2^n \equiv \frac{1}{n} x_2 \tag{6.27}$$

when n expansions supply the total requirement of $x_2 = (g_1 + g_2)(t_1 - t_{12})$. The present worth cost of these expansions will be

$$W_2(x_2, n) = C_2(x_2^n)\left\{ 1 + e^{-r[x_2^n/(g_1 + g_2)]} + e^{-r[2x_2^n/(g_1 + g_2)]} \right.$$

$$\left. + \cdots + e^{-r[(n-1)x_2^n/(g_1 + g_2)]} \right\},$$

or, collapsing the sum,

$$W_2(x_2, n) = C_2(x_2^n) \frac{1 - e^{-r[x_2/(g_1 + g_2)]}}{1 - e^{-r[x_2^n/(g_1 + g_2)]}}. \tag{6.28}$$

We know from Chapter 4 that if x_2^n happens to equal the solution of an infinite-horizon problem with this same growth rate $g_1 + g_2$, it will also be optimal for the finite-horizon problem. Otherwise, we rely on the generally observed shallowness of present worth cost with respect to small perturbations in size (e.g., see Chapter 4).

A useful observation may be made concerning the form of the present worth cost function (6.28). That is, when the total capacity x_2 is fixed, W_2 as a function of x_2^n is identical in form to the objective function of the simple, linear growth, repeated expansion problem of Chapter 3 [see Equation (3.2) and Figure 3.1]:

$$W_2 = (\text{constant}) \frac{C_2(x_2^n)}{1 - e^{-r[x_2^n/(g_1 + g_2)]}}. \tag{6.29}$$

If we ignore the integer restriction on n [Equation (6.27)], the optimal expansion size x_2^{**} that minimizes (6.29) is just the solution of a simple capacity expansion problem as studied in Chapters 3 and 4 [capacity cost $C_2(x)$ and growth rate $g_1 + g_2$]. Provided that (6.29) has only the one local minimum [true for $C_2(x) = A_2 + B_2 x$; e.g., see Figure 3.1], the actual optimal size will correspond to the value of n that yields either the next smaller or next larger size than x_2^{**}. That is, the optimal number of expansions, n^* will be given by

$$n^* = [x_2/x_2^{**}] \quad \text{or} \quad [x_2/x_2^{**}] + 1, \tag{6.30}$$

where the square brackets denote the greatest integer less than this number.

Example 6.8. For the data of Example 6.2 (see Table 6.1) and discounting rate $r = 0.07$ as before, what values of n, the number of standard expansions, should have been tried in Example 6.4? For the given data, the present worth cost (6.29) is

$$W_2 = (\text{constant}) \frac{1 + 0.003 x_2^n}{1 - e^{-(0.07)x_2^n/(40 + 120)}},$$

which takes on a minimum (e.g., by methods of Chapter 3 or 4) at $x_2^{**} = 1,133$. From (6.30), we thus see that $n^* = 1$ ($n^* = 0$ is not allowed) if $x_2 \leq 1,133$; $n^* = 1$ or 2 if $1,133 \leq x_2 \leq 2(1,133)$; and so forth. In terms of the initial deluxe expansion x_1, this corresponds [Equation (6.12)] to $n^* = 1$ if $x_1 \leq (40/120)1,133 = 378$; $n^* = 1$ or 2 if $378 \leq x_1 \leq 755$; and so forth. These ranges have been plotted at the bottom of Figure 6.6. In the context of Figure 6.6, the point of this exercise is that within each of the ranges of x_1 shown, we need to consider at most *two* curves corresponding to the two values of $n = n^*$ indicated. No other number of standard expansions can be optimal. //

Finally, we note that Equation (6.28) suggests that some values of x_2 may be more favorable than others. That is, if the x_2^n that minimizes (6.29) happens to be an exact integer multiple of x_2^{**}, then W_2 will not have to be increased by rounding n [Equation (6.30)]. In the problem of this chapter, the total standard capacity x_2 depends on the initial deluxe expansion x_1 [Equations (6.12)]. We therefore would expect choices of x_1 that yield these favorable values of x_2 to be good candidates for nearly optimal policies. Example 6.6 illustrates this effect.

Chapter 7

Uncertain Demand

In Chapter 5 we generalized our earlier discussion by allowing demand to be some arbitrary nonlinear function of time. Here we consider the much more likely situation that we do not *know* at the outset just what the pattern of demand will be. Our ability to study this kind of problem is highly limited by our inability to specify exactly what we mean by "not knowing" what the demand will be. We assume that capacity expansion decisions *are*, in fact, made, and that they are made on the basis of *some* kind of information or assumptions about future demand.

One way of dealing with our ignorance might be to consider sensitivities of our decisions with respect to the demand assumed. We have already explored this approach in Chapters 4 and 5. In Section 4.1.2 we considered how our decision (or its cost) would be affected by changes in the cost of the future, while in Section 5.3, we considered the effect on our initial decision of demand being arbitrarily specified beyond some horizon time T. Both of these investigations revealed a considerable lack of sensitivity to ignorance about the future for the cases studied. We could go on and do further studies along similar lines, perhaps gaining further insights. Instead, we take a different approach that allows us to quantify the effects of uncertainty.

We assume that our ignorance about future demand can be quantified by probability statements such as, "There is a 10% chance that it will be longer than a year before demand exceeds 1,000 units." In order to make the specification and subsequent analysis tractable, we stick to well-known random processes as models for the demand. A lingering doubt about this approach is that once we have made the necessary assumptions and specified the parameters of the random process, we have, in fact, assumed much more knowledge of the future than we had originally intended. Nevertheless, this approach does allow us to analyze capacity expansion problems with demand projections having a quantified uncertainty and to explore systematically the effects of that uncertainty.

We assume throughout this chapter that it is appropriate to minimize the expected value of the present worth cost. While the full implications of such an assumption are beyond the scope of this book, the interested reader may wish to review Section 2.3 for a brief discussion of some effects of uncertainty on decision making.

In Sections 7.1 and 7.2 we study a formulation in which demand is determined by the random inward and outward movement of individual customers. When we assume, in Section 7.1, that the rates of inward and outward movement do not depend on the number of customers in the system, we find that the *random problem is equivalent to a deterministic one with a growth rate that is higher than the expected growth*. We show in Section 7.2 that similar conclusions (but not linear growth) hold even when transition rates depend on the number of customers in the system. In Section 7.1 we also discuss interpreting the random demand model as simply a quantification of our uncertainty and not necessarily as the physical movement of customers.

In Section 7.3 we use the simple model of Section 7.1 to show that there can be a significant economy-of-scale effect due to reduction of uncertainty when we aggregate demand.

In Section 7.4 we briefly examine what happens when we make other, less tractable, assumptions about the demand process. We show, for example, that a general Markov process formulation gives us greater flexibility, but a considerably greater computational burden.

The reader should be warned that the assumption of random demand in a more complex version of the capacity expansion problem than the one studied in this chapter is likely to be much more difficult. This will be illustrated by the analysis of capacity expansion with congestion costs in the Appendix to Chapter 8.

7.1 A Linear Demand Case

Suppose the demand for some facility is determined by the random inward and outward movement of customers. That is, the additional demand arising over any time interval is the difference between the number of inward and outward moves during the interval. In this section we assume that inward and outward movements are governed by independent Poisson processes with arrival rates λ and μ, respectively. This process does not represent an actual demand pattern perfectly in that it allows negative demand (more customers might leave than have arrived). For now, we shall assume that there are enough customers initially in the system to make such depletions highly unlikely. Our generalization of this demand process in Section 7.2 eliminates the problem.

We assume that capacity will be added whenever demand first reaches the existing capacity level, as illustrated in Figure 7.1.

One way to attack this problem might be to use an average or expected value of growth rate. We shall show later that the average growth rate for this process is just the difference between the inward and outward movement rates:

$$\bar{g} = \lambda - \mu. \tag{7.1}$$

We might guess that since the actual expansions may take place either earlier or later than indicated by this growth rate, we should do fairly well simply by using it as a linear growth forecast for a deterministic problem. This is particularly the case in view of the previously cited insensitivity of decisions to changes in demand. In this section we shall demonstrate quantitatively the extent to which this conjecture is true.

We shall show that the solution of the problem with random demand is identical to one with an equivalent deterministic growth rate of demand $\hat{g}$. We shall show that this equivalent deterministic growth is always greater

Figure 7.1. Capacity expansions for random demand.

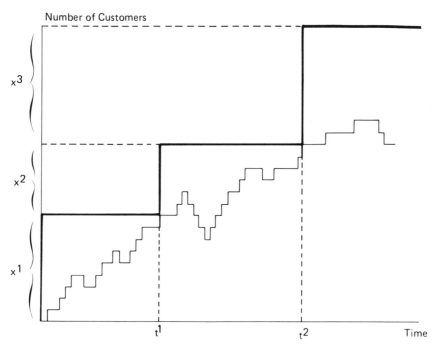

than the average growth; but unless there is a great deal of randomness (i.e., variance), the two are not very different.

7.1.1 Equivalent Deterministic Demand

Suppose we wish to evaluate a solution of the random demand problem specified by giving the sizes of subsequent expansions, $x^1, x^2, x^3, \ldots$ as shown in Figure 7.1. Its cost will be

$$W = C(x^1) + C(x^2)e^{-rt^1} + C(x^3)e^{-rt^2} + \cdots, \qquad (7.2)$$

where $t^1, t^2, \ldots$ are the times at which the additional demand first reaches $x^1, x^1 + x^2, \ldots$ customers as shown in Figure 7.1. The times $t^1, t^2, \ldots$ are random variables, but we assume that capacity costs are deterministic and independent of time, so the $C(x^1), C(x^2), \ldots$ can be treated as constants in finding the expected value of W:

$$E(W) = C(x^1) + C(x^2)E(e^{-rt^1}) + C(x^3)E(e^{-rt^2}) + \cdots. \qquad (7.3)$$

Each of the quantities $E(e^{-rt^i})$ is recognizable as the Laplace transform[1] of the time that demand will first reach some level. Thus, in order to calculate the expected present worth cost of any expansion sequence, all we need from the random demand process is Laplace transforms of first passage times to various demand levels.

This observation motivates us to define an *equivalent deterministic demand* as follows (this idea was also introduced in Section 2.3.3). Let t_n be the (random) time it will take to first reach a level of n customers. Define also a (nonrandom) time $\hat{t}_n$ by

$$e^{-r\hat{t}_n} \equiv E(e^{-rt_n}). \qquad (7.4)$$

Then the expected present worth cost of any expansion that is scheduled to take place when demand first reaches a level of n customers can be calculated equivalently by assuming that the expansion will occur at $\hat{t}_n$. Thus, we define a nonrandom demand process in which demand reaches n customers at $\hat{t}_n$, which we call the equivalent deterministic demand. By the above observations, *the solution of the deterministic problem using the equivalent deterministic demand also solves the random demand problem.*

Before proceeding with calculation of the equivalent deterministic demand, we are already in a position to make a significant observation about the effect of randomness. Let $\bar{t}_n$ denote the expected value of the time it will take to first reach a demand level of n customers. In Section 2.3.3, we used Jensen's inequality to show that

$$\hat{t}_n \leq \bar{t}_n. \qquad (7.5)$$

---

[1] Actually, not the whole transform, but only its value at the discounting rate r.

That is, the effect of randomness is identical to having customers arrive sooner; or, to put it another way, *the effect of randomness is equivalent to having more demand*.

7.1.2 Equivalent Growth Rate

Here we show that for the uniform demand process that we are studying, the equivalent deterministic demand defined in the previous section is actually linear. Thus, we can include the effects of randomness by simply solving a deterministic problem with a somewhat larger demand growth rate.

We decompose the time of first passage t_n to a demand level of n customers into

$$t_n = \tau_1 + \tau_2 + \cdots + \tau_n, \qquad (7.6)$$

where each τ_i is the time of first passage from $i-1$ to i customers as illustrated in Figure 7.2. Thus

$$E(e^{-rt_n}) = E(e^{-r\tau_1}e^{-r\tau_2}\cdots e^{-r\tau_n}). \qquad (7.7)$$

Since the random process we have defined is memoryless (i.e., future arrivals and departures are independent of past ones), the τ_i are statistically independent, which means that the expected value of the product in (7.7) is

Figure 7.2. First passage times.

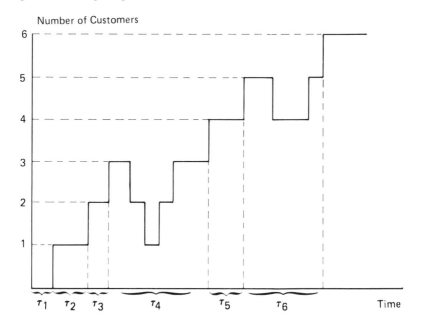

the same as the product of the expected values

$$E(e^{-rt_n}) = E(e^{-r\tau_1})E(e^{-r\tau_2})\cdots E(e^{-r\tau_n}). \tag{7.8}$$

Since the process transition rates are independent of the number of customers in the system, the τ_i are identically distributed random variables. Thus (7.8) becomes

$$E(e^{-rt_n}) = \theta^n, \tag{7.9}$$

where

$$\theta \equiv E(e^{-r\tau_1}). \tag{7.10}$$

In Section 7.2 [Equation (7.50)] we will show that the Laplace transform required in (7.10) is given by

$$\theta = \frac{(r+\lambda+\mu) - \sqrt{(r+\lambda+\mu)^2 - 4\lambda\mu}}{2\mu}. \tag{7.11}$$

Now, from the definition of the equivalent deterministic demand [Equation (7.4)],

$$e^{-r\hat{t}_n} = \theta^n, \tag{7.12}$$

or

$$\hat{t}_n = \frac{n}{(-r/\ln\theta)}. \tag{7.13}$$

That is, the time to reach a level of n customers in the equivalent deterministic demand process is proportional to n. That prompts us to define the proportionality factor as an equivalent growth rate

$$\hat{g} \equiv \frac{r}{-\ln\theta}. \tag{7.14}$$

Example 7.1. In Example 3.5 and again in Example 4.1, we considered a capacity expansion problem in which demand was growing at a rate of 1.5 thousand channels/year. Using a capacity cost of $(16+2x)$ for an x-thousand channel system and a discounting rate of $r=0.1$, we found it optimal to use systems with 13.2 thousand channels at a present worth cost of 72.5 thousand dollars. Suppose the growth rate of $g=1.5$ were actually the expected growth due to an expected connection rate of $\lambda=5.75$ and a disconnection rate of $\mu=4.25$ thousand channels/year. From (7.11),

$$\theta = \frac{(0.1+5.75+4.25) - \sqrt{(0.1+10)^2 - 4(5.75)(4.25)}}{2(4.25)} = 0.945,$$

and from (7.14),

$$\hat{g} = \frac{0.1}{-\ln\theta} = 1.78.$$

That is, the effect of this uncertainty is equivalent to having a demand growth rate of 1.78 instead of 1.50. If we go through the same calculations as we did in the deterministic case, only substituting $g = 1.78$, we get an optimal size of 14.6 thousand channels at a cost (expected value) of 80.8 thousand dollars—a rather modest change from the nonrandom case. //

7.1.3 Mean and Variance of Demand

Instead of thinking about uncertainty in terms of inward and outward movement of customers, it may be more meaningful to specify our uncertainty in terms of an expected value and variance of demand. In this section we develop expressions for the mean and variance of demand for the uniform inward/outward movement process we have been studying. These expressions point out the interesting property that the variability of the process as measured by standard deviation relative to mean *decreases* with time into the future.

The number of customers $n(t)$ at time t is the difference between the number of inward moves $n_i(t)$ and the number of outward moves $n_o(t)$:

$$n(t) = n_i(t) - n_o(t).$$

The expected number is

$$E[n(t)] = E[n_i(t) - n_o(t)] = E[n_i(t)] - E[n_o(t)].$$

The inward and outward processes are Poisson with parameters λ and μ, respectively, and therefore

$$E[n(t)] = (\lambda - \mu)t \equiv \bar{g}t, \qquad (7.15)$$

where $\bar{g}$ is an expected demand growth rate. The variance (surpressing t for notational convenience) is

$$\begin{aligned}
\mathrm{Var}[n(t)] &= E[n - E(n)]^2 \\
&= E\{[n_i - E(n_i)] - [n_o - E(n_o)]\}^2 \\
&= E\{(n_i - E(n_i))^2 + [n_o - E(n_o)]^2 - 2[n_i - E(n_i)][n_o - E(n_o)]\} \\
&= \mathrm{Var}[n_i(t)] + \mathrm{Var}[n_o(t)] - 2E\{[n_i - E(n_i)][n_o - E(n_o)]\}.
\end{aligned}$$

Since the processes are statistically independent, the last term becomes the product of the expected values, each of which is 0. Now, the variance of the number of events in a Poisson process is identical to the expected value; thus we get

$$\mathrm{Var}[n(t)] = (\lambda + \mu)t \equiv \sigma^2 t, \qquad (7.16)$$

where σ^2 is the variance per unit time of the demand.

In addition to this mean and variance, it is informative to calculate the expected value and variance of the time t_n to reach some level of demand n. This is a straightforward calculation since we have an expression for the Laplace transform of t_n. Standard probability theory tells us that

$$E(t_n) = -\frac{d}{dr} E(e^{-rt_n})\Big|_{r=0},$$
(7.17)

$$E(t_n^2) = \frac{d^2}{dr^2} E(e^{-rt_n})\Big|_{r=0},$$
(7.18)

and

$$\mathrm{Var}(t_n) = E(t_n^2) - \left[E(t_n) \right]^2.$$
(7.19)

We show the calculations only for the expected value. From (7.9),

$$\frac{d}{dr} E(e^{-rt_n})\Big|_{r=0} = n\theta^{n-1} \frac{d\theta}{dr}\Big|_{r=0}.$$

From (7.11), $\theta = 1$ at $r = 0$ and

$$\frac{d\theta}{dr}\Big|_{r=0} = \frac{1}{2\mu} \left[1 - \frac{r+\lambda+\mu}{\sqrt{(r+\lambda+\mu)^2 - 4\lambda\mu}} \right]_{r=0}$$

$$= \frac{1}{2\mu} \left[1 - \frac{\lambda+\mu}{\sqrt{(\lambda-\mu)^2}} \right]$$

$$= -\frac{1}{\lambda-\mu},$$

and so (7.17) gives us

$$E(t_n) = \frac{n}{\lambda-\mu}$$
(7.20)

Actually, this only holds for $\lambda > \mu$; otherwise, the expected value is infinite. Doing a similar calculation using (6.18) and (6.19) yields

$$\mathrm{Var}(t_n) = \frac{\lambda+\mu}{(\lambda-\mu)^3} n$$
(7.21)

(which, again, holds only for $\lambda > \mu$ and is infinite otherwise).

Equations (7.15) and (7.20) are both consistent with the intuitive idea that the expected growth is $\lambda - \mu$, the difference between the rates of inward and outward movement. The expressions for variance, (7.16) and (7.21), appear quite different; but suppose that we think of the variability of a random quantity by comparing its standard deviation (SD, square root of variance) to its mean. From (7.15) and (7.16),

$$\frac{\text{SD}[n(t)]}{E[n(t)]} = \frac{\sqrt{\lambda+\mu}}{\lambda-\mu} \frac{1}{\sqrt{t}}. \tag{7.22}$$

Similarly, from (7.20) and (7.21),

$$\frac{\text{SD}(t_n)}{E(t_n)} = \sqrt{\frac{\lambda+\mu}{\lambda-\mu}} \frac{1}{\sqrt{n}}. \tag{7.23}$$

Now, if we look at n and t such that $n=(\lambda-\mu)t$, we see that the two actually are telling us the same thing.

Equations (7.22) and (7.23) bring out a notable feature of this stochastic process—its variability, as measured by standard deviation relative to the mean, *decreases* with time. This is a property of any process whose value can be viewed as the sum of independent, identically distributed, events.

Example 7.2. In Example 7.1 we considered a demand process in which the arrival and departure rates were $\lambda=5.75$ and $\mu=4.25$ thousand channels. If we compute the variability with (7.22),

$$\frac{\text{SD}[n(t)]}{E[n(t)]} = \frac{\sqrt{5.75+4.25}}{5.75-4.25} \frac{1}{\sqrt{t}} = \frac{2.11}{\sqrt{t}}. \tag{7.24}$$

Thus, if we look at small t, say $t=1$ year, the variability is high—we have a standard deviation of more than twice the mean. If we look at, say, $t=9$ (or about one relief interval), the standard deviation is only about $\frac{2}{3}$ the mean, indicating considerably less variability. Suppose we wanted to model a much greater uncertainty than this. We might, for instance, specify that the standard deviation of the time required to reach 10 thousand channels should be twice the mean:

$$2 = \frac{\text{SD}(t_{10})}{E[t_{10}]} = \sqrt{\frac{\lambda+\mu}{\lambda-\mu}} \frac{1}{\sqrt{10}},$$

$$4 = \frac{\lambda+\mu}{1.5} \frac{1}{10}, \tag{7.25}$$

$$\lambda+\mu=60.$$

Keeping $\lambda-\mu=1.5$, yields $\lambda=30.75$ and $\mu=29.25$. Using these values to calculate equivalent growth (7.11) and (7.14) yields $\hat{g}=2.64$, which is substantially higher than the value of 1.78 obtained in Example 7.1. //

The very high inward and outward movement rates required to create the desired uncertainty in Example 7.2 should lead us to be cautious about interpreting our uncertainty in terms of customers physically moving in and out. In the following section, we get away from this interpretation and think of the random process simply as a way of modeling uncertainty (mean and variance).[2]

For later reference, we summarize the relationships between the inward/outward movement and the mean/variance views:

$$E[n(t)] = \bar{g}t = (\lambda - \mu)t \qquad \text{(expected number of customers),} \qquad (7.26)$$

$$\text{Var}[n(t)] = \sigma^2 t = (\lambda + \mu)t \qquad \text{(variance of number of customers),} \qquad (7.27)$$

$$E(t_n) = n/\bar{g} \qquad \text{(expected first passage time),} \qquad (7.28)$$

$$\text{Var}(t_n) = (\sigma^2/\bar{g}^3)n \qquad \text{(variance of first passage time),} \qquad (7.29)$$

or, solving for λ and μ instead,

$$\lambda = (\sigma^2 + \bar{g})/2 \quad \text{(inward movement rate),} \qquad (7.30)$$

$$\mu = (\sigma^2 - \bar{g})/2 \quad \text{(outward movement rate).} \qquad (7.31)$$

Note in (7.31) that σ^2 must be greater than $\bar{g}$. We have more to say about this in the next section.

7.1.4 A Diffusion Approximation

In many situations, individual units of demand are sufficiently small that demand is essentially a continuous quantity. We are then interested in the magnitude of the demand and not in the movements of individual customers. In this section we let demand be composed of more and more, smaller and smaller customers in such a way that the mean and variance of demand stay constant. The result is a *diffusion process*, although we do not establish this fact since it is not required for our analysis.

We develop an expression for the equivalent growth rate in terms of the mean and variance (Figure 7.3). We also find an approximate expression that shows how much additional growth can be attributed to uncertainty.

Suppose we scale the demand by letting $y = \alpha n(t)$, where α is a constant (e.g., when $\alpha = 0.5$, each unit of demand is actually two customers). We shall consider what happens when we let $\alpha \to 0$ and simultaneously adjust λ and μ to maintain a constant mean $\bar{g}t$ and variance $\sigma^2 t$ of demand:

$$\bar{g}t = E(y) = \alpha E[n(t)] = \alpha(\lambda - \mu)t, \qquad (7.32)$$

$$\sigma^2 t = \text{Var}(y) = \alpha^2 \text{Var}[n(t)] = \alpha^2(\lambda + \mu)t; \qquad (7.33)$$

or

$$\lambda - \mu = \bar{g}/\alpha, \qquad (7.34)$$

$$\lambda + \mu = \sigma^2/\alpha^2. \qquad (7.35)$$

---

[2] However, see Example 8.5 for a situation in which the interpretation of variance as ignorance may result in the curious observation that we may be better off being ignorant!

172

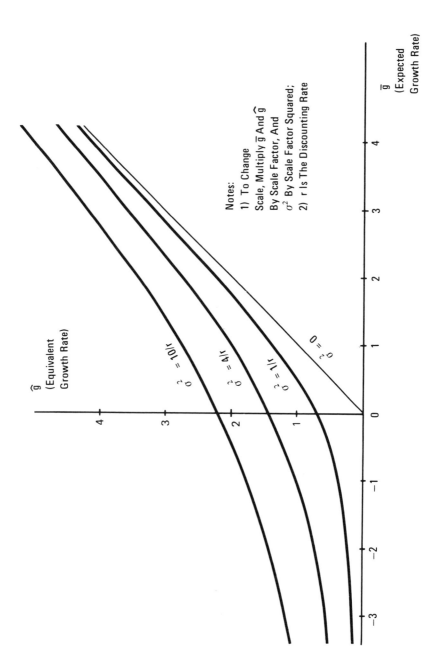

Figure 7.3. Equivalent growth rate versus expected growth rate.

We now wish to consider the time t_y to first reach a demand level of y. In terms of the original process, this means $n = y/\alpha$ customers. Thus, from (7.9) and (7.11),

$$E(e^{-rt_y}) = \left[\frac{(r+\lambda+\mu) - \sqrt{(r+\lambda+\mu)^2 - 4\lambda\mu}}{2\mu} \right]^{y/\alpha}. \qquad (7.36)$$

Solving (7.34) and (7.35) for λ and μ, and substituting into (7.36) eventually yields

$$E(e^{-rt_y}) = \left[\frac{(r\alpha^2 + \sigma^2) - \sqrt{(r\alpha^2 + \sigma^2)^2 - (\sigma^2)^2 + \alpha^2\bar{g}^2}}{\sigma^2 - \alpha\bar{g}} \right]^{(1/\alpha)y}. \qquad (7.37)$$

It is straightforward to take the limit as $\alpha \to 0$, for example using a series expansion for the square root and then for the quotient, to obtain finally

$$E(e^{-rt_y}) = e^{-ry/\left[(1/2)\left(\bar{g} + \sqrt{\bar{g}^2 + 2r\sigma^2} \right) \right]}. \qquad (7.38)$$

As we did before, we identify the equivalent growth rate:

$$\hat{g} \equiv \tfrac{1}{2}\left(\bar{g} + \sqrt{(\bar{g}^2 + 2r\sigma^2)} \right). \qquad (7.39)$$

Figure 7.3 plots $\hat{g}$ versus the expected growth rate $\bar{g}$ for various values of variance (actually, $r\sigma^2$).

It is interesting to examine the following approximation for (7.39). When $r\sigma^2$ is small compared to $\bar{g}^2$, the square root (note that only the positive root is used in these expressions) can be approximated by the first term of its Taylor series to obtain

$$\hat{g} \approx \frac{1}{2}\left[\bar{g} + \sqrt{\bar{g}^2}\left(1 + \frac{r\sigma^2}{\bar{g}^2} \right) \right] \qquad (7.40)$$

or

$$\hat{g} \approx \begin{cases} \bar{g} + \dfrac{r\sigma^2}{\bar{g}} & \text{if } \bar{g} > 0 \\[2mm] \dfrac{r\sigma^2}{|\bar{g}|} & \text{if } \bar{g} < 0. \end{cases} \qquad (7.41)$$

Thus the effect of randomness is taken into account approximately by using $r\sigma^2/|\bar{g}|$ as the equivalent growth rate if $\bar{g}$ is negative, and by adding this quantity to the expected growth if $\bar{g}$ is positive.

Example 7.3. How close is the diffusion approximation for the data of Example 7.1? There we had $\lambda = 5.75$, $\mu = 4.25$, and came up with $\hat{g} = 1.78$

when $r = 0.1$. Using (7.39) with $\bar{g} = \lambda - \mu = 1.5$ and $\sigma^2 = \lambda + \mu = 10.0$,

$$\hat{g} = \tfrac{1}{2}\left(1.5 + \sqrt{(1.5)^2 + 2(0.1)(10)}\,\right) = 1.78,$$

the same within two digits of accuracy. From the rough approximation (7.33), we obtain

$$\hat{g} \approx \bar{g} + \frac{r\sigma^2}{\bar{g}} = 1.5 + \frac{(0.1)(10)}{1.5} = 2.17,$$

which is not particularly close to the true value since $2r\sigma^2$ is not small enough compared to $\bar{g}^2$ for this example. //

An interesting final observation about this diffusion approximation is that (7.39) is valid for any nonnegative σ^2 value. This is *not* the case for the discrete inward/outward movement process as we pointed out in the previous section following Equation (7.31). There, the variance must at least equal the mean. We obtain this curious distinction between the two processes because the diffusion process is actually somewhat more general than the random inward/outward movement process. To obtain a similar property for the inward/outward movement process, we would have to let some inward movements occur with certainty (instead of at random) over time.

We are generally interested in cases with large variance, so that this restriction probably would not prevent us from interpreting a given mean and variance as an equivalent inward/outward movement of customers [Equations (6.30) and (6.31)]. In fact, Example 7.2 indicates that we sometimes may need disturbingly high inward/outward movements rates to model our intuitive uncertainty in demand.

7.2. When Demand is a Birth/Death Process

The demand process we studied in Section 7.1 is a birth/death process in which the transition rates are independent of the number of customers in the system. Here we show that the equivalent deterministic demand idea still holds even when we allow the transition rates to depend arbitrarily on the number of customers in the system. For example, we can assume that customers will not leave when there are none in the system or that customers will stop arriving when some total level is reached.

Our key observation here is that for any birth/death process, we can generate an *equivalent deterministic demand* problem whose solution also solves the stochastic case. As in the case of the equivalent growth rate, the equivalent deterministic demand always exceeds the expected demand, but in the general case, it is necessary to interpret expected demand in terms of the expected times of first passage to various demand levels and not in terms of the expected number of customers in the system.

We develop simple equations for generating the equivalent deterministic demand and, as a special case, show that Equation (7.11) holds for the birth/death process of Section 7.1.

7.2.1 Equivalent Deterministic Demand Generalized

In Section 7.1.1, we never had to assume that the transition rates were independent of the number of customers in the system; hence, all of that discussion carries over to the more general case. Accordingly, we let $\hat{t}_n$ [see Equation (7.4)] define an equivalent deterministic demand and $\bar{t}_n$ an expected demand as we did before. As in Section 7.1.1, the equivalent deterministic demand exceeds or equals the expected demand; and solution of the equivalent deterministic demand problem solves the stochastic demand case.

7.2.2 Calculating the Equivalent Deterministic Demand

As in the Section 7.1.2, we still can think of the time to first reach a level of n customers as the sum of successive first passage times [Equation (7.6)]. Since the general birth/death process is also Markov, these individual times are also independent; thus, the Laplace transform of the first passage time to n is again the product of the individual first passage times [Equation (7.8)]. With transition rates dependent on the number of customers in the system, the next step [Equation (7.9)] in Section 7.1.2 can no longer be taken. For notational convenience, we rewrite (7.8) as

$$e^{-r\hat{t}_n} \equiv E(e^{-rt_n}) = \theta_1 \theta_2 \cdots \theta_n, \tag{7.42}$$

where

$$\theta_i \equiv E(e^{-r\tau_i}) \tag{7.43}$$

To develop an expression for the θ_i, we have to use some properties of birth/death processes. We already have invoked the independence of successive first passage times. It is also well known that in any *state n* (i.e., when there are n customers in the system, regardless of how long they have been there), the time t until the next *event* (i.e., either an arrival or a departure) is an exponentially distributed random variable with mean $1/(\lambda_n + \mu_n)$, so that its probability density function is

$$\text{pdf}(t) = (\lambda_n + \mu_n) e^{-(\lambda_n + \mu_n)t}, \tag{7.44}$$

where λ_n and μ_n are the arrival and departure rates, respectively. Furthermore, the next event will be an arrival or a departure with probability

$$\Pr(\text{arrival}) = \frac{\lambda_n}{\lambda_n + \mu_n},$$

$$\Pr(\text{departure}) = \frac{\mu_n}{\lambda_n + \mu_n}. \tag{7.45}$$

We are now in a position to write a probability statement which is called *conditioning on the next event*:

$$f_{\tau_{n+1}}(\tau) = \left[(\lambda_n + \mu_n)e^{-(\lambda_n + \mu_n)\tau}\right]\left(\frac{\lambda_n}{\lambda_n + \mu_n}\right)$$

$$+ \int_0^\tau (\lambda_n + \mu_n)e^{-(\lambda_n + \mu_n)t}\left(\frac{\mu_n}{\lambda_n + \mu_n}\right)f_{\tau_n + \tau_{n+1}}(\tau - t)\, dt, \quad (7.46)$$

where

$f_{\tau_{n+1}}(\tau)$ is the probability density function of τ_{n+1} (the time to first reach $n+1$ customers starting at n); It is the probability that first passage from n to $n+1$ occurs at τ

$f_{\tau_n + \tau_{n+1}}(\tau)$ is the probability density function of $\tau_n + \tau_{n+1}$ (the time to first reach $n+1$ customers starting at $n-1$)

$(\lambda_n + \mu_n)e^{-(\lambda_n + \mu_n)\tau}$ is the probability that the next event (call it E_τ) occurs at τ

$\dfrac{\lambda_n}{\lambda_n + \mu_n}$ is the probability that E_τ is an arrival

$\int_0^\tau(\lambda_n + \mu_n)e^{-(\lambda_n + \mu_n)t}$ is the probability that E_t occurs at time t before τ

$\dfrac{\mu_n}{\lambda_n + \mu_n}$ is the probability that E_t is a departure

$f_{\tau_n + \tau_{n+1}}(\tau - t)\, dt$ is the probability that the first passage from the resulting state $n-1$ to $n+1$ occurs in the remaining time $\tau - t$.

A product of these terms may be expressed verbally by *and* and addition by *or*. In the interest of brevity, our explanatory notes on Equation 7.46 are a slight abuse of terminology since we are actually dealing with probability density functions and not probabilities. We are interested in the Laplace transforms of the first passage times

$$\theta_{n+1} \equiv E(e^{-r\tau_{n+1}}) \equiv \int_0^\infty e^{-r\tau}f_{\tau_{n+1}}(\tau)\, d\tau; \quad (7.47)$$

and so, from (7.46),

$$\theta_{n+1} = \frac{\lambda_n}{\lambda_n + \mu_n + r} + \mu_n \int_0^\infty e^{-r\tau}\int_0^\tau e^{-(\lambda_n + \mu_n)t}f_{\tau_n + \tau_{n+1}}(\tau - t)\, dt\, d\tau.$$

Changing the order of integration, substituting the variable $p = \tau - t$ for τ, and collecting terms gives

$$\theta_{n+1} = \frac{\lambda_n}{\lambda_n + \mu_n + r} + \mu_n \int_{t=0}^\infty e^{-(\lambda_n + \mu_n + r)t}\int_{p=0}^\infty e^{-rp}f_{\tau_n + \tau_{n+1}}(p)\, dp\, dt$$

$$= \frac{\lambda_n}{\lambda_n + \mu_n + r} + \frac{\mu_n}{\lambda_n + \mu_n + r}\int_0^\infty e^{-rp}f_{\tau_n + \tau_{n+1}}(p)\, dp. \quad (7.48)$$

The integral is just the Laplace transform of the sum of the two independent first passage times τ_n and τ_{n+1}; and so is the product of the two transforms. Thus

$$\theta_{n+1} = \frac{\lambda_n}{\lambda_n + \mu_n + r} + \frac{\mu_n}{\lambda_n + \mu_n + r} \theta_n \theta_{n+1}. \tag{7.49}$$

Finally, solving for θ_{n+1},

$$\theta_{n+1} = \frac{\lambda_n}{r + \lambda_n + \mu_n - \mu_n \theta_n}. \tag{7.50}$$

Example 7.4. In Section 7.1.2, we studied a special case of this birth/death process in which the arrival and departure rates were the same regardless of state $\lambda_n = \lambda$; $\mu_n = \mu$. The Laplace transforms of first passage times to the next higher state were, therefore, also independent of state: $\theta_n = \theta$, all n. In that case, Equation (7.49) becomes

$$\theta = \frac{\lambda}{\lambda + \mu + t} + \frac{\mu}{\lambda + \mu + r} \theta^2.$$

Solving for θ yields

$$\theta = \frac{(\lambda + \mu + r) - \sqrt{(\lambda + \mu + r)^2 - 4\lambda\mu}}{2\mu}. \tag{7.51}$$

It can be shown readily that $\theta \leq 1$ as required of a Laplace transform of a nonnegative random variable. (The other root of the quadratic equation turns out to be greater than 1.) //

Example 7.5. Suppose inward movements are generated uniformly, at random, by vacant premises of which there are a total of N, and outward movements occur uniformly, at random, among customers currently in the system. We can model such a situation by saying that when there are n customers in the system, the arrival rate is $\lambda_n = (N - n)\lambda$ and the departure rate is $\mu_n = n\mu$, where the constants λ and μ can be interpreted as

$\lambda = 1/E$(vacancy time of an unoccupied premises),

$\mu = 1/E$(time a customer stays in the system).

Since $\mu_n = 0$ for $n \leq 0$, we can simply iterate (7.50) to obtain all of the Laplace transforms desired.

To illustrate, let

$r = 0.1$ (discounting rate),

$N = 100$ (number of premises),

$\lambda = 0.042$ (inward movement rate per vacant premise),

$\mu = 0.028$ (outward movement rate per customer).

From (7.50),

$$\theta_1 = \frac{\lambda_0}{r + \lambda_0} = \frac{(100)(0.042)}{0.1 + 100(0.042)} = 0.9767,$$

$$\theta_2 = \frac{\lambda_1}{r + \lambda_1 + \mu_1 - \mu_1\theta_1} = \frac{99(0.042)}{0.1 + 99(0.042) + 0.028 - 0.028(0.9767)} = 0.9764,$$

$$\theta_3 = \frac{98(0.042)}{0.1 + 98(0.042) + 2(0.028) - 2(0.028)(0.9764)} = 0.9760,$$

From (7.42),

$$e^{-r\hat{t}_1} = \theta_1 = 0.9767,$$

$$\hat{t}_1 = -\frac{\ln(0.9767)}{0.1} = 0.2353,$$

$$e^{-r\hat{t}_2} = \theta_1\theta_2 = 0.9537,$$

$$\hat{t}_2 = -\frac{\ln(0.9537)}{1} = 0.4757,$$

$$\hat{t}_3 = -\frac{\ln[(0.9537)(0.9760)]}{0.1} = 0.7177,$$

$$\vdots$$

Note that these are roughly the times it would take for 1, 2, and 3 customers to enter the system at an arrival rate of about $(100)(0.042) = 4.2$ per year, as we would expect. Figure 7.4 plots $\hat{t}_n$ versus n (the curve labeled equivalent deterministic demand), but with n on the vertical axis since we are accustomed to looking at demand curves in this way. If we solve the deterministic problem with this demand, we shall have the solution of the stochastic demand problem. Since the curve is nonlinear, we should have to use the methods of Section 5.2 or 5.3. //

For purposes of comparison, it is useful to calculate the expected time of first passage

$$\bar{t}_n \equiv E(t_n) = E(\tau_1) + E(\tau_2) + \cdots + E(\tau_n). \tag{7.52}$$

We can get an expression for the expected time of first passage from n to $n+1$ customers from the Laplace transform (7.50),

$$\bar{\tau}_{n+1} = -\frac{d}{dr}\theta_{n+1}\bigg|_{r=0} = \frac{\lambda_n}{(r + \lambda_n + \mu_n - \mu_n\theta_n)^2}\left(1 - \mu_n\frac{d\theta_n}{dr}\right)\bigg|_{r=0},$$

or

$$\bar{\tau}_{n+1} = \frac{1}{\lambda_n}(1 + \mu_n\bar{\tau}_n), \tag{7.53}$$

179

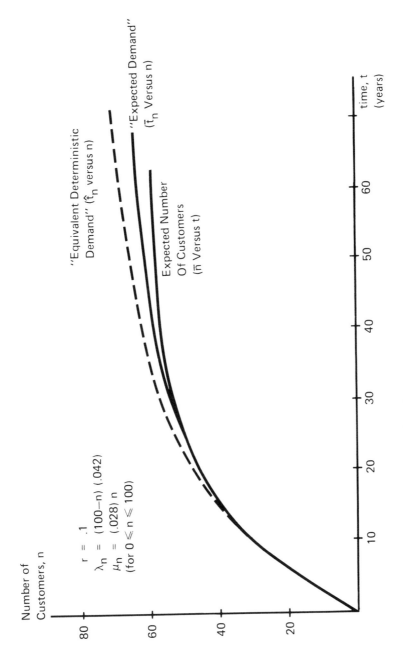

Figure 7.4. Demand curves for a birth/death process.

in the usual case. (When $\bar{\tau}_n = \infty$, it can be shown that $\bar{\tau}_{n+1} = \infty$ if $\mu_n > 0$ and $\bar{\tau}_{n+1} = 1/\lambda_n$ if $\mu_n = 0$.)

Note that for the special case of a uniform arrival and departure rate, $\lambda_n = \lambda$, $\mu_n = \mu$, so $\bar{\tau}_{n+1} = \bar{\tau}_n$, and (7.53) gives $\bar{\tau}_n = 1/(\lambda - \mu)$, which is consistent with (7.20).

Example 7.6. For the problem considered in Example 7.5,

$$\bar{\tau}_1 = 1/\lambda_0 = 1/(100)(0.042) = 0.2381,$$

$$\bar{\tau}_2 = \frac{1}{\lambda_1}(1 + \mu_1 \bar{\tau}_1) = \frac{1 + (0.028)(0.2381)}{(99)(0.042)} = 0.2421,$$

$$\bar{\tau}_3 = \frac{1 + 2(0.028)(0.2421)}{(98)(0.042)} = 0.2426.$$

The corresponding expected time $\bar{t}_n$ to first reach a level of n customers is the cumulative sum of these times. Table 7.1 compares these expected times to the equivalent deterministic times $\hat{t}_n$, calculated in Example 7.6. Of course, $\hat{t}_n < \bar{t}_n$, as required [see Equation (7.5)]. This is also apparent in Figure 7.4, which plots $\bar{t}_n$ versus n (the curve marked expected demand) with n on the vertical axis, as before. //

An important point to which we previously have alluded is that the expected demand defined by the expected first passage time $\bar{t}_n$ is *not the same* as the expected number of customers. In the special case of uniform arrival and departure rates studied in Section 7.1, the two did turn out identical. In general, however, to find the expected number of customers at time t, we would have to solve a system of first-order differential equations for the probabilities of having various numbers of customers in the system (the so-called Kolmogorov equations). The following example gives the expected number of customers versus time for the special case of Example 7.5. Derivations or further discussion of this topic would take us too far afield.

Example 7.7. Although we shall not derive it here,[3] the expected number of customers in the system at time t for the demand process of Example 7.5 is

$$E[n(t)] = N \frac{\lambda}{\lambda + \mu} [1 - e^{-(\lambda + \mu)t}]. \tag{7.54}$$

Figure 7.4 (the curve marked expected number of customers) plots $E[n(t)]$

---

[3] For example, see Feller, *An Introduction to Probability Theory and its Applications*, Volume I, 3rd ed., Wiley, 1968.

Table 7.1. Time to Reach n Customers (Examples 7.5 and 7.6)

n	$\bar{t}_n$ (sum of $\bar{\tau}_i$)	$\hat{t}_n$ (from Example 7.5)
1	0.2381	0.2353
2	0.4838	0.4757
3	0.7264	0.7171

versus t. Note that although we have drawn all of these as continuous curves, the other two, the equivalent deterministic demand and the expected demand, are actually only defined at integer values of n. //

7.2.3 Discussion

The birth/death model is very much a nonlinear generalization of the linear model of Section 7.1. It turns out that as in the linear case of Section 7.1, quite large inward/outward movement rates must be assumed to make the equivalent deterministic demand much different from the expected demand (e.g., in Figure 7.4 the two are nearly identical for practical purposes). An important distinction arises here between the expected demand, as defined by the expected first passage times, and the expected number of customers in the system. For the capacity expansion problem we have been studying, the former is a more relevant concept. (Although the expected number of customers in Figure 7.4 is also close to the other two curves, examples can readily be generated in which it is significantly different).

One final note is that although we have generalized to birth/death processes the idea that uncertainty is equivalent to higher demand, we *cannot* assume in general that uncertainty implies larger capacity expansions. In general, the equivalent deterministic demand is a nonlinear function; and, even though it is greater than the expected demand, we cannot infer that the optimal expansion sizes will necessarily increase. We can infer that the *expected cost* will be greater than the cost if we only had to serve the expected demand.

7.3 An Economy-of-Scale Effect

In Section 3.4, we discussed some economy-of-scale effects associated with serving a larger area (i.e., a higher growth rate). We defined an equivalent capacity cost c per unit time per customer in service (3.32), and explored its variation with growth rate (Figure 3.5). We considered two examples, one in which capacity was available in only one size, and another in which the size was assumed to be optimized for the particular growth rate under consideration. Here we generalize the latter case to see the effects of demand growth uncertainty on the equivalent capacity cost per unit time per customer in service.

One intuitively would expect to be less hurt by uncertainty if one served a larger area because some errors would tend to compensate each other.[4] To get a quantitative expression for this effect, we redefine the equivalent cost per unit time per customers in service c, originally defined by (3.23), for the stochastic demand process of Section 7.1:

$$E\left[\int_0^\infty cn(t)e^{-rt}\,dt\right] \equiv E\left\{\begin{array}{l}\text{present worth}\\\text{cost of}\\\text{providing all}\\\text{future capacity}\end{array}\right\}, \qquad (7.55)$$

where E denotes expected value and $n(t)$ is the (random) number of customers in the system at time t. That is, c is defined so that if we charge each customer c per unit time for the use of the facility, we can expect to just break even [this is analogous to its definition by (3.23)]. Taking the expectation inside the integral on the left-hand side, we can use $E[n(t)] = \bar{g}t$ [Equation (7.24)] and perform the integration. We can evaluate the right-hand side, according to the theory of Section 7.1 as if it were a deterministic problem, with $\hat{g}$ as the growth rate. Thus

$$c\frac{\bar{g}}{r^2} = \frac{C(x)}{1 - e^{-r(x/\hat{g})}},$$

or

$$c = \frac{r^2 C(x)}{\bar{g}\left(1 - e^{-rx/\hat{g}}\right)}. \qquad (7.56)$$

Now to see the effects of bigness, we suppose that the number of customers $n(t)$ actually is determined by summing the number from j different *statistically independent* areas, each having an expected growth rate of $\bar{g}_0$ and a variance per unit time of σ_0^2. The expected growth rate $\bar{g}$ and variance σ^2 of $n(t)$ is then given by

$$\bar{g} = j\bar{g}_0,$$

$$\sigma^2 = j\sigma_0^2 \qquad (7.57)$$

or combining

$$\sigma^2 = \frac{\sigma_0^2}{\bar{g}_0}\bar{g}.$$

---

[4]Recall, for example, that the effects of unsystematic randomness were eliminated by diversification in Section 2.3.2.

Table 7.2. Economy-of-Scale and Uncertainty

$\bar{g}$	$\sigma^2 = k\bar{g}$	$\hat{g}$ (7.58)	Optimal x (Section 3.1)	Present worth cost [Eq. (7.55)]	c [Eq. (7.56)]
			$k = 10/1.5$		
0.2	1.33	0.377	5.80	35.2	1.76
1.5	10.0	1.78	14.6	80.8	0.539
10	66.7	10.3	38.1	299	0.299
			$k = 60/1.5$		
0.2	8.0	0.740	8.76	48.3	2.42
1.5	60.0	2.64	18.2	105	0.700
10	400	11.7	40.8	332	0.332

Substituting into (7.39),

$$\hat{g} = \tfrac{1}{2}\left(\bar{g} + \sqrt{\bar{g}^2 + 2rk\bar{g}} \right), \tag{7.58}$$

where

$$k \equiv \sigma_0^2 / \bar{g}_0.$$

Example 7.8. In Example 3.12 we explored the economy-of-scale effects for a problem in which the capacity cost was $C(x) = 16 + 2x$ (x is thousands of channels) and the discounting rate was $r = 0.1$. We plotted c [calculated according to Equation (3.24) using an optimal x] versus g. The lowest curve in Figure 7.5 is identical to that one with $\bar{g}$ replacing g. That curve has been calculated assuming $k = \sigma_0^2/\bar{g}_0 = 0$ (no uncertainty), so that $\hat{g} = \bar{g}$ and (7.56) is identical to (3.24). The next curve uses $k = \sigma_0^2/\bar{g}_0 = 10/1.5$ (corresponding to the uncertainty assumed in Example 7.1), and the highest curve uses $k = \sigma_0^2/\bar{g}_0 = 60/1.5$ (corresponding to the uncertainty assumed in Example 7.2). Table 7.2 shows intermediate calculations for some of the values of $\bar{g}$. Note in Figure 7.5 that the economy-of-scale is more pronounced with more uncertainty. //

A word of caution is in order with respect to the assumption of statistical independence. The reason we do better with more aggregation in an uncertain situation is that the relative variance is reduced. This reduction of variance occurs only to the extent that the random quantities are independent. If the demand in various areas were perfectly correlated, for example, there would be no reduction of uncertainty with aggregation. Some correlation is likely, for instance, if the amount of demand depends on common factors such as the economic climate. One may be able to extend this analysis to such cases by using the diversifiable versus systematic risk concepts of Section 2.3.2.

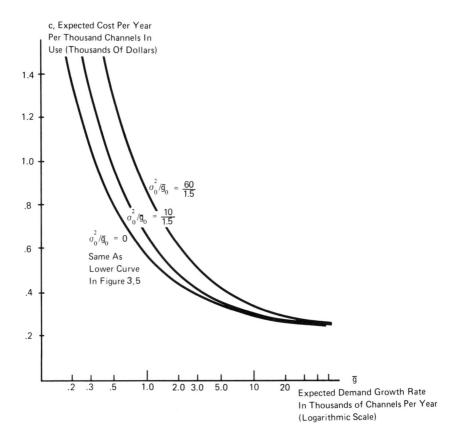

Figure 7.5. Economy-of-scale effect of uncertainty.

7.4 Extension to Other Demand Processes

All of our analysis so far has been limited to a very special demand process. It has been quite useful in giving us a particularly simple characterization of uncertainty, namely, that it is equivalent to having a deterministic demand that is somewhat greater than the expected demand. This characterization is undoubtedly sufficient for many applications. Perhaps even more significantly, it is simple enough to give us some insight into the impact of uncertainty (e.g., as in the economy-of-scale discussion of Section 7.3).

We must remember, however, that the equivalent deterministic demand concept strictly applies only when certain conditions hold. The following are a sufficient set:

1. The demand process is *memoryless* (or Markov).
2. It *changes continuously*. (In the discrete demand version, only one customer can enter or leave at a time.)

3. The *process transition rates are time invariant*.

4. Capacity *costs are time invariant*,[5] although they are allowed to depend on the number of customers in the system and even on the number of previous expansions that have taken place.

5. Capacity is infinitely durable,[6] so that future expansions will not include additional capacity to make up for older units wearing out.

If properties (1)–(4) did not hold, we still could define an equivalent deterministic demand, although probably with more computational difficulty. Such an equivalent demand still could be used to evaluate prespecified expansion policies of the type considered in this chapter—that is, install x^1, followed by x^2 when demand first reaches the additional level of x^1, and so forth. Unfortunately, such policies will not necessarily be optimal. If the demand process has memory, the optimal expansion will depend on information about how a certain level was reached and not just on the level itself. If jumps in demand are allowed, the optimal size will depend on both the existing level of capacity and on the number of customers in the system when capacity is first exhausted (these two are the same in the birth/death case). If either the process parameters or the capacity costs change with time, the optimal expansion will depend on both the number of customers and on the time the expansion is required. If capacity cannot be considered durable, there will be the equivalent of jumps in the demand when previously installed units wear out. Thus the apparent future demand will depend on the expansion sequence, which in turn will depend on the apparent future demand, complicating the problem considerably.[7]

Another problem with the equivalent deterministic demand concept is that it does not readily allow us to extend the problem definition to include other considerations such as operating costs[8] that may be incurred according to the number of customers in the system at a given time. A possibly useful approach in such circumstances might be to formulate a stochastic dynamic program. We illustrate with an example in which demand is assumed to be Markov, but in which jumps are allowed.

Suppose, when there are i customers in the system, transitions are allowed to various other levels of demand j at the rates λ_{ij} (in the birth/death process, $\lambda_{i,i+1} = \lambda_i$, $\lambda_{i,i-1} = \mu_i$, and all others are zero). Let $W(i, m)$ be the present worth cost of supplying all future facilities when

---

[5]Although a general price inflation may be includable through adjustment of the discounting rate (see Section 2.4).

[6]Or, equivalently, will be replaced by identical equipment at the end of its life, ad infinitum.

[7]In Section 11.1 we briefly discuss the nondurability complication in a deterministic demand context.

[8]To be discussed in Chapters 8 and 9.

there are i customers in the system with sufficient facilities to serve m. In the usual case, an expansion would be required immediately if $m \leq i$. If $m > i$, then we can condition on the next event as we did in Equation (7.46) to obtain

$$W(i, m) = \int_0^\infty \lambda^i e^{-\lambda^i t} \sum_j (\lambda_{ij}/\lambda^i) W(j, m) e^{-rt} \, dt,$$

where

$\lambda^i e^{-\lambda^i t}$ is the probability that the next event occurs at t

λ_{ij}/λ^i is the probability that there are j customers after the event.

Equivalently,

$$W(i, m) = \frac{1}{\lambda^i + r} \sum_j \lambda_{ij} W(j, m), \tag{7.59}$$

where $\lambda^i \equiv \sum_j \lambda_{ij}$. If $m \leq i$, then the optimal expansion is found from

$$W(i, m) = \min_x \left[C(x) + W(i, m+x) \right], \tag{7.60}$$

where $C(x)$ is the cost of a capacity expansion of size x.

Equations (7.59) and (7.60) give us a dynamic programming formulation analogous to that of Section 5.2. There are two very significant differences. One is that here the state variable is 2-dimensional (i and m) whereas in Equation (5.6) it is 1-dimensional (just time t; equivalently, (5.6) could have been written in terms of the number of customers). The other is that we can evaluate (5.6) by starting with the largest value of t and working backward. The W values required in the right-hand side thus always will be known. In (7.59), by contrast, we are liable to require values of W in the right-hand side that have not yet been calculated.

It turns out that the system (7.59), (7.60) is a Markov decision process that can be solved in a number of ways. In one solution method, known as the *value iteration* method, we start by guessing values of W for the right-hand side in (7.59). Then, in successive iterations, we use (7.59), (7.60) with the best current right-hand side of (7.59) to obtain improved estimates of $W(i, m)$. This procedure is analogous to that of Example 4.1. There is also a so-called *policy iteration* approach analogous to Example 4.2, although we shall not pursue it here.

An advantage of this formulation is the greater flexibility it allows. We illustrate by considering a situation in which there is an operating cost $v(i, m)$ per unit time when i customers are in the system and there is a total of m facilities available. Under these circumstances, when we condition on the next event we have to add in the expected operating cost incurred up to that event

$$\int_0^\infty \lambda^i e^{-\lambda^i t} \left[\int_0^t v(i, m) e^{-rp} \, dp \right] dt = \left(\frac{1}{\lambda^i + r} \right) v(i, m), \tag{7.61}$$

where the first integral is the probability that the event occurs at t and the second integral is the present worth of operating costs up to t. Now it may be optimal to add capacity even if $m > i$ (to reduce the operating cost), and so in place of (7.59), (7.60) we have

$$W(i, m) = \min_{x} \left\{ C(x) + \frac{1}{\lambda^i + r} \left[v(i, m+x) + \sum_{j} \lambda_{ij} W(i, m+x) \right] \right\}.$$
(7.62)

This is the most general formulation we have considered for the random demand case. The previous models of this chapter can be viewed as special cases. Nevertheless, it is clearly not universally applicable. For example, it does not allow the demand process parameters to change with time. In some cases of time-variation, it may be reasonable to assume that transition rates depend only on the number of customers in the system. For instance, the saturating demand process of Examples 7.5–7.7 (Figure 7.4), an apparently time-varying process, is modeled this way. In general, however, we may need to account for actual declines in demand over some period followed by increases over some other period. None of the models of this chapter strictly would be applicable in such cases. As a heuristic, however, we may be able to do a reasonably good job by hedging with an equivalent deterministic demand calculated according to some instantaneous means and variances of the process.

7.5 Summary

In this chapter we studied the effects of uncertainty in our knowledge of future demand on capacity expansion decisions. We assumed that our uncertainty could be described by specifying the parameters of a stochastic process. For mathematical tractability, we chose to focus our attention on a birth/death process, with most of the emphasis on uniform inward and outward movement rates. In this case, we were able to show that the effect of randomness is identical to the effect of a larger growth rate. Figure 7.3 shows the equivalent growth rate that should be used as a function of the expected growth rate for several values of variance. We discussed in Section 7.1.3 the use of this random process as simply a quantification of our uncertainty about future demand levels. Example 7.2 indicated that if we wish to model a great deal of uncertainty, we may not be able realistically to attribute that uncertainty to the random inward and outward movement of customers (we needed *very* large movement rates).

For a general birth/death process, our findings were similar to those for the special case. We showed how to generate an equivalent deterministic demand (not a linear growth, in general) whose solution is identical to that of the random problem.

Using the simple uniform transition model of Section 7.1, we showed in Section 7.3 that there may be a significant economy-of-scale effect due to demand uncertainty. If the demand processes of different regions are statistically independent, then the relative uncertainty will be reduced when those areas are aggregated, resulting in a lower cost.

Finally, we considered the difficulties in extending our analysis to more general demand models. We found, for instance, that we could get a dynamic programming formulation when demand was a general Markov process (i.e., more than one customer could arrive or depart at a time), but that its solution would be substantially more difficult than those considered in Chapters 4 and 5.

7.6 Further Reading

The original source for the simple model of Section 7.1 is

A. S. Manne, Capacity Expansion and Probabilistic Growth, *Econometrica* 29(4), October 1961, 632–649,

although Manne used only the diffusion process and interpreted the effects of randomness as a decrease in the interest rate rather than an increase in demand.

The extension to a birth/death process comes from

John Freidenfelds, Capacity Expansion when Demand is a Birth/Death Random Process, *Operations Research* 28(3), Part II, 1980, 712–721.

Many ideas expressed in this chapter have benefited from the work of W. L. G. Koontz and R. S. Shipley cited at the end of Chapter 9 and from unpublished work at Bell Laboratories by C. E. Warren and R. A. Skoog. (See also Skoog's book cited at the end of Chapter 11.)

The reader interested in Markov decision processes mentioned in Section 7.4 might consult a general operations research text, or, for more depth,

Ronald A. Howard, *Dynamic Probabilistic Systems, Volumes I and II*, New York, Wiley, 1971.

Chapter 8

Consideration
of Congestion Costs

Up to now we have taken a very simple view of demand and available capacity. Additional capacity was assumed to be required when demand reached existing capacity. Real problems are unlikely to be so cooperative —complications seem to always crop up. Often these complications will require the use of much more sophisticated models, as we shall discuss in later chapters. It turns out, however, that many complications can be modeled reasonably as an added cost penalty due to running low on capacity, which we shall call a *congestion cost*.

In Chapter 9 we shall discuss some situations in which capacity and/or demand are not actually as uniform as we have assumed; and we shall show that these phenomena can be viewed in terms of congestion costs building up as we run out of capacity. For example, additional demand may be served by costly imports for a time in lieu of adding capacity. In another example, associated with telephone networks, capacity and demand are actually geographically distributed. This results in an increasing incidence of blockages, or required rearrangements, as the total demand approaches total capacity. In electrical power generation, demand exhibits strong daily, weekly, and seasonal peaks that actually are served by generators with different operating costs. Our discussion of these problems in Chapter 9 will use the machinery developed in this chapter.

Here we add a congestion cost to our basic capacity expansion model and explore its impact on the expansion decision. We find that with this modification, it is no longer self-evident when to declare a shortage. That is, the decision of *when* to add capacity, as well as *how much* to add, must be determined on an economic basis.

We start in Section 8.1 with a case in which imports are allowed at a fixed cost per unit of demand per unit time. It turns out that *imports should be used until their annual cost equals or exceeds the equivalent annual cost of the next expansion* [Equation (8.4)]. The optimal expansion size is also larger in this case than it would be if imports were not allowed; furthermore, it is somewhat more difficult to compute.

In Section 8.2 we replace the constant import cost with a congestion cost that is allowed to vary with the amount of spare capacity in the system. Then expansion time is determined by the requirement that congestion cost reduction due to the expansion must offset the equivalent annual cost of the expansion [Equation (8.15)].

In general, optimal expansion sizes are more difficult to calculate when congestion costs are included because it may pay to install a system with greater capacity not only to take advantage of economies of scale in its initial purchase, as discussed in earlier chapters, but also to reduce the congestion cost. Section 8.3 illustrates that sometimes the problems of optimal expansion sizing and timing can be separated as a practical matter. That is, sometimes little is lost if the sizing decision is based on a rough approximation of the timing decision and its related congestion cost; and similarly, adequate timing decisions can sometimes be based on rough approximations of the optimal expansion size.

An interesting extreme case is one in which demand growth goes to zero. We show in Section 8.4 that in such a case, capacity expansion still may be attractive purely for purposes of reducing congestion costs.

In the appendix we consider the role of congestion costs in the random demand model of Chapter 7. The mathematics are more complicated, but qualitative observations are similar to those of the deterministic case. A curious phenomenon, however, is that in the random demand model including congestion costs, the expected total present worth cost may *decrease* with increasing variance in demand! Our discussion in the appendix argues that this observation does not really demonstrate that ignorance is bliss.

8.1 Imports Allowed

Suppose we modify the simple capacity expansion problem of Chapter 3 slightly. Suppose we allow importing (at a cost, of course) to postpone the addition of capacity. As we shall see in Chapter 9, "importing" may actually mean for example, using an alternative technology or temporarily losing sales.

Our model from Chapter 3 is that demand at time t is given by $D(t) = gt$, x units of additional capacity cost $C(x)$ [where we shall take $C(x) = A + Bx$ as a special case], and the discounting rate is r; we now postulate an importing cost of β per unit time per unit of capacity. That is, when

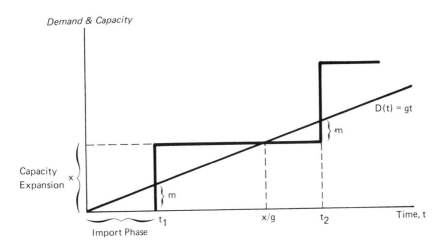

Figure 8.1. Use of imports to defer capacity expansion.

demand reaches existing capacity, we may import in lieu of immediate expansion, as illustrated in Figure 8.1.

The present worth cost $W(0)$, starting at a time when existing spare capacity has just exhausted, can be written

$$W(0) = \int_0^{t_1} \beta D(t) e^{-rt}\, dt + C(x) e^{-rt_1} + W_F(0) e^{-rx/g}, \qquad (8.1)$$

where the expansion that would have taken place at time 0 has been deferred to t_1 by importing at a present worth cost given by the first term (β per unit time per customer requiring the imports) and the cost of all future additions and imports from the time capacity next exhausts is given by $W_F(0)$ (see cost of the future formulation in Section 4.1). Note in (8.1) that imports are assumed to stop at t_1, when the expansion takes place. This will be the usual case when both the size x and the import phase t_1 are being optimized.

One reasonable way to solve (8.1) is to assume a *complete regeneration* at the time x/g, so that $W_F(0) = W(0)$ and we can solve for $W(0)$ to get

$$W(0) = \frac{\displaystyle\int_0^{t_1} \beta D(t) e^{-rt}\, dt + C(x) e^{-rt_1}}{1 - e^{-rx/g}}, \qquad (8.2)$$

the present worth cost if we used repeatedly an import phase of length t_1, followed by an expansion of size x, ad infinitum. It is now a straightforward optimization problem to find the x and t_1 that minimize $W(0)$. As a supplement to this straightforward approach, we look at (8.1) from the backward dynamic programming viewpoint of Section 4.1.

If the expansion size x is held constant, we can find the optimal importing phase t_1 by setting the derivative of (8.1) with respect to t_1 to 0:

$$0 = \frac{dW(0)}{dt_1} = \beta D(t_1)e^{-rt_1} - rC(x)e^{-rt_1}, \tag{8.3}$$

or

$$\boxed{\beta m = rC(x)}, \tag{8.4}$$

where the maximum import level $m \equiv D(t_1)$.

Equation (8.4) has the very appealing intuitive interpretation that *importing should continue until its cost per unit time reaches the equivalent annual cost of expansion*.[1] We note that this conclusion holds whether or not x has been optimized, except for the following limiting case. When β is small relative to $C(x)$, that is, when

$$\beta x \leq rC(x), \tag{8.5}$$

it is better to *import all additional requirements* than to add x units of capacity.

We now turn to finding the optimal expansion size x. For this purpose, we assume that the maximum import level m has been fixed, and we shift our time origin to the time of the initial expansion as shown in Figure 8.2. The present worth cost [in place of Equation (8.1)] is

$$W = C(x) + \int_{(x-m)/g}^{x/g} \beta(m + gt - x)e^{-rt}\,dt + W_F e^{-(r/g)x}. \tag{8.6}$$

Carrying out the integration, (8.6) can be written as

$$W = C(x) + \left(V_* + W_F\right)e^{-(r/g)x}, \tag{8.7}$$

where

$$V_* \equiv \frac{\beta g}{r^2}\left[e^{rm/g} - \frac{rm}{g} - 1\right]. \tag{8.8}$$

Now (8.7) is in the form of the simple sizing formulation of Section 4.1 [Equation (4.3)], but with $(V_* + W_F)$ as the future cost. That is, expansion x is deferring not only the usual future costs W_F, starting with the next expansion, but also the costs associated with the importing phase V_*. (Note that for a fixed maximum import level m, V_* is independent of the size x.)

---

[1]Recall that $C(x)$ is the present worth cost of providing x units of capacity (including income tax benefits of capital depreciation, replacement at the end of its useful life, and so forth, as discussed in Section 2.1.3. Thus, the present worth of an infinite annuity of $rC(x)$ is precisely $C(x)$.

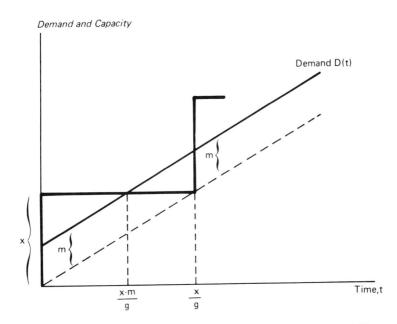

Figure 8.2. Capacity expansion with imports (time-shifted version of Figure 8.1.).

One observation we can draw from (8.7) is that *the optimal size with imports is larger than it would be without imports*. Also, it may appear from (8.7) that the present worth cost must increase when imports are allowed. This, of course, is not the case if the maximum import level has been optimized, since we could always have chosen to use zero imports. The present worth costs in (8.7) are referenced to a time at which an expansion is to take place. To compare legitimately the costs of using different import levels, it is necessary to use a common time reference point. A convenient one for this problem is a time when there is zero spare capacity in the system. The reader may wish to check that the present worth cost from such a time is

$$W(0) = (V_* + W)e^{-(r/g)m}. \tag{8.9}$$

In the following example, we show that Equation (8.7) can be used as the basis for an iterative algorithm much like those of Section 4.1.

Example 8.1. In Example 4.1 we considered a capacity expansion problem in which demand was given by $D(t) = 1.5t$, the cost of additional capacity was $C(x) = 16 + 2x$, and the discounting rate was $r = 0.1$. We found the optimal expansion size to be $x = 13.2$, yielding a present worth cost of $W = 72.5$. Suppose now that a capacity expansion is not required as soon as demand reaches existing capacity, but that a penalty cost of $0.8y$ per unit time is incurred whenever demand exceeds capacity by y units (i.e., $\beta = 0.8$). Starting with the earlier solution, we find the maximum import level m from (8.4):

$$m = \frac{1}{0.8}(0.1)\left[16 + (2)(13.2)\right] = 5.3.$$

From (8.8),

$$V_* = \frac{0.8(1.5)}{(0.1)^2}\left[e^{(0.1)(5.3)/1.5} - \frac{(0.1)(5.3)}{1.5} - 1\right] = 8.5.$$

The size x that minimizes W in (8.7) for the case of $C(x) = A + Bx$ is just [e.g., Equation (4.5)]

$$x = \frac{g}{r}\ln\frac{r(V_* + W_F)}{Bg}$$

$$= \frac{1.5}{0.1}\ln\frac{(0.1)(8.5 + 72.5)}{(2)(1.5)} = 14.9. \qquad (8.10)$$

But, of course, $W_F = 72.5$ is only an approximation for the problem at hand.

To get a new estimate of W_F, we assume that $W = W_F$ in (8.7) and solve for W_F (the policy iteration approach of Example 4.2):

$$W_F = \frac{C(x) + V_* e^{-(r/g)x}}{1 - e^{-(r/g)x}}$$

$$= \frac{16 + 2(14.9) + 8.5e^{-(0.1/1.5)14.9}}{1 - e^{-(0.1/1.5)14.9}} = 77.7. \qquad (8.11)$$

We now repeat the calculation of m using (8.4), V_* using (8.8), x using (8.10), and W_F using (8.11) until we get sufficiently close to the desired solution. Successive values are shown in Table 8.1. Also shown in the last column of Table 8.1 is the present worth cost, referenced to time 0

Table 8.1. Iterations for Example 8.1

Iteration number	m [Eq. (8.4)]	V_* [Eq. (8.8)]	x [Eq. (8.10)]	W_F [Eq. (8.11)]	$W(0)$ [Eq. (8.9)]
0	0	0	13.2	72.5	72.50
1	5.3	8.5	14.9	77.7	60.52
2	5.7	10.0	16.1	78.4	60.34
3	6.0	11.1	16.4	79.0	60.31
4	6.1	11.4	16.5	79.1	60.30
5	6.1	11.6	16.6	79.2	60.30
6	6.1	11.6	16.6	79.2	60.30

[Equation (8.9)] using the latest solution. Note that this cost changes only very slightly after the first one or two iterations. //

Figures 8.3–8.5 summarize the results of similar calculations for various values of the parameters. All quantities are plotted in terms of dimension-less ratios. Note that the optimal import interval (Figure 8.3) and the optimal expansion interval (Figure 8.4) become arbitrarily large as the import cost approaches the incremental expansion cost $[\beta/(rB) \to 1]$. This corresponds to using imports to satisfy all demand. Figure 8.3 indicates that the optimal import interval is strongly dependent on import costs. The optimal expansion size (Figure 8.4), however, is affected (increased) only when the parameters are such as to indicate a significant import phase.

Figure 8.3. Optimal import interval versus import cost for various economies-of-scale/growth rates.

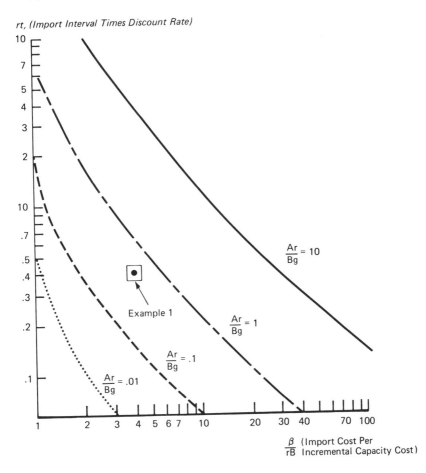

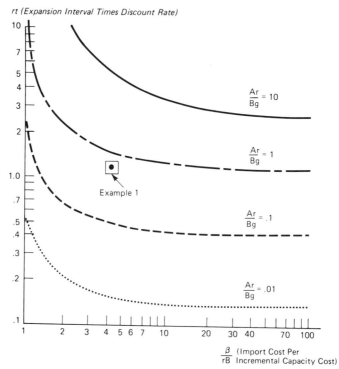

Figure 8.4. Optimal expansion interval versus import cost for various economies-of-scale/growth rates.

Figure 8.5. Present worth cost versus import cost for various economies-of-scale/growth rates.

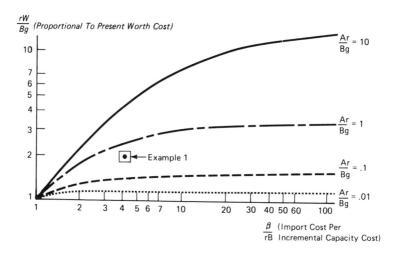

Figure 8.5 shows that the relative impact on present worth cost of the availability of imports is most important for the cases in which a large expansion interval is optimal. For example, when $Ar/(Bg)=10$, if imports are available at twice the marginal cost of expansion, $[\beta/(rB)=2]$, the present worth cost is proportional to 2; while if imports are unavailable [(look at $\beta/(r(B)=100]$, the present worth cost is proportional to about 13, a $6\frac{1}{2}:1$ ratio. In contrast, when $Ar/(Bg)=0.01$, the analogous ratio is barely larger than 1. That is, in the latter case little would be gained, proportionately, by the use of imports. Intuitively, the latter case is one in which capacity is added almost continuously in any case, and so little would change if it could be imported at a similar marginal cost.

8.2 Congestion Cost

In the previous section, we assumed that a cost (the importing cost) would be incurred as soon as there was a deficit in available capacity relative to demand. More typically, as we shall see in Chapter 9, running out of capacity is liable to be a gradual process marked by increases in operating costs, rearrangement costs, overtime penalties, and the like. Here we assume that these costs can be approximated by a congestion cost $v(s)$ per unit time, which is a function of the spare capacity s in the system (difference between available capacity and demand). In Section 8.1 we studied the special case in which

$$v(s) = \begin{cases} 0 & \text{for } s \geq 0 \\ -\beta s & \text{for } s < 0. \end{cases} \tag{8.12}$$

Nominally, we can think of $v(s)$ as a convex function that increases with decreasing s (i.e., the marginal congestion cost increases with more congestion).

In writing the expression (8.1) for present worth cost with imports, we assumed that spare capacity would go to 0 in each expansion cycle. We defined the present worth costs W and W_F for the time when spare capacity was 0. Here we cannot make such an assumption [$v(s)$ could rise precipitously as $s \rightarrow 0$, for example]. Figure 8.6 shows, schematically, a situation in which there is z spare capacity at time 0; an expansion of size x is to take place at time t_1, when there will be $s_* \equiv z - gt_1$ spare capacity; and further expansions will start at time $t_2 \equiv (z+x-s_{*F})/g$, when there will be s_{*F} spare capacity in the system. To start with, we think of the critical spare level for the second expansion s_{*F} and the present worth cost from that time on W_F as being known constants. We wish to find the optimal spare level s_* at which the initial expansion should take place and the optimal size x of that expansion. The present worth cost, which we

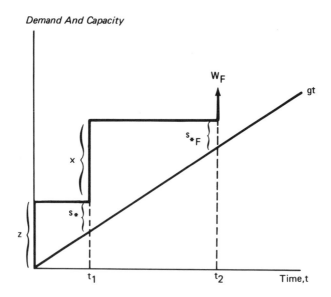

Figure 8.6. One cycle in a capacity expansion problem.

wish to minimize, is given by

$$W(z) = \int_0^{t_1} v[z - D(t)]e^{-rt}\,dt + C(x)e^{-rt_1}$$

$$+ \int_{t_1}^{t_2} v[z + x - D(t)]e^{-rt}\,dt + W_F(s_{*F})e^{-rt_2} \qquad (8.13)$$

[analogous to Equation (8.1) for the case with imports]. We next develop the equations corresponding to (8.13), (8.4), (8.7), and (8.8) for this more general case.

If the capacity size x is fixed (whether or not it is at its optimum), we may find the optimal time t_1 at which the expansion should take place by setting the derivative of (8.13) to 0:

$$0 = \frac{dW(z)}{dt_1} = v[z - D(t_1)]e^{-rt_1} - rC(x)e^{-rt_1} - v[z + x - D(t_1)]e^{-rt_1},$$

$$(8.14)$$

or

$$\boxed{v(s_*) - v(s_* + x) = rC(x)}\,,^2 \qquad (8.15)$$

---

[2] More precisely, if v is continuous, this is a *necessary* condition; and it turns out that if v is convex decreasing, this is also a sufficient condition.

where $s_* \equiv z - D(t_1)$ is the *critical spare level*. [These equations are generalizations of Equations (8.3 and (8.4)]. Thus, *the expansion should not be undertaken until its equivalent annual cost is just offset by the savings in congestion cost*.

We next consider the optimal expansion size x with the critical spare level s_* fixed (possibly at something other than its optimum).

Analogous to Equation (8.6) for the imports case, we rewrite the present worth cost (8.13) for the initial expansion time, so that $z = s_*$, $t_1 = 0$, and

$$W = C(x) + \int_0^{t_2} v\left[s_* + x - D(t) \right] e^{-rt} dt + W_F e^{-rt_2}, \qquad (8.16)$$

where now we have used just W for $W(s_*)$ and W_F for $W_F(s_{*F})$. A useful way of viewing the congestion cost (second term) is in terms of the costs incurred at various spare levels (instead of at various times). We therefore make the substitution of variable $y \equiv x - D(t) = x - gt$ for t in the integral; and with some rearrangement of terms, we obtain

$$W = C(x) + \left[V(x) + W_F e^{-(r/g)(s_* - s_{*F})} \right] e^{-(r/g)x}, \qquad (8.17)$$

where

$$V(x) \equiv \frac{1}{g} \int_{s_{*F} - s_*}^x v(s_* + y) e^{ry/g} dy. \qquad (8.18)$$

To simplify the expressions, we shall assume that $s_{*F} = s_*$. (In the repeated expansion case, this would be true for the optimal solution.) Thus, $t_2 = x/g$ and

$$W = C(x) + \left[V(x) + W_F \right] e^{-(r/g)x}, \qquad (8.19)$$

$$V(x) \equiv \frac{1}{g} \int_0^x v(s_* + y) e^{(r/g)y} dy \qquad (8.20)$$

[the analogues of Equations (8.7), (8.8)]. Expression (8.19) says that the present worth cost is given by the cost of the added capacity $C(x)$ at time 0 plus the future costs $V(x)$ and W_F incurred at the time of the next expansion x/g. Note that V is defined as the *future worth* of the annual congestion costs v incurred during the expansion cycle.

Finally, if we are to make present worth cost comparisons (for sensitivity studies, for example), it is necessary to relate the cost W given by Equation (8.19) to that given by (8.13). The cost in (8.19) is expressed *for an expansion time*, while the cost in (8.13) is expressed for a time when the system has z spare capacity. Thus, if we are to compare the relative costs of different expansion sizing and timing policies, it is the cost given by (8.13) that we must use. It is straightforward to check that the two are related by

$$W(z) = \left[V(z - s_*) + W \right] e^{-(r/g)(z - s_*)} \tag{8.21}$$

[the analogue of Equation (8.9)], where we have taken $z \geq s_*$. To reiterate the need for Equation (8.21), suppose that the present worth cost has been calculated for an expansion time for two different sizing and timing policies using (8.19) and (8.20). To compare the two policies, it is first necessary to refer them to the same time using (8.21).

We see from these expressions that, in general, the optimal expansion size depends intimately upon the congestion cost function. For any given set of data, of course we could find the optimal expansion time and size by minimizing W given by (8.13) with respect to t_1 and t_2 (by numerical means if necessary). Alternatively, we could try finding successively the size x that minimizes W in (8.19) and then the optimal critical spare level s_* in (8.15).[3]

In the following two sections we show that some insights can be gained by examining special cases of this congestion cost model.

8.3 Separation of Sizing and Timing Decisions

In more complex capacity expansion problems than the one that we have been considering in this chapter, it may be highly desirable to separate the sizing and timing decisions. That is, we may not wish to load down an already complex sizing model with detailed congestion cost calculations. We have hinted at this possibility in our solution algorithm for the importing problem illustrated in Example 8.1. The rapid convergence of that algorithm indicates that we could expect to obtain a very reasonable solution of the sizing problem using only a rough estimate of the timing problem (i.e., determination of the maximum import level).

In this section we shall explore some circumstances that allow a reasonable separation of the sizing and timing decisions and examine how properly to include the congestion cost effects in these circumstances. The following is a simple case in which complete separation is possible.

Example 8.2. Suppose the congestion cost when there is s spare capacity is given by

$$v(s) = \begin{cases} \infty & \text{for } s < s_1 \\ 0 & \text{for } s \geq s_1. \end{cases}$$

It should be intuitively clear that s_1 will be the critical spare level, that is, $s_* = s_1$ [in Equation (8.14) with $z > s_1$, the derivative will be negative when

---

[3]Further restrictions on C and v would be required to ensure that such a procedure always converges to the optimum.

$s < s_1$ and $+\infty$ when $s > s_1$]. From (8.20), $V(x) = 0$, and so (8.19) becomes the usual sizing equation [e.g., see Equation (4.3)]:

$$W = C(x) + W_F e^{-(r/g)x}.$$

Thus, an equivalent way of including the entire congestion cost effect is to use a modified demand function

$$D_1(t) \equiv D(t) + s_1,$$

defined so that a 0 spare level in the modified demand corresponds with an actual spare level of s_1. //

The next example can be viewed as a less extreme version of this one.

Example 8.3. Suppose the congestion cost when there is s spare capacity is given by

$$v(s) = v_0 e^{-\alpha s}, \tag{8.22}$$

with $v_0 = 20$ and $\alpha = 0.5$. As in Example 8.1, let capacity cost be $C(x) = A + Bx$ with $A = 16$, $B = 2$; let demand grow at $g = 1.5$; and let the discounting rate be $r = 0.1$.

Suppose we start with an expansion size of $x = 13.2$, which is optimal in the ordinary expansion problem using this data, but with no congestion cost. The optimal timing of this expansion is found using Equation (8.15):

$$v_0 e^{-\alpha s_*} - v_0 e^{-\alpha(s_* + x)} = rC(x), \tag{8.23}$$

or

$$s_* = -\frac{1}{\alpha} \ln \frac{rC(x)}{v_0(1 - e^{-\alpha x})}.$$

$$= -\frac{1}{0.5} \ln \frac{0.1(16 + 2(13.2))}{20(1 - e^{-0.5(13.2)})} = 3.1. \tag{8.24}$$

It is easy to check that the congestion cost after expansion, the second term in (8.23), is quite small and can be ignored. The congestion cost over an expansion cycle is given by (8.20), which integrates for this example to

$$V(x) = \frac{v_0 e^{-\alpha s_*}}{g(\alpha - r/g)} \left[1 - e^{-(\alpha - r/g)x} \right]$$

$$= \frac{20 e^{-0.5(3.1)}}{1.5(0.5 - 0.1/1.5)} \left[1 - e^{-(0.5 - 0.1/1.5)x} \right]$$

$$= 6.53 \left[1 - e^{-0.4333(13.2)} \right] = 6.51 \tag{8.25}$$

For expansion sizes x near 13.2, the factor in brackets is very nearly unity, and therefore $V(x)$ is virtually independent of x. Thus, we assume that V can be treated as a constant in the sizing Equation (8.19); consequently, the optimal size [from Equation (8.10)] is

$$x = \frac{1.5}{0.1} \ln \frac{0.1(6.51 + 72.5)}{2(1.5)} = 14.5.$$

Similarly, we can get a new estimate of W_F as in Equation (8.11):

$$W_F = \frac{16 + 2(14.5) + 6.51e^{-(0.1/1.5)14.5}}{1 - e^{-(0.1/1.5)14.5}} = 76.6.$$

It is straightforward to repeat the calculations for s_* using (8.24), V using (8.25), x using (8.10), and W_F using (8.11) to obtain the values shown in Table 8.2. The last column of Table 8.2 shows $W(5)$, the present worth cost from a time when the spare in the system is $z = 5$ [from Equation (8.21)]. As in Example 8.1 where we considered the case of imports, we find a rapid convergence to the optimal solution. //

In Examples 8.1 and 8.3, we have found situations for which the congestion cost (or import cost) basically can be tacked on as an added cost incurred just prior to each expansion (see Figure 8.7). While the congestion cost in these cases *does* depend on the expansion size (through s_* or m), the dependence is relatively weak. In turn, the optimal expansion size is relatively insensitive to changes in the congestion cost. [In Equation (8.19), the optimal size is not very sensitive to small changes in the future cost, as discussed in Section 4.1.] In general, the congestion cost may affect the optimal size more directly [e.g., when V is large relative to W_F and is a strong function of x in Equation (8.19)]. In extreme cases, congestion cost may be the sole determinant of expansion size and time, as we show in the following section.

8.4 A Zero-Growth Case

Suppose the demand growth rate g goes to 0. Then the present worth cost [Equation (8.13)] becomes

$$W(z) = \int_0^{t_1} v(z)e^{-rt}\,dt + C(x)e^{-rt_1} + \int_{t_1}^{\infty} v(z+x)e^{-rt}\,dt + W_F(z)e^{-\infty},$$

Table 8.2. Iterations for Example 8.3

Iteration number	s_* [Eq. (8.24)]	$V(x)$ [Eq. (8.25)]	x [Eq. (8.10)]	W_F [Eq. (8.11)]	$W(5)$ [Eq. (8.21)]
0	—	—	13.2	72.5	—
1	3.1	6.51	14.5	76.6	70.71
2	3.0	6.85	15.3	76.8	70.53
3	2.9	7.21	15.4	76.9	70.25
4	2.9	7.21	15.5	76.9	70.25

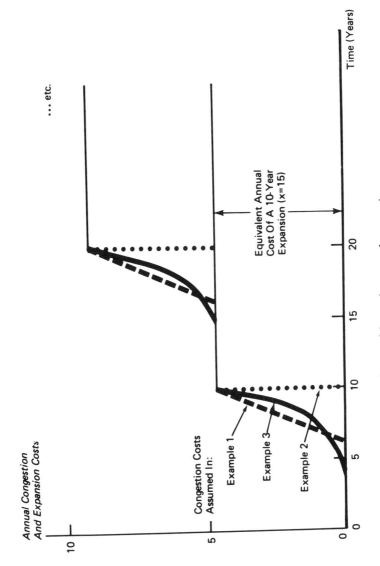

Figure 8.7. Congestion costs are incurred just prior to each expansion.

or

$$W(z) = \frac{v(z)}{r} + \left\{ C(x) - \frac{1}{r}[v(z) - v(z+x)] \right\} e^{-rt_1}. \qquad (8.26)$$

The first term is the present worth of congestion costs with z spare. (Recall that with no growth, the spare level stays at z unless it is changed by a capacity expansion.) The second term is the cost of an expansion $C(x)$ less the present worth of congestion cost savings due to the expansion, all discounted to time 0. Since the term in brackets is independent of time, the expansion will pay at time 0 if it pays at all; and clearly, the expansion will only pay if the right-hand side is negative:

$$rC(x) \le v(z) - v(z+x). \qquad (8.27)$$

In the previous section, we obtained a similar relationship [Equation (8.15)] for determining the critical spare level s_* given the expansion size x. Here, the *same* equation also determines the optimal size. Note that *because we have no growth, capacity expansion is being considered purely for the purpose of reducing the ongoing congestion cost.*

The solution of this problem is nicely illustrated graphically for the following special case. Consider a smooth, convex, decreasing congestion cost function $v(s)$, as shown in Figure 8.8, and let $C(x) = A + Bx$. Setting the derivative with respect to x of $W(z)$ [Equation (8.26)] to 0 yields

$$v'(z+x) = -rB, \qquad (8.28)$$

where the prime denotes derivative. This prompts us to define an optimal capacity *after* expansion $S^* \equiv z + x$, where $z + x$ satisfies the slope condition (8.28). Figure 8.8 illustrates that S^* is simply the point of tangency to the congestion cost curve of a line having slope $-rB$. For this special case, the relation (8.27) tells us that the expansion will pay if and only if

$$r[A + B(S^* - z)] \le v(z) - v(S^*),$$

or

$$v(z) \ge v(S^*) + r[A + B(S^* - z)]. \qquad (8.29)$$

As z varies, the right-hand side of (8.29) traces the upper dashed line shown in Figure 8.8. Thus, the critical spare level s_* at which equality holds in (8.29) is the intersection of this line with the congestion cost curve (see Figure 8.8). Clearly, the expansion will pay only if existing spare capacity z is below the critical spare level s_*. Furthermore, if an expansion is undertaken (whether it should have been done or not), sufficient capacity should be provided to bring the spare level up to S^*.

Example 8.4. Suppose that the congestion cost is given by $v(s) = 1/s$ (only positive spare capacity allowed), the capacity cost is $r[C(x)] = 1.6 + 0.2x$, and there is no growth ($g = 0$). At what level of spare would a capacity

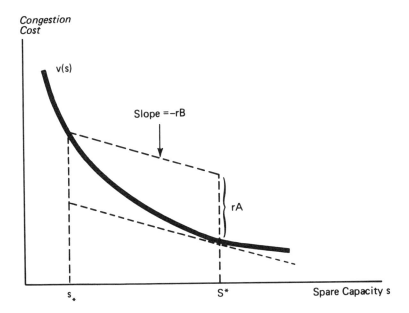

Figure 8.8. Capacity expansion to reduce congestion cost.

expansion be justified to reduce the congestion cost, and how much capacity should be added? We first determine S^* from (8.28): $-1/S^{*2} = -0.2$, or $S^* = 2.24$; thus, $v(S^*) = 0.45$. Then (8.29) at the critical spare level becomes

$$\frac{1}{s_*} = 0.45 + \left[1.6 + 0.2(2.24 - s_*) \right],$$

which rearranges into the quadratic equation

$$s_*^2 - 12.48 s_* + 5 = 0,$$

whose solution is $s_* = 0.41$. Thus, capacity expansion is not justified unless the spare level is less than $s_* = 0.41$; and if capacity is added, the spare level should be increased to $S^* = 2.24$. //

This section illustrates that congestion cost may have a significant impact on the optimal expansion size; and, in fact, in the limit of zero growth of demand, the optimal expansion size is determined purely by congestion cost. In a more general case, size would be determined by both the need to serve increasing demand and the desire to reduce congestion costs. Consequently, the analysis would be more involved than that of this section or Section 8.3, where we assumed that a separation of sizing and timing decisions was possible.

8.5 Summary

We have enhanced the basic capacity expansion model with the addition of a congestion cost. By congestion cost we mean a cost per unit time that is allowed to depend on the amount of spare capacity in the system. It is meant to capture whatever penalties there may be for running out of capacity. We shall show in Chapter 9 that this enhancement gives us considerable flexibility in modeling capacity expansion problems.

We have shown in this chapter that the existence of a congestion cost leads to a natural economic determination of *when* to undertake a capacity expansion; namely, when the equivalent annual cost of that expansion is offset by the resulting savings in congestion cost [Equation (8.15)]. Sizing is also affected by the existence of congestion costs. This is most vividly illustrated by the case in which demand growth is assumed to be zero (Section 8.4). It turns out that a capacity expansion may be warranted purely for purposes of reducing the ongoing congestion cost.

In general, when there is growth, an expansion has the effect of reducing congestion costs, and so may motivate somewhat larger sizes. In the special case for which congestion costs can be assumed infinite below some spare level s_1 and 0 above that level (Example 8.2), the full effect of the congestion cost can be included by a simple shift of the demand function (i.e., redefine demand so that s_1 corresponds to 0 spare). Even if the congestion cost does not fall off quite so rapidly, as a practical matter it may be reasonable to behave as if it did in calculating optimal expansion sizes. Examples 8.1 and 8.3 indicate that it may be possible to obtain good approximations to the optimal expansion size using only a rough approximation of the critical spare level at which the expansion should be undertaken (we called this *separation of sizing and timing*). This will be true whenever the congestion cost, when plotted as in Figure 8.7, rises sharply enough to constitute a small portion of the overall cost. Our discussion on separating sizing and timing decisions is really aimed at more complex capacity expansion models. It probably would not be worthwhile if the simple model of this chapter were our only goal.

In Chapter 9 we shall discuss how some capacity expansion problems can be viewed in terms of a congestion cost and illustrate the application of some ideas from this chapter.

8.6 Further Reading

The capacity expansion problem with imports allowed has been studied by

D. Erlenkotter, Optimal Plant Size with Time-Phased Imports, In *Investments for Capacity Expansion*, A. S. Manne (ed.), London, Allen & Unwin, 1967.

The appendix adapts to the notation of this book, the work of

A. S. Manne, Capacity Expansion and Probabilistic Growth, *Econometrica* 29(4), October 1961, 632–649.

Much of the outlook and formulation in this chapter bears similarities to S. A. Marglin's book cited in Section 2.11.

Appendix. Congestion Cost with Random Demand

Here we consider the effects of congestion cost when demand is assumed to be the random process studied in Section 7.1. We develop an expression (8.52) for the expected present worth cost of capacity expansion including congestion cost. We then show the results of sample calculations for an example in which the congestion cost is an import cost. The example turns out to be one in which expected present worth cost *decreases* for small increases in variance. Despite appearances, we argue that this does not really indicate that ignorance is beneficial.

The analogue of the present worth cost of the deterministic case [Equation (8.13)] is

$$E[W(z)] = E\left\{ \int_0^{t_1} v[z - D(t)] e^{-rt} \, dt \right\}$$

$$+ C(x)E(e^{-rt_1}) + E\left\{ \int_{t_1}^{t_2} v[z + x - D(t)] e^{-rt} \, dt \right\}$$

$$+ E\left[W_F(z) e^{-rt_2} \right], \tag{8.30}$$

where the process starts off at 0 with an initial level z of spare capacity; t_1 is the random time at which the process first reaches a level $z - s_*$ (i.e., when the spare level first drops to the critical level s_*, at which time an expansion will take place); x is the size of the expansion; and t_2 is the random time at which the process first reaches a level x (i.e., when the spare level is once more restored to its initial level z). In the deterministic case we were able to differentiate with respect to t_1 and obtain immediately the annual cost relation (8.15). Here, t_1 is a random variable and s_* is the analogous control variable, so that no such simple differentiation is possible. We can rewrite readily the second and fourth terms of (8.30) using the equivalent growth notion of Chapter 7 to obtain

$$E[W(z)] = E\begin{pmatrix} \text{congestion} \\ \text{cost} \\ \text{before expansion} \end{pmatrix} + C(x) e^{-r(z - s_* / \hat{g}_1)}$$

$$+ E\begin{pmatrix} \text{congestion} \\ \text{cost} \\ \text{after expansion} \end{pmatrix} + E[W_F(z)] e^{-r(x/\hat{g}_1)}, \tag{8.31}$$

where $\hat{g}_1$ is the equivalent deterministic growth rate of demand as determined by Equations (7.11) and (7.14) for discrete customers or by Equation (7.39) for continuous demand. The congestion cost terms require calculations we did not do in Chapter 7.

We shall go through a rather involved derivation that will show that these terms can be expressed as the integral of instantaneous congestion cost v times a factor $\hat{p}$ that is analogous to the simple present worth factor in the deterministic case [Equation (8.52)].

We begin by showing that both congestion cost terms require the same mathematical formula. In the third term of (8.30), making the substitution of variables $u = t - t_1$ in the integral gives

$$E\left(\begin{array}{c} \text{congestion} \\ \text{cost} \\ \text{after expansion} \end{array}\right) = E\left\{ e^{-rt_1} \int_0^{t_2 - t_1} v[z + x - D(t_1 + u)] e^{-ru} \, du \right\}. \quad (8.32)$$

Since our demand process has stationary independent increments, we know that for statistical purposes we may take

$$D(t_1 + u) = D(t_1) + D(u) = z - s_* + D(u), \quad (8.33)$$

and that

$$t_2 - t_1 = t_x, \quad (8.34)$$

where t_x is the time to first reach a level x starting from 0. Thus the integral in (8.32) is really independent of t_1, and we can write

$$E\left(\begin{array}{c} \text{congestion} \\ \text{cost} \\ \text{after expansion} \end{array}\right) = e^{-r(z - s_*)/\hat{g}_1} E\left\{ \int_0^{t_x} v[s_* + x - D(u)] e^{-ru} \, du \right\}. \quad (8.35)$$

Now the first term of (8.30) is identical in form with the expected value expression in (8.35) (just take $z = s_* + x$). Thus we shall have expressions for both congestion cost terms if we can find an expression for the expected congestion cost before expansion for arbitrary initial spare z. We next proceed with that task.

Consider, first, the case of discrete customers and $t_1 = \infty$ (i.e., what would the expected congestion cost be if no expansion were to take place?). Then

$$E\left[\begin{array}{c} \text{congestion} \\ \text{cost with} \\ t_1 = \infty \end{array}\right] = E\left\{ \int_0^\infty v[z - D(t)] e^{-rt} \, dt \right\}$$

$$= \int_0^\infty E\{v[z - D(t)]\} e^{-rt} \, dt$$

$$= \int_0^\infty \sum_{n=-\infty}^\infty \Pr[D(t) = n] v(z - n) e^{-rt} \, dt$$

$$= \sum_{n=-\infty}^\infty v(z - n) \int_0^\infty \Pr[D(t) = n] e^{-rt} \, dt. \quad (8.36)$$

For later reference, we define

$$p_n(t) \equiv \Pr[D(t) = n],$$

$$\hat{p}_n \equiv \int_0^\infty e^{-rt} \Pr[D(t) = n] \, dt. \quad (8.37)$$

We can readily solve for $\hat{p}_n$ from the birth/death equations for this process (derived in most standard probability texts):

$$\frac{d}{dt}p_n(t) = -(\lambda+\mu)p_n(t)+\lambda p_{n-1}(t)+\mu p_{n+1}(t). \qquad (8.38)$$

Taking the Laplace transform with the initial conditions $p_0(0)=1$ and $p_n(0)=0$, $n \neq 1$ (i.e., the process starts with 0 demand),

$$(r+\lambda+\mu)\hat{p}_0 = \lambda\hat{p}_{-1}+\mu\hat{p}_1+1,$$

$$(r+\lambda+\mu)\hat{p}_n = \lambda\hat{p}_{n-1}+\mu\hat{p}_{n+1}, \qquad n \neq 0. \qquad (8.39)$$

The solution of these difference equations turns out to be

$$\hat{p}_n = \begin{cases} k\theta^n & \text{if } n \geq 0 \\ k\delta^n & \text{if } n \leq 0, \end{cases} \qquad (8.40)$$

with

$$\theta \equiv \frac{(r+\lambda+\mu)-\sqrt{(r+\lambda+\mu)^2-4\lambda\mu}}{2\mu},$$

$$1/\delta \equiv \frac{(r+\lambda+\mu)-\sqrt{(r+\lambda+\mu)^2-4\lambda\mu}}{2\lambda}, \qquad (8.41)$$

$$k \equiv \frac{1}{\sqrt{(r+\lambda+\mu)^2-4\lambda\mu}}.$$

It is straightforward to check that this solution satisfies the difference equations. Furthermore, it is the only solution for which $\hat{p}_n \to 0$ as $|n| \to \infty$, as required by physical reasoning. Note that θ is the quantity that defines equivalent growth rate [see Equation (7.14)]. By analogy, $1/\delta$ can be viewed as defining another equivalent growth rate, but with λ and μ interchanged (an equivalent *downward* growth rate).

Since we are actually interested in the case for which congestion costs are accumulated only until time t_1 when demand first reaches a level $z-s_*$, we need to replace $p_n(t)$ and $\hat{p}_n$ by

$$p_{n,z-s_*}(t) \equiv \Pr\{D(t)=z-s_* \text{ and } D(T)<z-s_* \text{ for } T<t\}, \qquad (8.42)$$

$$\hat{p}_{n,z-s_*} \equiv \int_0^\infty e^{-rt}p_{n,z-s_*}(t)\, dt. \qquad (8.43)$$

That is, in place of (8.36) we need

$$E\begin{pmatrix} \text{congestion} \\ \text{cost} \\ \text{before expansion} \end{pmatrix} = \sum_{n=-\infty}^{z-s_*} v(z-n)\hat{p}_{n,z-s_*}. \qquad (8.44)$$

Fortunately, we can obtain an expression for $\hat{p}_{n,x}$ in terms of known quantities. We start with the identity

$$\Pr\{D(t)=n\} = \Pr\{D(t)=n \text{ and } D(t)<x \text{ for } T<t\}$$
$$+ \int_{T=0}^t f_{t_x}(T)\Pr\{D(t-T)=n-x\}\, dT, \qquad (8.45)$$

where $f_{t_x}(T)$ is the probability density function of the time of first passage to x. This decomposition says that demand at t could be n without ever having reached x or by having first reached x at some intermediate time T and then dropped back to n. Taking Laplace transforms of both sides and interchanging limits of integration in the last term gives

$$\hat{p}_n = \hat{p}_{n,x} + E(e^{-r t_x})\hat{p}_{n-x}. \tag{8.46}$$

Since we know the Laplace transform of the first passage time to x from Chapter 7 [Equation (7.9)] and we have expressions (8.40) for $\hat{p}_n$, we may solve for the desired $\hat{p}_{n,x}$:

$$\hat{p}_{n,x} = \begin{cases} k\theta^n - \theta^x(k\delta^{n-x}) & \text{if } 0 \le n \le x \\ k\delta^n - \theta^x(k\delta^{n-x}) & \text{if } n \le 0. \end{cases} \tag{8.47}$$

It is interesting to think of this equation in terms of the equivalent growth rates $\hat{g}_1$ and $\hat{g}_2$; these are defined by

$$e^{-r/\hat{g}_1} \equiv \theta,$$

$$e^{r/\hat{g}_2} \equiv \delta, \tag{8.48}$$

so that $\hat{g}_1$ is our previously defined quantity and $\hat{g}_2$ is a downward growth. Also, it is convenient to go to a continuous process, carefully taking the limit as in Section 7.1.4 to obtain

$$\hat{g}_1 = \frac{\sqrt{\bar{g}^2 + 2r\sigma^2} + \bar{g}}{2},$$

$$\hat{g}_2 = \frac{\sqrt{\bar{g}^2 + 2r\sigma^2} - \bar{g}}{2}, \tag{8.49}$$

$$k = \frac{1}{\hat{g}_1 + \hat{g}_2},$$

with $\bar{g}$ and σ^2 the mean and variance of demand per unit time as discussed in Sections 7.1.3 and 7.1.4. In terms of these quantities (8.47) becomes

$$\hat{p}_{n,x} = \frac{1}{\hat{g}_1 + \hat{g}_2} \begin{cases} e^{-r(n/\hat{g}_1)} - e^{-r[(x/\hat{g}_1)+(x-n)/\hat{g}_2]}, & 0 \le n \le x \\ e^{r(n/\hat{g}_2)} - e^{-r[(x/\hat{g}_1)+(x-n)/\hat{g}_2]}, & n \le 0. \end{cases} \tag{8.50}$$

Also, with continuous demand, the sum in the expected congestion cost (8.44) becomes an integral:

$$E\begin{pmatrix} \text{congestion} \\ \text{cost} \\ \text{before expansion} \end{pmatrix} = \int_{-\infty}^{z-s_*} v(z-n)\hat{p}_{n,z-s_*}\, dn. \tag{8.51}$$

Putting all of this together, we can write the present worth cost (8.31) as

$$E[W(z)] = \int_{-\infty}^{z-s_*} v(z-n)\hat{p}_{n,z-s_*}\, dn + C(x)e^{-r(z-s_*)/\hat{g}_1}$$

$$+ e^{-r(z-s_*)/\hat{g}_1} \int_{-\infty}^{x} v(s_*+x-n)\hat{p}_{n,x}\, dn + E[W_{\mathrm{F}}(z)]e^{-r(x/\hat{g}_1)}. \tag{8.52}$$

In comparing this with the deterministic case [e.g., Equation 8.13], we see that $\hat{g}_1$ replaces $\bar{g}$ and $\hat{p}$ replaces a present worth factor in the congestion cost integrals. [It can be shown readily that $\hat{p}$, defined by Equation (8.50), converges to a simple present worth factor when $\sigma^2 \to 0$.]

Solution approaches similar to those discussed in the text may apply to this random model, but the reader should be warned that the situation is liable to be somewhat more complex. For example, we do not, in general, obtain a simple expression such as Equation (8.15) for determining the optimal critical spare level. We give no further discussion of how to minimize (8.52). We turn instead to an interesting phenomenon that can be demonstrated readily for the special case in which congestion cost is an import cost.

For the case of imports, we can rewrite Equation (8.52) using $z = 0$, $s_* = -m$, and $v(s) = -\beta s$. Carrying out the integration in the first term and noting that the third term vanishes, we get

$$E[W(0)] = \frac{\beta \bar{g}}{r^2} \left[\frac{\hat{g}_1^2 e^{r(m/\hat{g}_1)} - \hat{g}_2^2 e^{-r(m/\hat{g}_2)}}{\hat{g}_1^2 - \hat{g}_2^2} - \frac{rm}{g} - 1 \right] e^{-r(m/\hat{g}_1)}$$

$$+ C(x) e^{-r(m/\hat{g}_1)} + E[W_F(0)] e^{-r(x/\hat{g}_1)}. \tag{8.53}$$

Example 8.5. Consider a random demand version of Example 8.1. That is, discounting rate, $r = 0.1$, capacity cost $C(x) = 16 + 2x$, importing cost $\beta = 0.8$, and the expected growth rate $\bar{g} = 1.5$. Example 8.1 shows that in the zero-variance case, the optimal solution is to use a maximum import level of $m = 6.1$ and an expansion size of $x = 16.6$, for a present worth cost of $W = 60.30$. With positive variance, we wish to minimize expected cost as given by (8.53). Making the same assumption as in Example 8.1, that is, $E[W_F(0)] = E[W(0)]$, we can solve (8.53) explicitly for $E[W(0)]$ to obtain

$$E[W(0)] = \frac{\left[\bar{V}(m) + C(x) \right] e^{-r(m/\hat{g}_1)}}{1 - e^{-r(x/\hat{g}_1)}}, \tag{8.54}$$

where

$$\bar{V}(m) \equiv \frac{\beta \bar{g}}{r^2} \left[\frac{\hat{g}_1^2 e^{r(m/\hat{g}_1)} - \hat{g}_2^2 e^{-r(m/\hat{g}_2)}}{\hat{g}_1^2 - \hat{g}_2^2} - \frac{rm}{g} - 1 \right]. \tag{8.55}$$

It is interesting (and straightforward) to find the expected present worth cost using (8.54) and (8.55) for the expansion policy that was found to be optimal with no variance (i.e., $m = 6.1$, $x = 16.6$). The upper curve of Figure 8.9 plots this cost versus variance. Note that the curve *decreases* for small values of variance before rising again as variance gets large! The effect is even more pronounced if we assume that the expansion policy will be tailored to the variance. The lower curve of Figure 8.9 shows the smallest expected present worth cost that can be obtained at each value of variance by selecting the import level and expansion size to minimize (8.54). For example, when the variance is 3, it turns out that $E[W(0)] = 60.03$ if we use $m = 6.1$

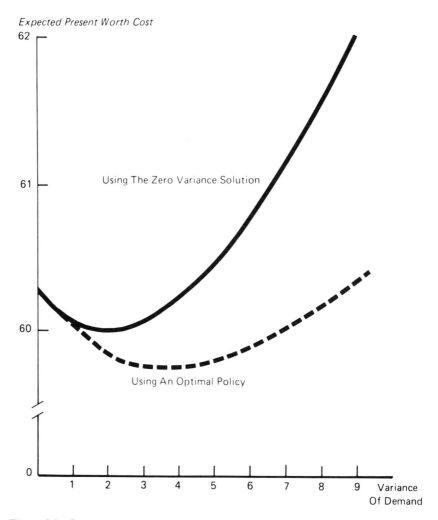

Figure 8.9. Cost versus variance.

and $x = 16.6$ in (8.54). By doing some searching, we find that $E[W(0)]$ achieves its minimum value of 59.76 when $m = 7.3$ and $x = 17.3$. It is possible to do some systematic searching analogous to the methods used in the deterministic case in the main body of the chapter. As we already have noted, however, it is not possible to use a relation as simple as (8.4) or (8.15) to determine the maximum import level for a fixed expansion size. //

Thus we have an illustration that the expected present worth cost may *decrease* with more variance in demand. This contrasts with our observation in Chapter 7, where imports were not allowed, that expected present worth cost necessarily *increases* with variance in demand. It may seem surprising that we should expect to benefit from more uncertainty (which we often intuitively think of as ignorance) about the demand. We should bear in mind, however, that this uncertainty has been modeled by a specific inward/outward movement process (see the discussion at the beginning of Chapter 7). This example has demonstrated that when shortages are allowed to be temporarily served by imports, we may be better off to take our chances on a process in which demand may decrease or increase rather than be forced to serve the expected demand. The example also serves to point out that demand variance is not necessarily a very good measure of our ignorance. If we view the variance simply as a physical measure (or estimate) of the volatility of the process, the mystery disappears. We are *not* rewarded for ignorance.

Chapter 9

When to Declare a Shortage

In Chapter 8 we added to our basic simple capacity expansion model a term congestion costs for. We found that congestion costs not only influence the optimal expansion *size*, but also serve to define an optimal expansion *time*. The question of expansion time hardly even arose in our earlier models—we obviously wanted to expand only when it became necessary, which is whenever we first experienced a shortage. In Chapter 8, congestion cost largely remained an abstract entity. Here we will consider some specific capacity expansion problems that can be modeled in this way.

Before proceeding, it is worth reflecting on why we would want to focus on costs that are a function of spare capacity. In any applications, there are probably many different types of associated costs; however, not all are relevant to capacity expansion decisions. For example, if capacity always exceeds demand, costs that are strictly a function of demand (such as raw material used per item of manufacture) need not be included, since they are unaffected by our expansion decisions.[1] Similarly, costs strictly associated with capacity in place probably need not be considered separately. These costs can probably best be included in the purchase cost of capacity. However, costs that depend on both the amount of capacity *and* the demand are not so easily shrugged off. These are the costs that our congestion cost format tries to capture.

In Section 9.1 we describe some phenomena that can be viewed as temporary imports, including the use of an alternative technology in a

---

[1] In Example 9.1, capacity need not always meet demand, and so raw material costs *are* relevant.

telephone example (Example 9.3) and the case of lost sales (Example 9.4).

We describe a blockage model from another telephone application in Section 9.2. This serves to illustrate that what we nominally call capacity and demand are not necessarily simple, uniform quantities. In this case, it is necessary to deal with their geographic dispersion.

In Section 9.3 we describe a model of electric generating capacity. Here again, the capacity is not uniform—some generating plants cost more to operate than others. Furthermore, demand for power exhibits very strong daily, weekly, and seasonal fluctuations, making it nonuniform as well (peaks in demand can be served by different machines).

Finally, in the summary in Section 9.4, we discuss various other considerations that may enter into deciding when to declare a shortage. For example, shortage may be defined by regulatory or reliability requirements and not directly by economics at all.

9.1 Temporary Imports

In many applications, deficits in capacity temporarily can be served by imports; the larger the deficit, the greater the imports required. In some instances, these imports literally may be shipments of goods from abroad, as, for example, in studies of the aluminum production capability of India.[2] Since we have assumed a cost minimization criterion for our capacity expansion studies, we are really only interested in the importing *cost*; and so we can view various other phenomena as imports as well. Generally, whenever we can associate a constant charge β per unit time per unit of demand in excess of existing capacity, we shall refer to that charge as the *importing cost*. In Section 8.1 we analyzed the availability of this kind of importing capability.

The following examples sketch some situations that could be treated as imports by the above definition.

Example 9.1. The XYZ Chemicals firm uses stainless steel tubing in many of its plants; and so maintains a production capability for the tubing. It is currently producing at its full capacity of M feet/year, and its use is projected to grow at the rate of g feet/year/year. In formulating expansion plans, the firm has been considering machines of various output capacities. It has ignored the material and labor costs of manufacture, m dollars/foot, as being common to all of the machines under consideration. It now wishes to consider the possibility of buying tubing, perhaps temporarily, from an outside supplier at c dollars/foot. How should the firm calculate its importing cost? The actual importing cost β, which we have defined as the cost per unit time per unit of demand in excess of available

---

[2] See the work edited by A. S. Manne cited in Section 3.6.

capacity, would be just $\beta = c$. Thus, if the firm does not expand, at time t from now its demand will exceed its supply by gt feet/year, and it will be spending $(gt)(c)$ dollars/year on importing the tubing. If the firm wishes to analyze importing and/or expansion alternatives in the same study, however, it must also deal with the material and labor costs of manufacture. To be consistent, it is necessary either to include these with its expansion costs, which the firm has not done, or to deduct them from the outside purchase cost (these costs would not be incurred for the purchased tubing), and so the firm should use an importing cost of $\beta = c - m$. //

Example 9.2. Suppose additional warehouse space can be rented at $15/square foot/year. If this warehouse space is equivalent to space we are planning to add, then we can treat $\beta = 15$ as an importing cost. We should be careful, however, that is is really equivalent for our purposes. Is it available when and where we need it in the proper dimensions, and so on? //

Example 9.3. In the local feeder portion of the telephone transmission network, which we shall study in Chapter 10, communication paths generally consist of a pair of copper wires per customer. The capacity of a link of the feeder network is ordinarily expanded by installing an optimally sized (see the EFRAP problem in Chapter 10) bundle of wire pairs called a cable. In lieu of adding cable, it is sometimes possible to provide service with pair gain systems, electronic devices that allow additional communication paths to share wire pairs already in use (by multiplexing or switching). Many of these systems can be installed and removed in small bundles, and so used only temporarily whenever demand exceeds available capacity. Furthermore, their cost per unit time is roughly proportional to the number of units in service.[3] In these instances, use of the *alternative technology* of pair gain devices is analogous to importing. //

Example 9.4. Suppose, as an alternative to building another factory, that we simply can let some demand go unmet for a while. Then the lost sales (net of expenses) are essentially an importing cost. In such a situation, however, we may have to consider also the potential permanent loss of some customers who switch to other brands. If we were considering the expansion of a public facility such as water or sewerage supply, we may wish to impose a social cost for unsatisfied demand in place of lost revenues. //

---

[3] Real situations can get much more complex, of course, as illustrated in the article by Koontz and Shipley cited at the end of this chapter.

Example 9.5. What if goods can be produced using slack capacity at other locations and shipped to the one under consideration (the goods may be electrical power, for example). For moderate import levels, we simply could ship from the nearest alternative location, and β would be the transportation cost (assuming similar manufacturing costs at all locations). As the capacity of the nearest facility is exhausted, however, we would have to ship at higher cost from other facilities, and so on. In that case, the cost of imports with demand growing linearly over time might look like the flat kinked curve in Figure 9.1. If demand is also growing at the nearest location, more would have to be supplied over time from the other at a higher cost (dashed curve). Due to the nonlinearity, this cost might be better viewed as a general congestion cost rather than an importing cost. More generally, we probably should be looking at possible expansion of all of the capacities at all of the locations with all transportation costs considered. Such problems are discussed briefly in Section 11.2. //

Example 9.6. Suppose a machine (e.g., the tubing machine of Example 9.1) is operating at its nominal capacity, but that a higher production level can be obtained with overtime work. To the extent that additional production can be achieved at a constant extra overtime charge per unit, this use of overtime can be viewed as importing. In a situation such as this, if we try to squeeze too much extra production out of existing facilities, the extra cost per unit probably will increase due to factors such as breakdown of

Figure 9.1. Transporting from alternative facilities.

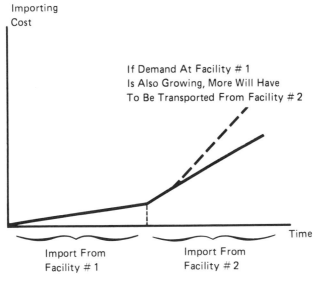

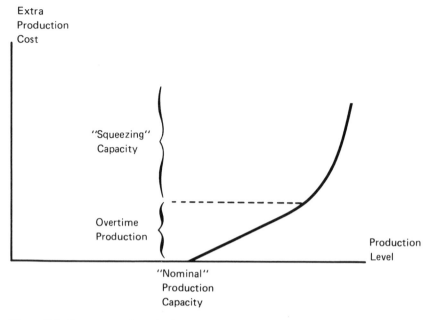

Figure 9.2. Extra cost of producing at higher than nominal capacity.

machines during production hours (see Figure 9.2). Instead of a linear importing cost, we then will be dealing with a nonlinear congestion cost. //

We now leave these samples of linear importing costs (which may become nonlinear in extremes) and consider some other possible consequences of running out of capacity.

9.2 Blockage Cost

In our simple capacity expansion models we have assumed a *uniformity* of capacity and of customers that may be a poor approximation in some circumstances. Here we explore the problem in terms of a specific application.

9.2.1 Multipled Connection of Feeder

In Chapter 10 we shall study a rather complex capacity expansion problem for the local feeder portion of the telephone network. Here we examine some aspects of that problem which we shall be unable to include in the complex model of Chapter 10.

The feeder network connects each customer, via a pair of copper wires, to a switching machine in the central office. The wire pairs are added to the network in bundles called cables that generally are placed on pole lines

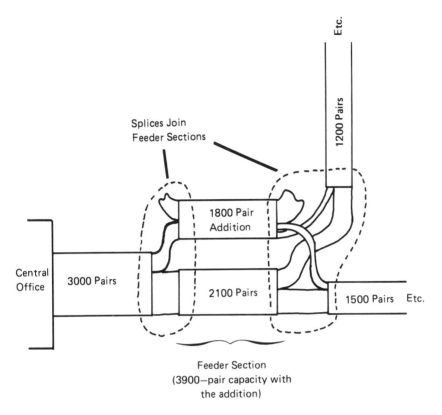

Figure 9.3. Cable is added to a feeder section and spliced, pair by pair to other cables at the end points.

or in underground conduit along *sections* of the feeder as illustrated schematically in Figure 9.3. In the highlighted feeder section, the capacity was 2,100 pairs, and we have illustrated the addition of an 1,800-pair cable (so that current capacity is 3,900 pairs). This is the view of the feeder that we take in Chapter 10 for the purpose of studying capacity expansions.

Here we take another view for the purpose of studying what happens as we run out of capacity. Figure 9.4 traces a *pair group* from the central office to a geographical region called an *allocation area*. Each wire pair in the group stands ready to provide a complete electrical connection to a customer in the area. The pairs in this group possibly *could* be used to serve customers in another allocation area, but that would require a network rearrangement—some pairs would have to be cut and spliced to others. Note that some spare pairs that may have been added to a feeder section, but not yet spliced into the network (because there is not yet anything to splice them to in adjacent sections) do not appear in any of these pair groups.

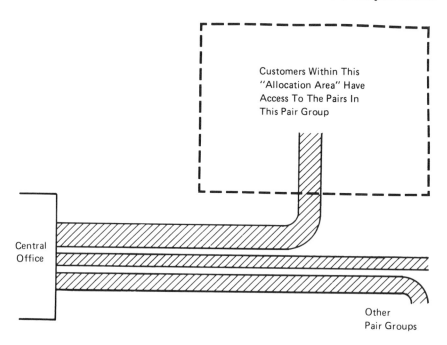

Figure 9.4. Feeder cable pairs can be viewed as falling into pair groups that serve certain geographical areas.

In their respective allocation areas, the pairs of a pair group are connected to *terminals*[4] that are accessible to individual customers in some small neighborhood. In the *multiple-connection* method, which is a commonly used one, each pair is connected to more than one terminal (i.e., *multipled*), so that it is accessible to customers in the more than one immediate neighborhood. Figure 9.5 illustrates schematically (5-pair terminals are shown, but 10–50-pair terminals would be more realistic; also, each pair typically may appear in 1–6 different terminals). Assuming single-party service, any wire pair can only be used for one customer at a time.[5] Why, then, do we connect each pair to several terminals? The answer is simply that we do not know precisely where the pair can be used best over time. We may have a good idea of how many feeder pairs are needed in the allocation area, but due to customer movement, are generally much more uncertain as to the precise needs in the smaller area served by a terminal. Why, then, do we not simply make every pair available in

---

[4]I have simplified the discussion considerably here by ignoring the intervening *distribution* cables—see the overview article on loop plant by B. L. Marsh cited at the end of this chapter.

[5]Of course, we may want to use pair gain systems as discussed in Example 9.3, when their cost is less than the marginal blocking cost defined below.

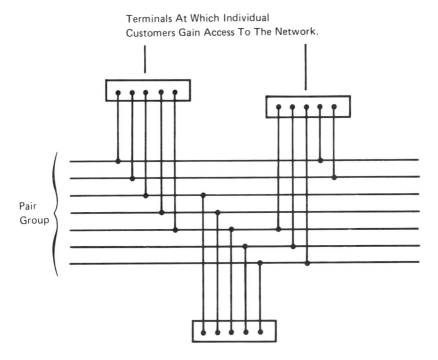

Figure 9.5. Multiple connection of feeder cable.

every terminal? This may be reasonable in some cases, but often would be a costly waste of hardware.

9.2.2 Blockages

When there is plenty of spare capacity (i.e., many less customers than feeder pairs), generally we would expect to find a spare pair accessible to any given terminal. With less spare, we would begin to run into situations in which all of the feeder pairs available at a given terminal are already in use either at that terminal or at some other terminal. Then, even though there are unused feeder pairs available in the pair group, a customer arriving at the given terminal would be *blocked* from obtaining an immediate connection. Note that we are *not* hypothesizing that there are necessarily more customers than terminations at that terminal. In fact, the connection can often be made by a relatively simple transfer of a customer from another terminal (called a *line-and-station transfer*) as illustrated in Figure 9.6. Note that the customer served from terminal B originally assigned to pair 5 has been transferred to pair 6 (also requiring a change at the central office). This frees pair 5 for use in terminal A. The multiple

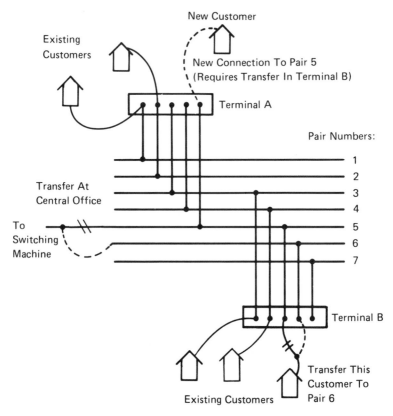

Figure 9.6. Line-and-station transfer—connecting new customer in terminal A requires the transfer of a customer in terminal B.

connection configuration is designed to make this kind of transfer routine; nevertheless, transfers impose a cost on the system. Since we expect the number of blockages to decrease with more feeder capacity, we may wish to consider the effect of blockage costs in expansion decisions.

We next develop simple formulas for estimating blockage rates. These are based on some strong assumptions and so should not be taken *too* seriously, but will give us a more concrete picture of increasing blockage rates with decreasing spare capacity.

Suppose there are n total feeder pairs in the pair group, w of them are assigned to customers (i.e., are working), and each terminal has k pairs. Assume, in addition, that there has been a complete mixing in the following sense: *The pairs in any given terminal can be viewed as a random selection of all pairs in the group.* A terminal is blocked if all k pairs to which it is connected are working (somewhere, not necessarily in that terminal). One way to develop the probability that a terminal is blocked is to consider an experiment in which we select k pairs sequentially and independently from a bin in which there are a total of n, w of which are working. The probability that all k are working is

$$\text{Pr(blockage)} = \left(\frac{w}{n}\right)\left(\frac{w-1}{n-1}\right)\cdots\left(\frac{w-k+1}{n-k+1}\right). \qquad (9.1)$$

If k is small relative to n and w, which it typically is in the current application, it is a very good approximation to write

$$\text{Pr(blockage)} \approx \left(\frac{w}{n}\right)^k \qquad (9.2)$$

(i.e., to ignore changes in the successive factors due to changes in the numerator and denominator—this corresponds to selection with replacement). Furthermore, we shall be interested most in blockages when the network starts to fill up—that is, when w gets close to n. Let $s \equiv n - w$ be the spare pairs available. If s is small, then:

$$\text{Pr(blockage)} \approx \left(1 - \frac{s}{n}\right)^k \approx (e^{-s/n})^k = e^{-(k/n)s}. \qquad (9.3)$$

Thus, according to this model, *the probability of blockage is approximately exponential in the spare capacity* (see Figure 9.7). Note that blockages decline dramatically with more spare in the system. Also, there are less blockages with larger terminal sizes.

Since we are interested in costs associated with running out of capacity, we can think of

$$\left(\begin{array}{c}\text{cost per}\\\text{unit time}\end{array}\right) = \left[\begin{array}{c}\text{rate at which}\\\text{customers enter}\\\text{the system}\end{array}\right] \times \text{Pr(blockage)} \times \left(\begin{array}{c}\text{cost of a}\\\text{blockage}\end{array}\right). \qquad (9.4)$$

Recall, for example, in Chapter 7 that we discussed models in which customers entered and left the system at random. Here, in effect, we are assuming also that the customers are entering and leaving *different parts* of the system, giving rise to the blockage phenomenon. In a simple model, we may wish to assume a constant inward movement rate λ and blockage cost C_B, so that, with Equation (9.3), the blockage cost per unit time $v(s)$ when there are s spare pairs is

$$v(s) = \lambda C_B e^{-(k/n)s}. \qquad (9.5)$$

Example 9.7. A feeder section currently has 10,000 pairs feeding through it. Customers are connected in multiple using predominately 16-pair terminals. It is projected that customers enter at a rate of about 500/year, and leave at a rate of about 400/year, for a net gain of about 100/year. Blockages resulting from our inability to serve a given customer immediately from his terminal are estimated to cost about $50/occurrence. A 1,200-pair capacity expansion costing $1,500 (equivalent annual cost) is

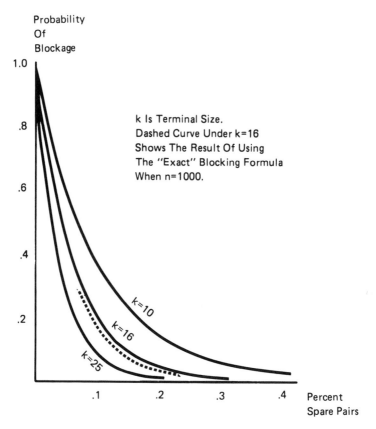

Figure 9.7. The probability of blockage versus spare for various terminal sizes.

planned for this section. When should this additional cable be placed? From (9.5), the congestion cost is

$$v(s) \approx (500)(50)e^{-(16/10,000)s}$$

(we shall ignore changes in the 10,000-pair cross section as cable is added.) At the critical spare level, the reduction in congestion cost due to the expansion just equals the annual cost of doing the expansion [Equation (8.15)]:

$$25,000e^{-0.0016s_*} - 25,000e^{-0.0016(s_* + 1,200)} = 1,500,$$

which can be solved readily for s_* to obtain $s_* = 1,659$. That is, this expansion should be undertaken when there is about 17% spare capacity in the system.

Suppose there were some unusual circumstance associated with this expansion that caused its cost to double from $1,500 to $3,000. Redoing the above calculation with 3,000 replacing 1,500 in the right-hand side, we obtain $s_* = 1,226$, which corresponds to about 12% spare capacity in the cross section. Note that at the net growth rate of 100 pairs per year, this corresponds to doing the expansion about 4.3 years later than in the previous case. It pays to incur the blockage costs longer because of the relatively less attractive cost of expansion.

It may be desirable also to include congestion cost considerations in determining the optimal size (here we were simply given the 1,200-pair cable). Example 8.3 illustrates an iterative procedure for a congestion cost function of this form. //

In a more sophisticated model, we may want to take into account different kinds of blockages (we may not be able to make some connections unless we do two line-and-station transfers, for example) whose relative rates of occurrence might change as we run out of spare; we may want to relax the complete mixing assumption; we may want to take into account the potential need for more drastic network rearrangements as we run out of spare. These complications certainly would change the calculations, but probably would not change the general observation that running out of capacity will be marked by rising blockage costs.

9.3 Operating Cost

Another phenomenon we are likely to encounter in running out of capacity is a rise in operating cost. We have alluded already to such possibilities in Example 9.6 (payment of overtime). Here we illustrate by looking at an important aspect of electrical power generation, that of serving demand that peaks severely over the daily, weekly, and yearly cycles.

9.3.1 The Demand Curve

The demand for electrical power varies considerably over time of day, day of week, and time of year. Figure 9.8 shows typical daily demand patterns for a high-usage and a low-usage day. The curve at the right is called the load–duration curve. It shows the fraction of the year that the load will be at the indicated level. (It is a sum or integral of all of the daily curves.) The vertical axis on all of the curves measures power output. Enough generating capacity must be available to serve that requirement. Thus, if demand is always to be met, the total capacity required is given by the maximum of the load–duration curve. We have indicated horizontal bands in Figure 9.8 labeled base load, medium load, and peak load. These are broad subdivisions indicating the use of different types of machines. The base load is served by machines with the lowest operating cost per unit of energy

226

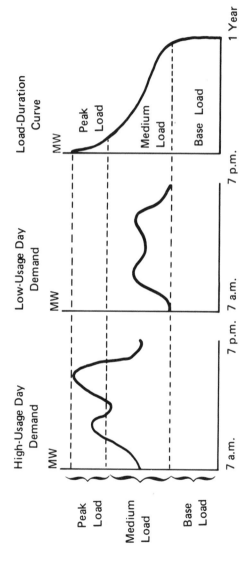

Figure 9.8. Load–duration of electrical power demand.

delivered.[6] These may include nuclear plants and large new fossil-fuel plants. The medium load would be handled with smaller and/or older fossil-fuel plants that have a higher operating cost; and the peak load would be handled with gas turbines, or possibly with reductions in power delivered (called brownouts) in extreme cases. In some cases, peak power may be handled by purchasing (importing) power from other regions. The area under the load–duration curve between bands is the total energy generated by the different capacities. Note that the base-load plants, which are the least expensive to operate, are applied over the portion of the load–duration curve that results in the largest area; the medium-load plants are applied over the portion that will encompass the next largest area; and so on. The reason for having these different types of plants is that the ones that are inexpensive to operate are more expensive to buy and install (if a plant were more expensive in both respects, it would be priced out of the market). Also, there are typically some older plants in use that are not as efficient as their modern counterparts.

Finally, in addition to this daily and seasonal fluctuation in demand, we must also consider long-term growth. A way of depicting such growth is shown in Figure 9.9. We have plotted the load–duration curve to the left of the demand curves to define the curves labeled 1%, 10%, and so forth. For instance, the 50% curve indicates how much power will be required over 50% of the year (i.e., capacity used to serve this demand will sit idle for the other 50% of the year).

9.3.2 Operating Cost Versus Base-Load Capacity

Suppose we are considering expansion of the base-load generating capacity. Since the base-load units are the least expensive to operate, we can expect a savings in operating cost with more base-load capacity; and we know from Chapter 8 that this savings may be important in the expansion sizing and timing decisions. To express this problem in the language of Chapter 8, we need to define an appropriate congestion cost that decreases with additional spare base-load capacity. The following example illustrates this point.

Example 9.8. Consider the simplified load–duration curve shown in Figure 9.10. Suppose that peak-load generating plants[7] are capable of supplying up to 600 MW of power at a cost of $100,000/MW/year;[8] medium-load

---

[6]Hydroelectrical plants are a special case that must be considered separately since they have not only a *power* limitation, but a total energy output limitation as well (e.g., see the article by D. Anderson cited at the end of this chapter).

[7]This may include importing power from distant plants with slack capacity, for example.

[8]This figure is usually given in $/MW-hr, which is this divided by the number of hours in a year: $100,000/8,766 = $11.4/MW-hr.

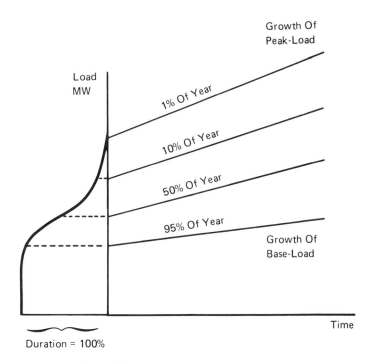

Figure 9.9. Demand over time.

plants can generate up to 1,200 MW at a cost of \$40,000/MW/year; and that base-load plants can generate power at a cost of \$10,000/MW/year.[9] We wish to find how much it would cost to generate the power under the load–duration curve of Figure 9.10 for various possible levels of base-load generating capacity. The solution is a matter of straightforward arithmetic with this simple load–duration curve. For instance, suppose the base-load capacity is 400 MW. Then the energy supplied by base-load units is the area of the rectangle below the lower horizontal dashed line in Figure 9.10:

$$\text{base-load energy} = (400 \text{ MW}) \times (1 \text{ year}) = 400 \text{ MW-years.}$$

The energy supplied by medium-load units is the area under the curve between the two horizontal dashed lines:

medium-load energy

$$= (200 \text{ MW}) \times (1 \text{ year}) + (800 \text{ MW}) \times \tfrac{1}{2}(1 \text{ year} + 0.333 \text{ years})$$

$$= 733 \text{ MW-years.}$$

---

[9]In a more realistic example, the various existing generating capacities would be stacked on the load–duration curve in order of increasing operating cost.

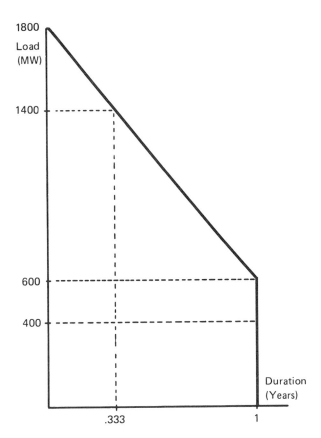

Figure 9.10. A simplified load–duration curve.

Similarly, peak energy is the area above the upper dashed line:

$$\text{peak-load energy} = (400 \text{ MW}) \times \tfrac{1}{2}(0.333 \text{ years}) = 67 \text{ MW-years}.$$

The corresponding total annual operating cost is

$$\text{total operating cost/year} = (400 \text{ MW-years})(0.01 \times 10^6 \text{ \$/MW-years})$$
$$+ (733)(0.04 \times 10^6) + (67)(0.10 \times 10^6)$$
$$= \$40.0 \times 10^6,$$

which is plotted in Figure 9.11. The rest of the points on the curve in Figure 9.11 are found in a similar manner.[10] This curve is essentially congestion cost as defined in Chapter 8 when we are considering the expansion of base-load capacity. //

---

[10] The curve is quadratic with parameters changing at base-load = 600 MW, at which time the peak-load capacity is no longer used.

230

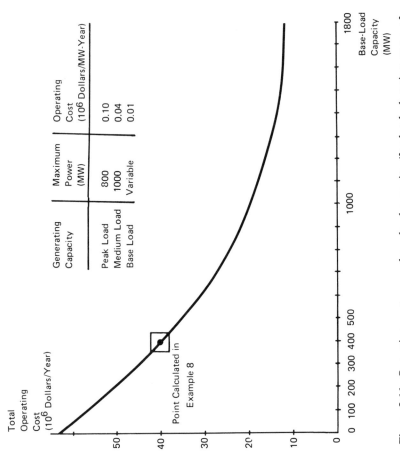

Figure 9.11. Operating cost versus base-load capacity (for load–duration curve of Figure 9.10).

9.3.3 Expansion of Base-Load Capacity

Once we have obtained a congestion cost relation (such as Figure 9.11) that shows us how the operating cost will decline with the addition of base-load capacity, we are in a position to examine its effect on our capacity expansion problem. The next two examples illustrate, first with a static case (no growth), and then with a special case that considers growth.

Example 9.9. Consider the congestion cost curve of Figure 9.11, which we have redrawn in Figure 9.12. (The horizontal axis is expressed in terms of spare base-load capacity; we have taken 600 MW as the nominal amount.) Suppose that demand is assumed to have no long-term growth; and that base-load capacity can be added at an equivalent annual cost of $(3.0 + 0.03x) \times \$1$ million for x MW. How low would our existing base-load capacity have to be before we would consider adding capacity to reduce operating costs; and how much would we add? Section 8.3 solves this problem, as illustrated in Figure 8.8. The dashed parallelogram in Figure 9.12 indicates the solution (the angled lines have a slope of 0.03 and the vertical distance is 3.0). The two arrows point to the critical spare before expansion $s_* = -165$ MW (which corresponds to a base-load capacity of 435 MW) and an optimal spare after expansion $S^* = 135$ MW (which corresponds to a base-load capacity of 735 MW). Thus, if an expansion is undertaken, sufficient capacity should be added to end up with 135 MW spare over the nominal 600-MW base load. Furthermore, addition of capacity is not warranted unless existing spare is at least 165 MW below the nominal 600-MW base load. //

Example 9.10. Consider next the situation of Example 9.9, but with base-load demand projected to grow at a rate of 100 MW/year. Suppose further that a maximum size limitation of 500 MW is imposed for purposes of reliability. (If too large a generating unit breaks down, it could cause the whole system to crash.)

We start with a quick curve lookup based on the analysis of Section 8.1. From Example 9.9, the ratio $rA/(gB) = (0.1)(3)/(100)(0.03) = 0.1$. Although this is not an importing problem, the $v(s)$ curve is nearly a straight line over fairly wide ranges of values, and so we treat its slope as an importing cost. In Figure 9.12 the slope of the $v(s)$ curve for low values of s is approximately $\beta \approx 0.05$, so that $\beta/(rB) \approx 0.05/0.03 = 1.67$. From Figure 8.4, we read off the optimal expansion

$$\frac{rx}{g} \approx 0.75,$$

which makes $x \approx 750$ MW. This is only a rough determination since Figure 8.4 does not apply strictly to this case. Nevertheless, we take it as sufficient evidence that the optimal expansion size is the maximum allowed, that is,

232

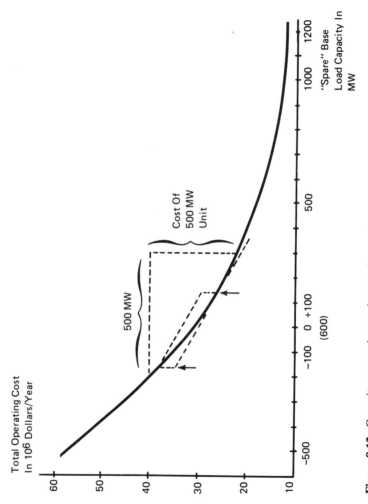

Figure 9.12. Capacity expansion and operating cost.

the 500-MW unit. To determine when the unit should be put into operation, we apply the relationship (8.14), which says that the reduction in congestion cost due to the expansion must just equal the equivalent annual cost of the expansion. A graphical determination of the critical spare level at which this occurs is shown in Figure 9.12. The solution is to expand when there is a spare of $s_* = -200$ MW (leaving 300 MW after the expansion) relative to the base-load demand. Note that we have assumed no change in the shape of the operating cost curve with growth. This corresponds to having the base load (which starts at 600 MW in Figure 9.10) and the peak load (which starts at 1,800 MW in Figure 9.10) both growing at the same rate of 100 MW/year. //

We have not *really* studied the dynamic case here. Due to the limit on expansion size, we were able to solve the problem essentially as a static one. Because the operating cost does change over a wide range of base-load capacities, the dynamic problem probably would not be separable in the sense of Section 8.3, so that we could not expect to obtain very good results by ignoring changes in congestion costs due to changes in expansion size.[11] That is, the sizing algorithm probably would have to take very specific account of congestion costs and so would be more involved than the examples we considered in Chapter 8.

The reader should be cautioned that these expansion problems involving electrical power generation have been *very much simplified*. As such, the approaches indicated here are valuable in gaining insight, and perhaps in guiding more sophisticated algorithms.

9.4 Summary

We have discussed several situations that can be modeled in terms of congestion costs. Their common feature is that capacity and/or demand are not really as uniform as required in our simple model of earlier chapters. In Section 9.1, capacity is allowed to be of two types—regular and imports. In Section 9.2, telephone feeder cable capacity and demand are actually distributed geographically, so that only *part* of the capacity is easily available to any given customer. In Section 9.3, electrical generating capacity consists of a mixture of machines with different operating costs; and demand must be distinguished as to whether it is base load, peak load, and so forth.

Casting these problems in terms of congestion costs allows us to use the theory developed in Chapter 8 to determine *when to declare a shortage*.[12]

---

[11]In Equation (8.19), $V(x)$ is truly a function of x, and so cannot reasonably be assumed to be constant when we are looking for an optimal x, as it was in Example 8.3.

[12]Of course, we know from Chapter 8 that the problems of determining optimal expansion size and time are generally interrelated.

That is, an expansion should be undertaken when its equivalent annual cost is offset by the savings in congestion cost.

In these examples we have stuck deliberately to effects whose costs are readily quantifiable. It is not difficult to think of situations in which the congestion cost *idea* fits qualitatively, but in which actual costs may be practically impossible to assess. Consider, for example, a water reservoir system in which running out of capacity may mean occasionally supplying water with slightly more impurities or having to legally restrict usage. How does one attribute costs to such events? In other cases, running out of capacity may increase the risk of having a disaster. In the telephone problem of Section 9.2, blockages are more likely to occur with less spare capacity, but no individual blockage constitutes a disaster. In electrical power, operating very close to capacity *may* increase the risk of a serious power outage. What are the costs associated with such an outage? Who would bear those costs? The difficulty of answering such questions has led to various simpler definitions of when to declare a shortage. For example, a regulatory agency may rule that sufficient electrical generating capacity must be provided to maintain the probability of massive outage at some selected low level. A firm may decide to take no chances on losing good will by being unable to meet its manufacturing commitments and so may expand its facilities well before overtime work shifts are required, even though it may appear to be optimal to defer the expansion temporarily by using existing facilities more intensively.

Thus, it may be that overriding factors obviate the need for explicitly modeling congestion costs. Even in these cases, the intuitive idea of congestion costs may be useful in arriving at reasonable definitions of what constitutes a shortage of capacity. An interesting exercise in some cases might be to try to *infer* implicit congestion costs from the alternative definition of shortage.

9.5 Further Reading

The telephone feeder cable expansion problem which was discussed at several points in the chapter is introduced in

B. L. Marsh, The Telephone Loop Plant—An Overview, *1976 International Conference on Communications*, Conference Record, IEEE Catalog Number 76 CH 1085-0 CSCB.

The application of pair gain systems, discussed in Example 9.3, is studied by

W. L. G. Koontz and R. S. Shipley, Application of Pair Gain Systems in an Environment of Stochastic Demand, *Proceedings of the Sixth Annual Pittsburgh Conference on Modeling and Simulation*, published by the Instrument Society of America, April 1975, 315–320.

and the multipled feeder blocking model, based on unpublished work by E. P. Klein, is discussed in

M. J. Krone, Congestion Effects in Telephone Cable Networks, *1976 International Conference on Communications*, Conference Record, IEEE Catalog Number 76 CH 1085-0 CSCB.

Further depth on these and other problems in the loop plant portion of the telephone network may be found in the special issue on the Loop Plant, *Bell System Technical Journal* 57(4), April 1978.

A great deal has been written on various aspects of electricity generation. A good review of some of these approaches and a copious bibliography may be found in

D. Anderson, Models for Determining Least-Cost Investments in Electricity Supply, *Bell Journal of Economics and Management Science* 3(1), Spring 1972, 267–299.

Chapter 10

Sizing Local Telephone Network Feeder Cables

Here we take a very careful look at a real capacity expansion problem—that of determining the optimal size of cables to install in expanding the capacity of feeder routes in a portion of the telephone network. In a sense, much of the material in this chapter is outside the mainstream of this book.

The rest of the book is devoted to the study of various general aspects of capacity expansion through detailed analysis of simple models. Here we retain more realism, and therefore more complexity, in the problem formulation. The kind of straightforward and complete analysis we did earlier is no longer possible. The problem is sufficiently complex to raise questions whether *exact* solutions can even be found in finite time. Nevertheless, the problem is one that actually arises, and is "solved" routinely (i.e., sizing decisions are made) in the normal course of business by telephone planners and engineers.

This chapter describes the sizing algorithm that has been implemented in a computer program offered to Bell System companies. The overall algorithm turns out to be complex indeed, but many of the heuristics described here are motivated by the simple models and analyses of the earlier chapters.

In the first section (Section 10.1), we describe the problem. We show in Section 10.2 that a special case can be solved by a slight generalization of the earlier simple model results. Section 10.3 describes the more complex combination of algorithms actually used in the computer program. Some discussion of the role of complex versus simple capacity expansion models is given in Section 10.4. Finally, Section 10.5 points to some further reading on the feeder cable sizing problem.

10.1 Telephone Feeder Routes

A telephone communication path between two customers generally consists of several very different links. Each of the customers is connected via the *local network* (also known as the loop or exchange plant) to the *wire center* serving his geographic region. Wire centers are interconnected via the *interoffice network*.

Since we shall be studying capacity expansion in the local network, we shall give only very brief descriptions of the rest of the path to provide some context (for more detail see Skoog's book cited at the end of Chapter 11). In the local network, each customer's telephone is connected to a switching machine at his wire center via a pair of copper wires, by and large dedicated to his sole use. The switching machines are capable of completing an electrical path between customers served by the same wire center or of connecting a customer via the interoffice network to a switching machine at another wire center, which in turn may connect to still another until the desired path is complete. Unlike the local network, the communication channels in the interoffice network are not dedicated to individual customers, but are used as needed for any communications between the wire centers that they connect. Therefore, the interoffice network generally consists of concentrated, high-volume links, which naturally call for quite a different technology than the local network. In place of a single pair of wires serving a single customer, many communication channels may be electronically *multiplexed* over one or two pairs. In higher-volume applications *microwave* radio or *waveguides* may provide the required links.

Because of the geographically dispersed nature of the local network, this highly developed electronic technology is generally not applicable.[1] In the local network, *cables* consisting of various numbers of wire pairs are placed sometimes on poles (*aerial* plant), sometimes directly buried or plowed into the ground (*buried* plant), and sometimes into an underground conduit duct previously constructed for the purpose (*underground* plant). Conduit ducts are essentially just empty pipes, a number of which are buried at one time to avoid digging up the street upon later cable additions. The wire pairs of adjoining cables are *spliced* together (see Figure 9.3 for a schematic depiction) to provide continuous, individual electrical paths[2] between the wire center and each customer in the geographical area it serves.

The local network can be subdivided broadly into two categories, the *feeder* and the *distribution* plant. Distribution is the portion of the network

---

[1] But see the discussion of pair gain systems in Example 9.3.

[2] At least they are individual at any given time—see Section 9.2 for a discussion of the multiple connection strategy. Also, in a party line, several customers share a single connection to the wire center.

closest to the customer. A short aerial or buried *drop wire* runs from each customer's premises to a nearby *distribution terminal*, which is spliced to several pairs of some distribution cable (often in multiple with other distribution terminals as discussed in Section 9.2.1). This gives the customer access to a wire pair in the local network.

Distribution cables serve small, well-defined geographical areas. Due to the limited number of customers in such small areas and to the economies-of-scale in placing additional cable, it generally pays to place as much as ultimately will be needed according to planned land usage and occupancy projections. This is not to say that all distribution cable is placed at one time, but only that when distribution cable is first needed in some area, enough is placed to serve the projected ultimate demand for that area.

Going toward the central office, distribution cables are spliced together to form larger cables. At some point, it becomes worthwhile to install fewer pairs in a cross section than ultimately will be required and to plan for future capacity expansions. From that point to the central office, the network is designated *feeder* rather than distribution.

In practice, the distinction between distribution and feeder is not determined purely on the economic grounds that we have indicated. There are, it turns out, great administrative and operational advantages to defining and maintaining a fairly rigid separation. The connection and disconnection of customers, record keeping, and certain maintenance operations are simplified if a sharp division is made between feeder and distribution plant.[3]

The feeder network can be viewed as consisting of *sections* or links defined by major branch points as illustrated in Figure 10.1[4] (also shown are *allocation area* boundaries, which indicate the geographical areas served by the different portions of the feeder network). These feeder sections will be the focus of our capacity expansion models. Wire pairs feeding through a given section may be serving customers from diverse geographical areas, some nearby, and some far away. Because of electrical resistance, distant customers need a coarser gauge of conductor (i.e., thicker wires) than nearby customers. Finer-gauge cables are less costly, and so generally are preferred where they meet the resistance requirements, but when there are both fine- and coarse-gauge demands, it may be less expensive to use the coarse-gauge cable for both.

A general assumption we shall make for purposes of mathematical tractability is that capacity expansion calculations can be done *indepen-*

---

[3]In recent years the division has become quite sharp with the increasing usage of the *serving area interface* hardware as discussed in some of the articles cited at the end of this chapter.

[4]This is, of course, not the only way in which it can be viewed. For example, see the discussion in Section 9.2 contrasting Figure 9.4 with Figure 9.3.

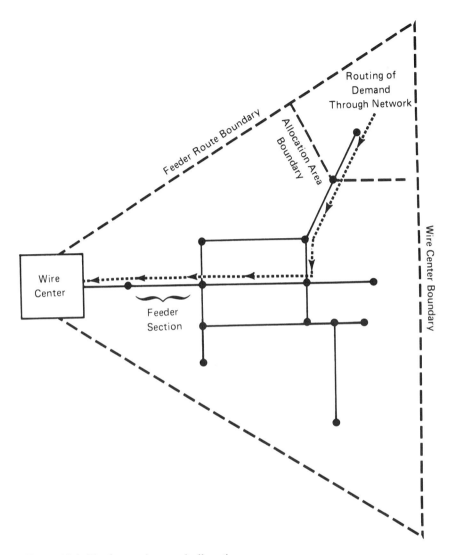

Figure 10.1. Feeder sections and allocation areas.

dently for each feeder section. The sections are not actually independent since cable in adjacent sections must be spliced together (see Figure 9.3), and the splicing configurations associated with some capacity expansion patterns may be more desirable than others. The assumption is reasonable, however, because splicing and rearrangement costs are generally quite small compared to expansion costs. Another implication of treating sections independently is that routing of demand through the feeder network is fixed, or at least predetermined. For instance, we cannot consider the possibility of temporarily serving customers along a *different path* through the network to postpone the need for an expansion in some section. This limitation is not serious for our application because it turns out that there are strong practical reasons for establishing fixed routing schemes. We also assume that demand is deterministic (and linear in the long run). In general, we allow for demand in up to four gauges (capacity types), where any demand can be met by capacity of its own or coarser gauge. Each cable placed to satisfy this demand uses up a cable space. This demand for cable spaces generally is satisfied by constructing conduit[5] (another type of capacity). In practice, cable sizes are limited to a standard set readily available from the manufacturer.

Finally, we assume that the congestion cost effects discussed in Chapters 8 and 9 (particularly Section 9.2) can be adequately taken into account by a suitable modification of the demand (e.g., as was possible in Example 8.2). In practice, this is often done by scaling the demand by a *fill-at-relief* fraction (for example, 0.8 or 0.9); so that a shortage is declared when demand reaches the fill-at-relief fraction (for example, 80 or 90%) of existing capacity. We assume henceforth that demand has been adjusted to include a suitable margin of spare at capacity expansions.

10.2 One Gauge and Conduit

We start by considering a special case that is easy to solve. Suppose only one gauge of cable is required, and that demand for it is linear, but that conduit must also be provided. Without the conduit, of course we would have the simple capacity expansion problem of Chapters 3 and 4. Conduit is quite expensive, however, and so has a strong influence on the solution.

Our solution algorithm is a generalization of the backward dynamic programming algorithm given in Section 4.1.1. Let W_n designate the present worth cost of optimally providing all future capacity starting with a shortage of cable and n spare conduit ducts. Then for $n \geq 1$, we can write

$$W_n = \min_x \left[C(x) + W_{n-1} e^{-rx/g} \right], \qquad (10.1)$$

where r is the discounting rate, g the demand growth rate, x the cable size for the current shortage, and $C(x)$ its cost. If W_{n-1} is known, this minimization is straightforward. For example, if $C(x)$ can be expressed as $A + Bx$ and we assume that x can take on any value, by setting the

---

[5]Sometimes it may be feasible to build another pole line instead. Since pole lines are generally much less expensive, they would usually be preferred on the basis of cost alone. Also, sometimes it is possible to create another cable space by removing a small existing cable. Of course, the capacity of the cable that is removed must be made up by new cable added. Finally, it may be possible to allocate additional right-of-way for direct burial of another cable; but only a limited number of cables may be buried without constructing a conduit system due to splicing and maintenance problems.

derivative to 0 it can be shown readily that the minimizing x, namely, x_n^*, is given by [Equation (4.5)]

$$x_n^* = \frac{g}{r} \ln \frac{rW_{n-1}}{Bg}. \tag{10.2}$$

When spare conduit spaces go to 0, suppose another conduit system must be built at a cost of $C_{\text{COND}}(n)$ for n ducts. The optimal number of ducts will satisfy

$$W_0 = \min_n \left[C_{\text{COND}}(n) + W_n \right]. \tag{10.3}$$

Note that we are assuming the same regeneration property for conduit systems as we have for other capacity. That is, after construction of the new conduit system in the right-hand side of (10.3), future costs will be given by the same W_n as before.

The following example illustrates how to solve this system of equations by guessing an initial W_0 and then successively iterating (10.1) and (10.3).

Example 10.1. Suppose the discounting rate is $r = 0.1$, the demand growth rate $g = 200$ pairs/year; cable costs $C(x) = A + Bx = 1.5 + 0.005x$ dollars/foot, and conduit costs $C_{\text{COND}}(n) = 10 + n$ dollars/foot. What size conduit system should be constructed, and what size cables should be installed? The first three columns of Table 10.1a show the results of iterating (10.1) starting with a wild guess of $W_0 = 1,000$ (the optimum ultimately turns out to be 31.3). Thus, for example, when 4 ducts remain, the present worth cost of all future expansions would be \$23.2 per foot, and it would be optimal to install a 2,333-pair cable. Note that sizes have been limited to a maximum of 3,000 pairs. The last row of Table 10.1a shows the values to which the size and cost W_n converge. These are, of course, just the size and present worth cost we would have obtained if we had ignored conduit. In fact, (10.1) corresponds to the value iteration method of solving the simple capacity expansion problem illustrated in Example 4.1. The last two columns of Table 10.1a show the solution of (10.3) using the W_n values of column 3. For general cost functions, there could be multiple local minima in the values of column 5. In those cases, it would be necessary to generate this table for all feasible values of n. Here, it turns out that the sum of W_n and $C_{\text{COND}}(n)$ is unimodal, so that the first local minimum is the global minimum. This minimum is \$34.4/foot for a 6-duct conduit using the first 6 cable sizes of column 2 (of course the 1,376-pair cable should be installed *first*, when there are 6 spare spaces). Using $W_0 = 34.4$ as a new estimate of the overall cost, we repeat the calculations in Table 10.1b. This time a 3-duct conduit is optimal with the cable sizes shown in column 2, for a total present worth cost of 31.3. Since this is not very different from the total cost of 34.4 obtained in the last iteration, we expect that this solution is nearly correct. Table 10.1c, starting

Table 10.1a. Optimal Sizes When $W_0 = 1,000$

1	2	3	4	5
		Cost W_n when		Sum of
number	optimal	n-ducts	Cost $10 + n$ of	columns
of ducts	size x_n^*	remain	building an	3 and 4
n	[Eq. (10.2)]	[Eq. (10.1)]	n-duct conduit	[Eq. (10.3)]
1	3,000	239.6	11	250.6
2	3,000	70.0	12	82.0
3	3,000	32.1	13	45.1
4	2,333	23.2	14	37.2
5	1,680	19.9	15	34.9
6	1,376	18.4	16	34.4 minimum
7	1,218	17.6	17	34.6
8	1,129	17.1	18	35.1
$\vdots$	$\vdots$	$\vdots$	$\vdots$	$\vdots$
∞	1,004	16.5	∞	∞

Table 10.1b. Optimal Sizes When $W_0 = 34.4$

1	2	3	4	5
		Cost W_n when		Sum of
number	optimal	n-ducts	Cost $10 + n$ of	columns
of ducts	size x_n^*	remain	building an	3 and 4
n	[Eq. (10.2)]	[Eq. (10.1)]	n-duct conduit	[Eq. (10.3)]
1	2,295	23.0	11	34.0
2	1,664	19.8	12	31.8
3	1,368	18.3	13	31.3 minimum
4	1,213	17.6	14	31.6

Table 10.1c. Optimal Sizes When $W_0 = 31.3$

1	2	3	4	5
		Cost W_n when		Sum of
Number	optimal	n-ducts	Cost $10 + n$	columns
of ducts	size x_n^*	remain	building an	3 and 4
n	[Eq. (10.2)]	[Eq. (10.1)]	n-duct conduit	[Eq. (10.3)]
1	2,282	22.9	11	33.9
2	1,658	19.8	12	31.8
3	1,365	18.3	13	31.3 minimum
4	1,212	17.6	14	31.6

with $W_0 = 31.3$, confirms this suspicion. Since the total cost is the same (within one decimal place) as the estimate of W_0, we declare the problem solved, the solution being to install a 3-duct conduit and a 1,365-pair cable now and to install a 1,658-pair cable and a 2,282-pair cable at the next two shortages. //

The algorithm of Example 10.1 is a generalization of the value iteration approach in Section 4.1.1. A policy iteration algorithm analogous to that of Section 4.1.1 could be defined readily.

Before leaving this special case of the feeder expansion problem, we make some observations.

1. In practice, the algorithm of Example 10.1 would have to be modified to take into account the fact that cables only come in discrete sizes. This simply means that (10.1) will have to be minimized by trying some available sizes and not just by using the size obtained from (10.2).

2. The approach can be modified readily to include cases in which something unusual will happen in the short run. For example, it is sometimes possible to defer the costly construction of conduit by placing a directly buried cable now, and building a conduit with the *next* expansion. (There is generally a limit to the number of cables that can be buried directly without overly congesting the right of way.)

Finally, we note that the rapid convergence observed in calculations on these simple problems is a prime motivating factor for the solution approach described for the much more complex EFRAP algorithm to be discussed next.

10.3 The Exchange Feeder Route Analysis Program (EFRAP) Sizing Algorithm

The feeder sizing problem becomes much more difficult to solve as we retain more of its realistic features. In this section we describe a version of the problem and a solution algorithm that was developed for the use of operating companies in the Bell System.

The point of this section is not to give all of the details of a large, complex computer program (which would be impossible in so short a space anyway), but rather to illustrate a solution strategy that may have wider applicability.

Due to added complexities, it turns out that none of our simple solution methods is quite applicable to this version of the problem. We chose, instead, a "branch and bound search" algorithm structure, which gives us great flexibility in treating complicating factors. However, to make the algorithm run fast enough to be practical for field use, we needed to trim drastically the amount of searching it could potentially do. Using our experience with simpler capacity expansion problems, we designed fast procedures for obtaining approximate solutions that serve as bounds for cutting down on the search. In our implementation, we relied on these approximations to the extent that the solution finally obtained is not guaranteed to be exactly optimal. Exact optimality is sacrificed for computational speed. The solution is a compromise between a methodical search of an astronomical number of solution possibilities and the use of simple heuristics, or approximate solutions, alone.

In Section 10.3.1 we present the problem to be solved and discuss why it is difficult. In Section 10.3.2 we describe the algorithm overall; and in Section 10.3.3 (and the appendices) we give some details about the approximate solution methods it uses. Section 10.3.4 further discusses the nature of the problem by applying the algorithm to a sample problem. Section 10.3.5 describes the use of the algorithm in a computer program offered to telephone operating companies.

10.3.1 The problem

We need to supply demand for additional cable pairs in up to four different gauges of wire, where a coarser-gauge wire (to which we will give a lower index number) can be used in place of the required gauge. Symbolically, we may write

$$\sum_{i=1}^{j} D_i(t) \le \sum_{i=1}^{j} X_i(t), \qquad j = 1, 2, 3, 4, \tag{10.4}$$

where

$D_i(t)$ is the cumulative demand for gauge i at time t

$X_i(t)$ is the sum total of all capacity of gauge i in place at time t.

Each cable placed, regardless of its size, is assumed to use up one of a finite number of cable spaces. When there are no more cable spaces, it is assumed that a new conduit system must be built to provide additional cable spaces (i.e., cable spaces are another type of capacity that must be provided).

We assume that *the only important costs are the present worth costs of buying and installing the cable and conduit.* We note that this implies free rearrangement of demand temporarily served by coarser gauge. This is the same assumption we made in the two-type expansion problem of Chapter 6. The problem, as posed here, is *much more difficult* than the two-type problem studied in Chapter 6, or the problem of one gauge with conduit of Section 10.2. The extra complications are summarized as follows.

1. There are up to four cable types rather than just two. For each type above two, the dynamic program of Chapter 6 would gain another dimension in its state space. This would be computationally disastrous. The approximation approach of Section 6.3 might still be useful but certainly would be more complex. (One of the approximate solution methods to be described in Section 10.3.3 is reminiscent of the approach taken in Section 6.3.)

2. Additional conduit must be built as cable spaces get used up. We already have seen the strong influence of conduit on the optimal size of cables in the simple, one-gauge case studied in Section 10.2. It seems that it would at least be necessary to add yet another dimension to the state space of the dynamic program of Section 6.3 to account for conduit.

3. Cables only come in discrete sizes. This would actually be helpful in the dynamic programming approach since it would provide a natural discretization when optimizing over the size. Strictly speaking, the approximations of Section 6.3 would no longer work, since it may be virtually impossible to obtain coordinated strategies as defined there. That is, with only discrete sizes available, it may not be possible to return periodically to a condition in which there is no spare of either type of capacity.

4. We wish to allow for the possibility of *nonlinear demand* projections over the early part of the study. Some users of the program feel capable of doing better than a simple growth rate estimate for demands in the near term. For example, when it is known that a new wire center will be established five years from the present, it can be predicted accurately that there will be sudden changes in demand as some customers are rerouted at that time. The dynamic program of Chapter 6 critically depends on having linear demand. The approximation approach might still be useful (i.e., the idea of an effective demand given coarser-gauge expansions), but would not be as straightforward.

10.3.2 Solution Strategy

We have already observed that dynamic programming probably will not be useful for this problem. Nevertheless, we shall find a viewpoint like that of dynamic programming to be of considerable value. Note that under the assumptions we have made, it does not pay to expand capacity unless some *shortage* exists. Thus, given some initial levels of existing capacity, both cable and conduit, we know that it is not optimal to add more capacity until at least one of the inequalities (10.4) is upset. It t' is the smallest time at which at least one inequality is upset, and j is the lowest-numbered inequality that is upset, we say that *the next shortage is at t' in gauge j*. This means that at t' a cable of gauge j or coarser (lower numbered) must be added (and possibly conduit also if there are no more spare cable spaces). The calculation of shortages is thus a natural extension of the formulas given in Chapter 6.

By analogy with the formulation in Chapter 6, we can think symbolically of a dynamic program for solving this problem:

$$W(X, t) = \min_a \left[\left(\begin{array}{c} \text{cost of} \\ \text{action } a \end{array} \right) + W(X', t')e^{-r(t'-t)} \right], \qquad (10.5)$$

where

$W(X, t)$ is the present worth cost of all future capacity starting with a shortage at time t and existing capacity X, where X is a vector representing all cable and conduit

a is the addition of capacity that will alleviate the shortage (i.e., cable in the gauge of shortage or coarser plus conduit if necessary)

X' is available capacity of all types following action a

t' is the time of the next shortage following action a.

We do not use this dynamic program directly because of the dimensionality problems already noted (i.e., the vector X is 5-dimensional). We use it instead to make an important observation. The optimal action a, the capacity expansion we are interested in, depends on *future costs* and not explicitly on future actions. We have seen that the optimal present worth cost in capacity expansion problems tends to be relatively insensitive to precisely which actions are taken, and so we should be able to find good approximations for W for the right-hand side of Equation (10.5). This basic idea is borrowed from the cost of the future approach for solving the simplest capacity expansion problems (Section 4.1), and the problem of single gauge plus conduit of Section 10.2.

For our computational algorithm, we actually view the recursive Equation (10.5) as defining a *decision tree* of the form shown in Figure 10.2. Each node corresponds to the next shortage given the available capacity of the parent node, as modified by the capacity expansion associated with the link entering the node. Each path down this tree is a sequence of capacity expansions that will satisfy the demand. Our problem is thus to find the path with minimum present worth cost. Note that if demand is assumed to stop growing in some finite time, the tree will be finite; while if growth goes on forever,[6] so does the decision tree (a possible cause of alarm, depending on the search strategy employed).

A commonly used tactic in searching decision trees is called *branch-and-bound*. The idea is to disqualify from further consideration as many nodes and all of their successors as possible by calculating bounds on the best possible solution that could be obtained starting from a given node. The procedure starts with an upper bound W_U on the cost of the solution. A handy way of obtaining such a bound would be to generate any reasonable path through the tree and take its cost. Also required at each node is some lower bound W_L on the total costs yet to be incurred from this node

---

[6]In Section 4.2 we showed that, at least for the simple capacity expansion problem, early decisions are essentially unaffected by growth sufficiently far into the future. To the extent that the effect carries over to this case, assumptions about growth into the very distant future should not affect the solution very much.

247

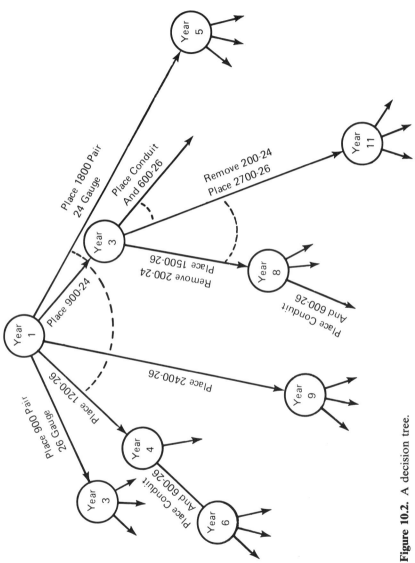

Figure 10.2. A decision tree.

onward. Further searching of the successors of this node is clearly unwarranted if

$$W_a + W_L \geq W_U, \qquad\qquad (10.6)$$

where W_a is the cost of all actions leading up to the node in question; that is, every path through this node is more expensive than the one that costs W_U. The success of branch-and-bound searches depends critically upon finding good bounds that can be calculated without too much computation.

Our approach is somewhat like branch-and-bound, but we trim the tree far more drastically than it would be possible to do using any bounds we were able to devise. Instead of generating lower bounds on the costs from some node, we make a rough estimate of the *total cost* of all further additions from that node (our so-called tail-end approximation). A prespecified fraction (0.95 works well) of that cost is then treated as a lower bound. The amount of searching is further reduced by avoiding branching altogether after the first two levels (i.e., cables satisfying the first two shortages) of the decision tree. Beyond the first two levels, a single sequence of sizing decisions is generated using our so-called elaborate heuristics for successive shortages up to 45 years. Beyond that, the tail-end heuristic provides an estimate of all further costs. Since the tail-end lower-bound approximation is not always very accurate, it is not used during the first two levels of explicit search ($W_L = 0$). Also, since the tail-end approximation is very much geared to linear growth of demand, it is not used if the shortage time of the node in question is within the initial nonlinear demand growth region specified by the user.

In summary, our solution strategy has three stages: an explicit enumeration of all alternatives at the first two levels; a completion of the two-level subsequence to 45 years using the elaborate heuristics; and a tail-end approximation that estimates any remaining costs after 45 years and also provides lower-bound estimates in the linear growth portion of the decision tree after the first two levels.

10.3.3 The Solution Heuristics

The *tail-end approximation* starts by solving independently four simple, linear growth capacity expansion problems (as in Chapters 3 and 4), one for each cable gauge. Heuristics are used to approximate the effects of interactions between the gauges and to estimate the demand for conduit. Another simple, linear growth capacity expansion model estimates the cost of conduit. All of these costs are put together to estimate the total cost of all future expansions starting with any given levels of capacities and demands in the various gauges. A feasible capacity expansion sequence is never generated, and so this procedure is used *only* to estimate cost. It is very fast, requiring negligible computer resources in our implementation.

Further details about the heuristics used may be found in Appendix 1 at the end of this chapter.

A more *elaborate heuristic procedure* is used to generate near-optimal sequences of expansions. A nominal expansion (to be described shortly) is generated for each shortage. Then, based on the following observations, a limited search is made to find improvements.

1. The optimal cable is most often in the same gauge as the shortage. Coarser gauges are more costly and finer gauges will not eliminate the shortage. The nominal expansion is thus in the gauge of shortage.

2. The optimal cable gauge is sometimes coarser than the gauge of the shortage in the presence of increasing demand for that coarser gauge;[7] and so coarser-gauge cables must be tried also.

3. The optimal cable size in the presence of increasing demand for finer gauges than that being placed and/or imminent exhaust of spare spaces tends to be larger than it would be otherwise (e.g., see Section 10.2); thus, smaller sizes need not be tried.

4. Removing a small cable to free up a cable space is nearly always less costly than building a new conduit right away, and so a removal is done whenever removable cables[8] have been specified by the user of the program, and a removal will postpone conduit construction.

The nominal size is determined by solving an auxiliary one-capacity-type problem. An effective nonlinear demand (reminiscent of that used in Section 6.3) in the gauge of the shortage is constructed that recognizes the effect of existing coarser gauge capacity (see Appendix 2 at the end of the chapter). Since this nonlinear problem must be solved a great many times in the course of the overall algorithm's search, it is done using the equated cost approximation mentioned in Section 4.3 (see Appendix 2).

This nominal cable size in the gauge of the shortage can be expected to be a reasonable choice when there is no demand in other gauges and no impending conduit shortage; that is, at least one more cable in the gauge of the shortage can be accommodated in the existing spare cable spaces. If these conditions do not hold, alternatives to the nominal cable are evaluated via the following look-ahead technique.

The nominal cable is added tentatively to the available facilities. Subsequent shortages and their corresponding nominal cable additions are

---

[7]This is nicely illustrated by the two-type capacity expansion problem of Chapter 6. Note in Figure 6.2 that the portion to the right of the origin corresponds to a shortage in coarse gauge, while that to the left of the origin corresponds to a shortage in fine gauge. But for fine-gauge shortages with a small spare level ($s_{12} < 140$), it turns out optimal to use deluxe capacity (i.e., coarse gauge).

[8]Only existing cables specified in the program input are considered for removal.

calculated. New conduit is assumed to be added as needed. The sequence generated following the initial tentative placement of the nominal cable both suggests the alternatives to be evaluated and serves as the basis for present worth cost comparisons.[9] If the next shortage following the tentative placement is in the same gauge as the tentative placement, and conduit is not required, no further alternatives are evaluated. It is assumed that anything that could be gained by altering the tentative placement could be gained in this case by altering the next decision in the same way at a lower present worth cost.

If the next shortage following the tentative placement is in a coarser gauge, then it may be advantageous to use a cable of that coarser gauge in place of the one tentatively placed (see observation 2). The algorithm tries cables at least as large as the one picked by the look-ahead algorithm in the coarser gauge. It completes the nominal sequence for each of these and replaces the cable tentatively placed if a present worth cost improvement results. It continues trying successively larger cables as long as there is improvement.

If the next shortage following the initial tentative placement is of finer gauge and/or requires the construction of conduit, it may be advantageous to place a cable larger than the nominal one, but in the same gauge (observation 3). Successively larger cables are tested against the cable tentatively placed as in the coarser-gauge case above until no further improvement results.

10.3.4 Sample Problem

Consider a 1,000-foot section of feeder with demand in 24 and 26 gauge ($i = 1$ and 2, respectively) and initial capacities as given in Table 10.2a. Also given in Table 10.2a are equivalent levelized *annual costs* of cable and conduit per foot. These have been calculated according to the methods of Section 2.1, including the effects of plant life, return on investment (discounting rate of $r = 0.07$), income taxes, and so forth. These data are not quite in the required form. Table 10.2b shows the result of some adjustments. The initial spare cable and growth rates reflect an assumed *fill at relief* of 0.85 to account for the fact that capacity needs to be added before the system is 100% full. The selection of some constant factor such as 85%, based on judgment and experience, is an admittedly crude way of recognizing the effects of congestion costs as discussed in Chapters 8 and 9 (see particularly Section 8.2 relative to the telephone feeder cable problem). In 24 gauge, for example, spare = $600 - 375/0.85$ and adjusted growth rate = $40/0.85$. Also shown in Table 10.2b are equivalent one-time costs in

---

[9]These will not be exact comparisons, since the sequences of sizes being generated are not optimal (but hopefully, not too far from optimal).

Table 10.2a. EFRAP Sample Problem Data

Capacity type	Initial		Demand growth rate	Equivalent annual cost of capacity
	Capacity	Demand		
1 (24 gauge)	600 pairs	375 pairs	40 pairs/year	$0.1 + 0.0005x$
2 (26 gauge)	2,100 pairs	1,742 pairs	120 pairs/year	$0.1 + 0.0003x$
conduit	6 ducts	3 ducts	to be estimated	$1 + 0.1N$

Table 10.2b. Adjusted EFRAP Data

Capacity type	Spare initially available	Adjusted demand growth rate	Capacity cost
1 (24 gauge)	159	47	$1,430 + 7.14x$
2 (26 gauge)	53	141	$1,430 + 4.29x$
conduit	3	—	$14,300 + 1,430N$

place of the equivalent annual costs per foot. These are found by taking the present worth of the corresponding annual cost as an infinite annuity (i.e., dividing by the discounting rate), and multiplying by 1,000, the feeder section length.

Cable may be assumed to be available in 300-pair increments ranging from 300 to 1,800 pairs for the 24 gauge and 300 to 3,000 for the 26 gauge.[10]

Several versions of the algorithm were applied to this sample problem for illustrative purposes. Table 10.3 summarizes the results. First, the tail-end heuristic was applied right at the beginning with no searching. It produced a present worth cost of 31,500, about 10% higher than the best ultimately achieved, but of course did not indicate any feasible sizing decisions. This good an estimate of cost with so little computational effort cannot be counted on in general, particularly if demands are nonlinear. Next, the elaborate heuristic procedure was applied with no branch-and-bound searching. Table 10.3 shows the first two sizing decisions. It should be noted that the initial shortage is in 26 gauge, but that a 24-gauge cable (1,800 pairs) turns out to be optimal (e.g., see Chapter 6 for a discussion of this phenomenon). The cost produced by this heuristic is 30,900, about 8% higher than the best ultimately achieved. This kind of performance is not atypical for the elaborate heuristic, and such a performance is considerably more reliable than that of the tail-end approximation. Nevertheless, there are many circumstances in which it cannot do as well, for example, for

---

[10]The upper limit is set by the maximum diameter cable that will fit in a conduit duct. Recall that coarser gauge means larger-diameter cable pairs.

highly nonlinear demand. The next four rows show the results of applying the branch-and-bound enumeration for one, two, three, and four levels of the decision tree. Note how dramatically the computer time rises with only a very modest improvement in the solution. Depending on the particular data, there may be considerably more improvement as more enumeration is performed. Experience has indicated, however, that there are generally diminishing returns beyond about two or three levels of search.

This kind of experimentation is what led to the decision to use two enumerating levels in the production program. With two levels, the 2–3 CPU seconds of computation required per feeder section are still a small part of the total cost of using the program, and the solutions obtained are, for the most part, indistinguishable from the optimum for practical purposes.

Some further observations can be gleaned from this example with the following series of computer runs. Suppose we vary the initial decision over all available 24-gauge cables. How will the cost vary? Figure 10.3 shows the results of the following computations. The initial decision was externally specified to be one of the sizes indicated on the abscissa. For each of those sizes the six versions of the algorithm used to generate Table 10.3 were exercised, and the present worth costs (including the cost of the externally specified initial decision) plotted. Note that *the optimal present worth cost, measured proportionately, tends to be very insensitive to the initial decision.* This is *not* to say that present worth cost differences in absolute terms are unimportant, but that much of the present worth cost is simply unavoidable (compare Section 3.1).

Each of the curves in Figure 10.3 can be viewed as being generated by the minimization indicated in Equation (10.5); the actions are the various 24-gauge cables listed on the abscissa, and the total present worth cost (left-hand side) is listed on the ordinate. Each curve is the result of a different approximation for W in the right-hand side of (10.5), the higher-numbered ones being the more accurate. Note that rougher approximations seem to yield similar optimal initial decisions. This is the kind of

Table 10.3. Computation Summary

Levels	1st decision	2nd decision	Present worth cost	CPU[a]
tail end	—	—	31,500	negligible
elaborate	1,800–24	1,800–26	30,900	1
1	1,500–24	2,100–26	29,800	11
2	1,200–24	2,100–26	29,100	54
3	1,500–24	2,100–26	28,600	324
4	1,500–24	2,100–26	28,600	1,275

[a]All CPU times are scaled in terms of the time for the elaborate heuristic alone, which was 0.04 seconds.

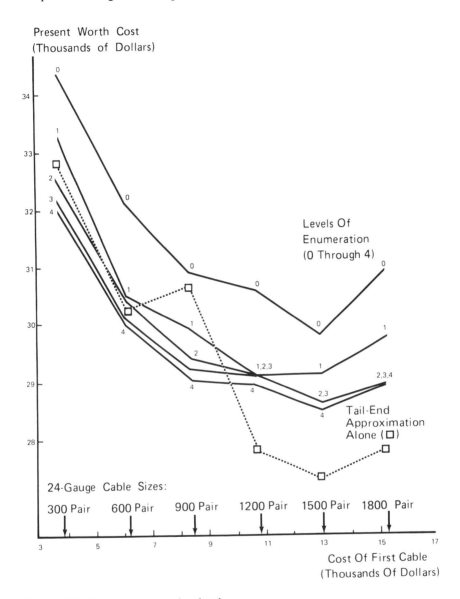

Figure 10.3. Various enumeration levels.

behavior that we would expect from a study of simple capacity expansion models. (The reader may wish to compare Figure 4.1, for example.)

10.3.5 Application

The algorithm described here has been implemented in a computer program (called EFRAP), which is offered as part of a line of engineering program services to the Bell System telephone operating companies by Western Electric Co.

This program and its earlier versions have been used widely since 1964 in so-called planning studies; that is, in studies of the long-term economic impact of projected growth in telephone feeder cable requirements. Feeder cable networks of 100 and more sections are analyzed with a single run of the program in a batched processing mode. More recently, the cable sizing algorithms described here have been implemented in a time-shared processing computer program designed to analyze one feeder section at a time. This time-share program permits the use of these algorithms on day-to-day engineering problems. In these problems, it is often necessary to evaluate alternatives that appear to be more practical than the optimal solution. For example, the cost of splicing cables between adjacent sections is not included in the algorithm. In some specific instances, it may be possible to save significantly on splicing costs if the cable sizes and gauges of certain sections are modified from the EFRAP solution. The time-share computer program provides a convenient way of estimating the present worth cost differences with specified alternatives for the initial decision. The telephone company engineer can then judge whether splicing or other savings offset the penalties for using a nonoptimal cable.

10.4 Discussion

This chapter examines an application of capacity expansion methods. The primary application, of course, is to the telephone feeder cable and conduit sizing problem. It is perhaps disappointing that our simple models could not be used directly.[11] Unfortunately, this is likely to be the case in *any* application. As a rough first approximation, we may estimate a linear growth rate of demand and a capacity cost function to get an idea of optimal expansion sizes. Sometimes that may be all that is necessary; but if we dig a bit deeper, we are bound to find a myriad of complicating circumstances. Even if we take only the more important ones into account, we are likely to have defined a capacity expansion problem that is unique to the one situation and, moreover, may be nearly impossible to solve. The actual application of the simple capacity expansion models is then to help find reasonable solutions of the derived complex expansion problem.

It is not likely that the actual sizing algorithm described in Section 10.3 will be useful for any other capacity expansion problem. It may be

---

[11]At one time, feeder cable sizing curves, based on a model essentially identical to our simplest model, were in common use in the Bell System. Also, currently there are manual methods for sizing based on the model of one gauge plus conduit of Section 10.2 (i.e., methods for determining a cable size without making a computer run).

however, that the *approach* taken there will be. The overall solution strategy (Section 10.3.2) with some other solution heuristics (Section 10.3.3) may be a good way to attack other capacity expansion applications. A thorough understanding of the simple capacity expansion models should be helpful in judging which aspects of a problem are likely to be the most important and in designing useful solution heuristics.

10.5 Further Reading

The reader may learn more about the technical problem of the local telephone network (sometimes known as the loop plant) by referring to the articles by Marsh, Koontz, and Shipley, or Krone cited at the end of Chapter 9. Also, the *Bell System Technical Journal* has devoted its April 1978 issue to problems in the loop plant. Section 10.2 was taken largely from the special issue article by

John Freidenfelds, A Simple Model for Studying Feeder Cable Sizing, *Bell System Technical Journal* 57(4), April 1978, 807–824.

The Exchange Feeder Route Analysis Program Sizing Algorithm description of Section 10.3 was taken from

John Freidenfelds, and C. D. McLaughlin, A Heuristic Branch and Bound Algorithm for Telephone Feeder Capacity Expansion, *Operations Research* 27(3), 1979, 567–582.

The dynamic programming view [Equation (10.5)] of our approximation algorithm is similar to what Erlenkotter calls an "incomplete dynamic programming" approach in

Donald Erlenkotter, Capacity Planning for Large Multilocation Systems: Approximate and Incomplete Dynamic Programming Approaches, *Management Science* 22(3), November 1975, 274–285.

A branch-and-bound approach to the capacity expansion decision is also employed by

D. T. O'Laoghaire, and D. M. Himmelblau, *Optimal Expansion of a Water Resources System*, New York, Academic Press, 1974.

A complex river basin and water usage model make O'Laoghaire and Himmelblau's problem difficult to solve by dynamic programming.

Appendix 1. Tail-End Approximation

Given some initial level of spare capacities in each of the gauges s_1, s_2, s_3, s_4; the number of initially spare cable spaces, N; and the knowledge that we are in the linear growth portion of the demand; we wish to find a quick approximation to the cost of providing all further capacity.

If we did not have to worry about the effects of conduit (see Section 10.2), we might consider supplying each of the four demands with cable of their own gauge, ignoring interactions between gauges (see Chapter 6) at the outset. From Chapters 3 and 4, we know that it is easy to find the minimum present worth cost of supplying each of the demands, $i = 1, 2, 3, 4$, independently:

$$W_i = \min_x \frac{A_i + B_i x}{1 - e^{-rx/g_i}}. \tag{10.7}$$

Designate the minimum, occurring at x_i^*, by W_i^*. If cables of this size were actually placed, cable spaces would be used up at the average rate of

$$g_c \equiv \sum_{i=1}^{4} g_i / x_i^*. \tag{10.8}$$

Treating this as a linear, continuous demand for conduit ducts, we find the optimal conduit size from

$$W_c = \min_N \frac{\alpha + \beta N}{1 - e^{-rN/g_c}}, \tag{10.9}$$

which we again designate by N^*, W_c^*. A method much like this is used for all conduit sizing in the algorithm; that is, no searching is done to improve the conduit sizing decision.

If it is assumed that the sequences of cables x_i^* start at the time of the first shortage in gauge i based on initial spare capacity alone, then the present worth cost of cable is

$$W_{\text{cable}} = \sum_{i=1}^{4} W_i^* e^{-r\tau_i}, \tag{10.10}$$

where

$$\tau_i \equiv \sum_{j=1}^{i} s_j \Big/ \sum_{j=1}^{i} g_j. \tag{10.11}$$

The times calculated this way may underestimate the times of next shortage by ignoring possibilities of temporarily using the excess capacity of coarser-gauge cables yet to be placed. A rough way to take this into account is to use, instead,

$$\tau_i' \equiv s_i / g_i + \sum_{j=1}^{i-1} \frac{1}{2} x_j^* \Big/ \sum_{j=1}^{i} g_j. \tag{10.12}$$

The first term is the time to use up existing spare in its own gauge, while the second assumes that, on average, the coarser-gauge cables placed will be about half-full when that occurs and so will defer the shortage. We actually calculate both times, τ_i and τ_i', and use the maximum.

We use the same approach to estimate the present worth cost of conduit:

$$W_{\text{COND}} = W_c^* e^{-r\tau_N}, \tag{10.13}$$

where

$$\tau_N \equiv \frac{N}{g_c}\left[1 + \frac{2-(1/2)^{N-1}}{N}\right]. \tag{10.14}$$

The factor N/g_c is simply the time at which we would run out of cable spaces if they were being used up at the rate g_c. The factor in brackets is an oversizing factor that recognizes that it will be optimal to place larger cables in the last few spaces to defer conduit construction (see, for example, Section 10.2). This particular factor is based on the assumption that the last cable will be 100% larger than it would have been without considering conduit, the second to last 50% larger, the third from last 25% larger, and so forth. Also, if there is a great deal of spare cable in one or more of the gauges, this equation will underestimate the time at which conduit will first be needed. Since conduit construction is such a large expense, another adjustment is used to recognize that demand in any gauge does not start using up cable spaces until the initially available spare in that gauge is exhausted.

Appendix 2. Equated Cost with Multigauge Demand

In the case of a single demand type, the equated cost is defined as (see Section 4.4)

$$\varepsilon \equiv \min_x \frac{A + Bx}{\int_0^\infty \min(D(t), x)e^{-rt}\,dt}, \tag{10.15}$$

where we have assumed 0 initial spare capacity. It was shown in Section 4.4 that in case $D(t) = gt$, this gives precisely the correct size.

In the presence of coarser gauge, we modify the criterion as follows:

$$\varepsilon_i = \min_x \frac{A_i + B_i x}{\int_0^\infty \min(\theta_i(t), x)e^{-rt}\,dt}, \tag{10.16}$$

where the function $\theta_i(t)$ consists of the demand in gauge i (the gauge of shortage) that cannot be served by the currently available capacity. That is,

$$\theta_i(t) \equiv \max\{0, D_i(t) - X_i - s_i(t)\}, \tag{10.17}$$

where X_i is the initially available capacity in gauge i and $s_i(t)$ is the spare in gauges coarser than i. That is, $s_1 \equiv 0$; and for $i = 2, 3, 4$,

$$s_i(t) \equiv \max\{0, s_{i-1}(t) + X_{i-1} - D_{i-1}(t)\}. \tag{10.18}$$

Inspection of these definitions will show that the effective demand $\theta_i(t)$ is defined in a similar manner to that of Section 6.3 for standard capacity in the two-type expansion problem. The difference is that here we do not take into account the effects of future additions of coarser-gauge cable on the effective demand—only that in existence at the outset.

Chapter 11

Other Capacity
Expansion Problems

There are many capacity expansion problems in addition to the ones we have studied so far in this book. This chapter describes some important ones, suggesting how they may be solved, giving some references to the literature, and indicating areas of further work.

Section 11.1 points out that expansion is often undertaken in conjunction with replacement of some part of existing capacity. Unless *all* existing capacity is assumed to be replaced, the resulting problem turns out to be very difficult.

Section 11.2 discusses a class of capacity expansion problems in which the location of projects is important. In these models, capacity may be added at alternative locations and production transported to other locations at a cost. Decision variables may include the location, size, and installation time of additional facilities.

The expansion of capacity in networks has many of its own unique features. Section 11.3 shows some analysis motivated by telecommunications transmission networks and road networks.

Section 11.4 considers whether the capacity expansion problem may not have a wider bearing on economic problems such as estimating a firm's annual construction budget, studying the growth of capital in an economy, and pricing the output of a regulated utility.

Section 11.5 gives a brief summary, and Section 11.6 indicates where the reader may learn more about these problems.

11.1 The Expansion/Replacement Decision

Thus far, we have virtually ignored the problem of replacing worn-out or obsolete capacity. Here we briefly explore the interaction of the replacement and expansion decisions. Section 11.1.1 presents a simple equipment replacement model and discusses its relation to our simple expansion model. In Section 11.1.2 we speculate on how the effects of combining replacements with expansions might be modeled in some problems. Finally, in Section 11.1.3, we give a mathematical programming formulation that encompasses both the replacement and expansion decisions. Although it is extremely flexible in its ability to include various complications, it is generally difficult to solve.

11.1.1 An Equipment Replacement Model

In our paradigm, a unit of capacity, once added, will last forever. A more realistic assumption leading to the same mathematical result is that as units wear out, they will be replaced by identical units, ad infinitum. As long as capacity cost includes the eventual replacement plus, if necessary, a provision for deteriorating efficiency toward the end of a unit's life, we can *say* it is the cost of perpetual capacity. In some situations, this may be a reasonable approximation of reality. For example, each added facility may be built into some larger system, making it attractive to replace worn-out units with exact duplicates. The actual timing of replacements is then a separate optimization problem whose form happens to be much like our simple capacity expansion problem.

Example 11.1. Suppose a communication facility of size x is to be added to accommodate growing demand. Suppose further that this facility is built into the communications network in such a way that it will be replaced at the end of its life by like equipment (same type, same size, etc.). If its life is L, then the present worth cost of having this equipment forever is

$$C = \frac{I(L)}{1 - e^{-rL}}, \tag{11.1}$$

where $I(L)$ is the present worth cost over its life L of installing and maintaining a unit of this size, including such effects as salvage and income tax considerations (see Section 2.1). The denominator reflects the repetition of these costs every L years; thus, C is the present worth cost of the equipment, which we have been using all along in this book.

Now it may be that longer-life equipment can be bought at a premium. In that case, we would choose the equipment for which

$$C = \min_{L} \frac{I(L)}{1 - e^{-rL}}, \tag{11.2}$$

which is identical in form to Equation (3.12) in the simple capacity expansion problem. That is, the problem of determining the *cost* of x units of additional capacity may itself be an optimization problem similar in form to the capacity expansion problem in which that cost is destined to be used.

A further observation may be made from Equation (11.1). If we are dealing with equipment that is inherently long lived, the assumption that it will be replaced by identical equipment at the end of its life is not likely to have a crucial impact on today's decisions. For example, if the discounting rate is $r = 0.1$ and the life is $L = 40$ years, the denominator turns out to be about 0.98. In other words, all but about 2% of the equipment cost C is the cost of the initial installation in this case. Thus, for long-lived equipment, the assumption of infinitely repeated installations can be viewed as little more than a mathematically convenient way of being consistent with the infinite study horizon. //

A great deal of study has gone into equipment replacement problems. Various authors have considered the effects of changes in operating costs or decline in output with age. Others have considered the impact of new and better equipment coming on the market.

Furthermore, many of the equipment replacement models reported in the literature make provision for capacity expansion as well, in the sense that new machines are allowed to be larger than the ones they replace. Most of these models, however, do not fit our standard capacity expansion paradigm because they make the assumption that *all capacity is renewed at a replacement point*. Thus, these models are more suited for studying the optimal behavior of, for example, a small entrepreneur (who operates a single machine and periodically trades it in for a newer, possibly better, possibly bigger one) than they would be for analyzing the optimal expansion of an electric utility.

11.1.2 Combining Replacements With Expansions

Our simplifying assumption that capacity lasts forever is clearly not always reasonable even when many vintages of capacity are to be in existence at any given time. It is often the case that replacement of the productive capacity of some obsolete or inefficient existing equipment can be undertaken simultaneously with a capacity expansion, making it possible to install a single larger facility with lower unit cost.

Example 11.2. In Chapter 3 we solved a simple capacity expansion problem (Example 3.5) with the following data: discounting rate $r = 0.1$; demand grows linearly at $g = 1.5$/year; and capacity costs $C(x) = 16 + 2x$. The optimal solution was found to be $x^* = 13.2$ for a total present worth cost of $W^* = 72.5$. Suppose an expansion of capacity is required at time 0 and that an existing unit of size $x_R = 10$ happens to be just slated for retirement at time 0 also. Suppose further that it is technically feasible to make up for the retired capacity in the size of the new unit being added for expansion. If we assume that in the future our regular simple model holds (i.e., all retired capacity is replaced in kind), then we can look at this as a problem with linear demand growth except for an initial jump to make up for the unit being retired. We know from Section 5.1 that the optimal size of the initial expansion in such a case is just what it would have been for the linear demand plus an amount to make up for the jump. The cost of the optimal solution can thus be written (see Section 4.1)

$$W = C(x_R + x^*) + W_F e^{-r(x^*/g)}, \qquad (11.3)$$

where W_F is the cost of all future expansion. If the retired unit had to be replaced in kind, the total cost would have been

$$W' = C(x_R) + C(x^*) + W_F e^{-r(x^*/g)}. \qquad (11.4)$$

The savings in present worth cost, the difference between these two expressions, is

$$\Delta W = C(x_R) + C(x^*) - C(x_R + x^*) = A = 16, \qquad (11.5)$$

which is quite substantial compared to the total present worth cost of 72.5 for this problem. //

Generalizations of the approach taken in this example are suitable when added facilities are expected to have long lives. That is, we can explicitly put jumps in the demand at the times in the future when existing units will be retired, but ignore the specific impact of the eventual retirement of units being added. Figure 11.1 illustrates for a situation in which three existing units are scheduled to be retired. The capacity expansion problem then reduces to one of the type we have been studying. Of course, even if demand is projected to grow linearly, the effective demand, including the capacity of retired units, will be nonlinear during the explicit retirements phase, as shown in Figure 11.1. As a final comment on this problem, we might guess from our experience with nonlinear problems in Chapters 5 and 6 that the optimal capacity expansions will probably tend to coordinate with the jumps, as illustrated by the initial expansion shown in Figure 11.1.

This kind of predetermination of retirements may be unsatisfactory for some problems because it fails to consider the possible dependence of the retirement decision on planned expansions. An example of this kind of interdependence is the removal of existing cables in the telephone feeder capacity expansion problem of Chapter 10. There we also considered the retirement (removal) only of prespecified cables. No times had been specified, however, at which these cables were to be removed. The removal

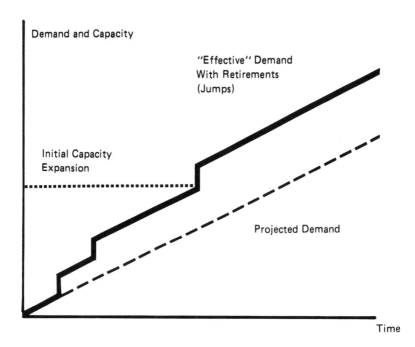

Figure 11.1. The retirement of existing units can be viewed as giving rise to effective jumps in the demand function.

decision was an *economic choice*. Removal of small cables to make room for larger ones was considered only when additional conduit would otherwise have to be built. Thus the retirement/expansion decisions were bound together inextricably.

11.1.3 An Integer Programming Formulation

When the retirement and expansion decisions cannot be separated as they were in Examples 1 and 2 above, the capacity expansion problem tends to get much more difficult. Here we show how such problems can be cast in an integer programming formulation. We also indicate that while this approach makes it possible to include easily many complications, the resulting optimization problem appears to be hard to solve.

We start with a simple version that does not include retirements and show how retirements and other complications can be formulated by modifying the coefficient matrix. Suppose we allow only a finite number of capacity expansion sizes, $x_1, x_2, \ldots, x_n$, costing $C_1, C_2, \ldots, C_n$; and that capacity expansion is to be considered only at a finite number of times, $t_1, t_2, \ldots, t_m$, at which times $D_1, D_2, \ldots, D_m$ capacity is required. Let y_{ij} be a variable whose value is only allowed to be 0 or 1, and which is 1 only if capacity of size x_j is to be added at time t_i. Then the capacity expansion problem is to minimize present worth cost subject to meeting all demand:

$$\text{minimize} \quad \sum_{i=1}^{m} \sum_{j=1}^{n} C_j e^{-rt_i} y_{ij}$$

$$\text{subject to} \quad \sum_{j=1}^{n} \sum_{k=1}^{i} x_j y_{kj} \geq D_i, \qquad i=1,\ldots,m. \tag{11.6}$$

(Recall that the C, t, x, and D values are all *data*; and the y are variables to be determined.)

Example 11.3. Consider the satellite problem of Example 4.6, with the following data: discounting rate $r=0.1$; available sizes $x_j=6$, 12, or 18 thousand channels with corresponding costs $C_j=28$, 40, or 52 thousand dollars; to be placed at times $t_i=0, 4, 8, 12$, or 16 years to meet a demand of $D_i=6,12,18,24,30$ thousand channels (capacity must be installed at $t=0$ to last at least until $t=4$, etc.). Equations (11.6) for this example are shown in Table 11.1a, where numerical entries are the nonzero coefficients of the variables listed at the bottom. Thus, for example, $y_{32}=1$ would correspond to placing a unit of size 12 in year 8 at a present worth cost of 18.0 (i.e., $40e^{-0.1(8)}$). //

This example illustrates a potential difficulty with the formulation. The number of variables and constraints increases rapidly as we consider more time periods or more capacity sizes. This might not be such a big concern

Table 11.1a. Capacity Expansion With Durable Equipment (Example 11.3)

Min	28	18.8	12.6	8.4	5.7	40	26.9	18.0	12.0	8.1	52	34.9	23.4	15.7	10.5	
	6					12					18					≥ 6
	6	6				12	12				18	18				≥ 12
	6	6	6			12	12	12			18	18	18			≥ 18
	6	6	6	6		12	12	12	12		18	18	18	18		≥ 24
	6	6	6	6	6	12	12	12	12	12	18	18	18	18	18	≥ 30
	y_{11}	y_{21}	y_{31}	y_{41}	y_{51}	y_{12}	y_{22}	y_{32}	y_{42}	y_{52}	y_{13}	y_{23}	y_{33}	y_{43}	y_{53}	

Table 11.1b. Including Finite Life and Varying Availability of Capacity over Time (Example 11.5)

Min	28	18.8	12.6	8.4	5.7	40	26.9	18.0	12.0	8.1	52	34.9	23.4	15.7	10.5
	6					6					18				
	6	6				12	6				14	18			
		6	6			12	12	6			10	14	18		
			6	6			12	12	6		6	10	14	18	
			6	6			12	12	6		2	2	10	14	18

if the problem did not require *integer* solutions; that is, if we could solve it by ordinary *linear programming* methods (see, for example, the formulation in Section 4.3).

Example 11.4. What is the solution of Example 11.3 if we do not restrict the y to take on integer values? It should be clear that y_{ij} for $j = 1$ or 2 would never be in the solution at nonzero level, since we can always get the same effect by increasing the corresponding y_{i3} at less cost. That is, without the integer restriction, we always would prefer to buy a smaller fraction of a larger facility, since it is available at a lower unit cost ($52/18 < 40/12 < 28/16$). Also, the y_{i3} would be just large enough to satisfy the inequalities, since the cost coefficients decrease with i (e.g., $34.9 < 52$). Thus, the solution would be: $y_{13} = y_{23} = y_{33} = y_{43} = y_{53} = 6/18 = 1/3$, at an objective function value of: cost $= 52(1/3) + 34.9(1/3) + 23.4(1/3) + 15.7(1/3) + 10.5(1/3) = 45.4$. Unfortunately, it is not physically possible to buy $1/3$ of the largest system at a time. We already know from Example 4.6 (the solution for $T = 20$ years) that the optimal solution of this problem is to use a system of size $x = 12$ (an 8-year system) followed by one of size $x = 18$ (a 12-year system). In terms of our current formulation, the optimal solution is: $y_{12} = 1$, $y_{33} = 1$, the rest 0, at an objective function value of: cost $= 40 + 23.4 = 63.4$. Thus the solution with fractional y values is literally worthless in obtaining the actual solution. //

This example illustrates that formulation (11.6) is a genuine integer programming problem. General-purpose algorithms exist for such problems, but their solution is not easy (e.g., see Wagner, cited in Section 2.11).

The beauty of this formulation is that at no extra cost, we can include all sorts of complications, such as the replacement of capacity. The following example illustrates how simple changes in the coefficient matrix can be used to model the *finite life of individual units being installed*, *unavailability of the entire capacity at once*, and *deterioration of capacity over time*.

Example 11.5. In the satellite problem whose integer programming formulation is given in Table 11.1a, suppose the 6 thousand-channel system has a life of only 2 periods, the 12 thousand channel system has only 6 thousand channels available in the first period and dies after 3 periods, while the 18 thousand channel system deteriorates at the rate of 4 thousand channels per period after the first period. All of these complications are included in the modified constraint matrix of Table 11.1b. //

It also only requires changes in the coefficients in the right-hand side to model arbitrary, *nonlinear demand*. Various effects such as assumed *availability of bigger or cheaper equipment in future periods* can be included with similar ease. With the use of some additional constraints, we can model *precedence restrictions* on equipment installation; for example,

$$\sum_{k=1}^{i} y_{k2} \leq N \sum_{k=1}^{i} y_{k1}, \quad \text{all } i, \tag{11.7}$$

with N some large number, will ensure that equipment number 2 does not get installed before equipment number 1.

If we wished to model replacement decisions more explicitly, recognizing that the life of a piece of equipment reflects an *economic* choice, we could include variables for equipment to be used over alternative lives as if they were a different piece of equipment. (Their cost coefficient would reflect changes in maintenance cost, tax effects, etc.) An effect that may bear significantly on replacement decisions, but that does not fit so neatly into this framework, is the congestion cost studied in Chapters 7 and 8. Since the congestion cost is likely to depend on *all* of the capacity available in each period, it is not separable into coefficients of the individual y_{ij}, and so would have to be included as a nonlinear function. No doubt, we could devise larger models with more integer variables and more constraints in which the objective function would be linear in the variables, but such an exercise is unlikely to prove fruitful.

In summary, the great advantage of integer programming formulations is that many effects can be included readily by only changing the data. The disadvantages are twofold. First, integer programming problems are generally hard to solve; and second, their solution tends to provide little insight into the nature of the problem being solved. A possible exception to the latter point is that we might be able to establish the difficulty of some capacity expansion problem by proving its equivalence to some other problem of known difficulty, such as the traveling salesman problem (discussed in any operations research text). Of course, we must be careful not to jump to rash conclusions on the basis of any single integer programming formulation. Recall that a slightly different formulation in Section 4.3 solves the special case of durable capacity by purely linear programming methods (i.e., not requiring explicit integer restrictions). Examples 11.3 and 11.4 show that integer restrictions *are* required under the current formulation. Perhaps there are still other formulations that allow some of the extensions considered here, but do not require explicit integer restrictions, or are easier in some other sense.

11.2 Transportation/Sequencing/Timing/Sizing

In planning the expansion of manufacturing capacity, the *location* of additional facilities is often a major concern. If the output of the manufacturing facility is to be used at other than its own location, a *transportation* cost is incurred. The problem is to find the *optimal locations* at which to provide additional capacity, the *optimal size* of the expansions, and the *optimal times* at which the expansions should be undertaken to minimize the overall cost of added facilities and transportation. We explore this problem by considering, in turn, the following. In Section 11.2.1, we consider a simple expansion sequencing problem in which there are n projects having predetermined sizes and costs that are to be added over time to serve the demand. Then, in Section 11.2.2, we add a transportation charge and consider the optimal timing as well as sequencing. Finally, in Section 11.2.3, we consider the optimal sizing of these projects.

11.2.1 The Simple Expansion Sequencing Problem

Suppose we are given a set of potential projects with capacities $x_1, \ldots, x_n$ that cost $C_1, \ldots, C_n$ to install and maintain forever. These capacities are to be installed to satisfy some nondecreasing demand function $D(t)$ at minimum present worth cost. Of course, if the demand eventually exceeds the total capacity available, $\Sigma_{i=1}^n x_i$, then something else eventually will have to be done. Our problem is limited to deploying the given projects at minimum cost. In some applications, such as the addition of reservoirs to a water system, the assumption of predetermined expansion sizes may be reasonable. In others, it may be a very rough approximation.

When there are n projects, there are $n!$ possible sequences. For moderately large n, this is a sufficiently large number to make a direct search infeasible; for example, if $n = 16$, $n!$ is more than 20 trillion. The following dynamic programming approach will reduce the search considerably. Let P denote some subset of projects and $\tau(P)$ the time at which demand first exceeds the total capacity of the projects in P. Designate by $P-i$ the set that contains all of the projects of P except project i. For all sets P containing j projects, let $W_j(P)$ designate the cost of optimally sequencing those projects. That cost can be found from

$$W_j(P) = \min_{i \in P} \left[W_{j-1}(P-i) + C_i e^{-r\tau(P-i)} \right], \qquad (11.8)$$

which uses the optimal cost of sequencing sets of $j-1$ projects. Thus, starting with $W_0(\text{empty set}) = 0$, we can successively generate W_j for larger and larger subsets of projects until the optimal sequence for all n projects is found.

This is in the form of a standard forward dynamic program such as we have used in Section 4.2, for example. A similar backward dynamic program can also be formulated. The difficulty with this dynamic program is that the state variable is a *subset of projects P*; and for moderately large number of projects, there can be a great many such subsets. For n projects, there are $n!/(j!(n-j)!)$ sets of j projects (the number of distinct combinations of j objects chosen from n). For $n = 16$, this takes on a maximum, at $j = 8$, of 12,870. Practical solution algorithms would probably rely on approximations rather than perform this amount of computation to find the exact minimum. Furthermore, added complications in a more realistic formulation may make a dynamic programming formulation such as (11.8) even more expensive computationally or invalidate it altogether.

The special case of this problem in which demand is assumed to be linear, that is, $D(t) = gt$, turns out to have a very simple solution, which suggests some approximations for the nonlinear case. With linear demand, it turns out to be optimal to order the projects according to their annual cost defined as

$$\mathrm{AC}(i) \equiv \frac{rC_i}{1 - e^{-rx_i/g}}. \qquad (11.9)$$

This is the constant cost per unit time whose present worth over the expansion interval is the same as the equipment cost C_i; that is,

$$\int_0^{x_i/g} \mathrm{AC}(i) e^{-rt} \, dt = C_i. \qquad (11.10)$$

To see why it is optimal to sequence the projects according to their annual cost, note that the total present worth cost of any expansion sequence is the discounted integral of these annuities (see Figure 11.2). Changing the order of any of the projects does not change their respective expansion intervals, nor does it change their annual charges $\mathrm{AC}(i)$. Since the discount factor decreases with time, *the present worth over all projects will be minimized if the projects are arranged in order of increasing annual charge* (i.e., 3, 1, 4, 2 in Figure 11.2). This argument using annual charges is taken from the article by Smith cited in Section 5.6.

With nonlinear demand, we can define a similar quantity,

$$\mathrm{AC}(i) \equiv \frac{rC_i}{1 - e^{-r\tau(i)}}, \qquad (11.11)$$

where $\tau(i)$ is the expansion interval corresponding to project i. However, now it is no longer true that $\tau(i)$ and $\mathrm{AC}(i)$ are independent of their positions in the expansion sequence, and so a simple ordering of projects according to $\mathrm{AC}(i)$ may not be optimal (as illustrated in Example 11.6). Nevertheless, it may be acceptable as an approximation.

If a better approximation is desired, we might consider *all pairs* of projects and choose the pair that produces the lowest equivalent constant annual cost over the combined expansion interval. Similarly, for a *jth-order approximation*, we could select the initial expansion sequence such that

$$\mathrm{AC}_j^* \equiv \min_P \frac{rW_j(P)}{1 - e^{-r\tau(P)}}, \qquad (11.12)$$

where $W_j(P)$ is the minimum present worth cost of sequencing the j projects in subset P, defined recursively by Equation (11.8). Note that when $j = 1$, $W_1(i) = C_i$, and so AC_1^* just gives the minimum annual cost over individual projects [Equation (11.11)]. Both dynamic program (11.8)

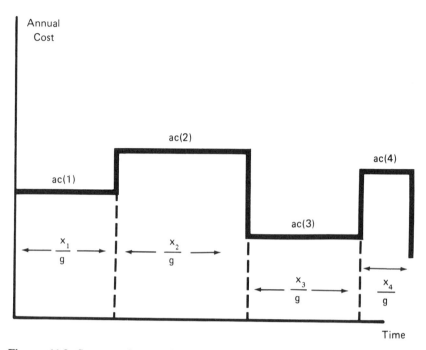

Figure 11.2. Stream of annual costs corresponding to expansion sequence x_1, x_2, x_3, x_4.

and the use of this approximation (11.12) are illustrated with a small sequencing problem in the following.

Example 11.6. Consider this simple sequencing problem. Three projects are available having capacities and costs shown in Table 11.2. Also given in Table 11.2 is demand $D(t)$ at all of the relevant points. (Think of it as varying linearly between those points.) Table 11.3 shows the dynamic programming iterations [Equation (11.8)]. For example, in the second row of iteration $j=2$, the optimal sequence is being sought for projects 1 and 3. Together, these projects provide a capacity of $3+12=15$ (Table 11.2), which will serve demand over the next 20 years (demand function in Table 11.2). In accordance with the dynamic programming equation (11.8), we try, in turn, sequencing each of the projects under consideration ($i=1$ and $i=3$) last. When $i=1$, the present worth cost is

$$W_1(3) + C_1 e^{-r\tau(3)} = 52 + 25e^{-0.1(5.5)} = 66.42,$$

where $\tau(3)$ and $W_1(3)$ are read from the third row of the previous iteration ($j=1$). Similarly, when $i=3$, the present worth cost is 74.46. Thus, the minimum present worth cost using projects $P=\{1,3\}$ is $W_2(P)=66.42$. The

Table 11.2. Data for Example 11.6: Demand versus Time and Available Projects

Time t (years)	0	0.5	5	5.5	20	30	35
Demand $D(t)$	0	3	9	12	15	21	24

Project i	1	2	3
Capacity	3	9	12
Cost	25	43	52

equivalent constant annual cost over the combined life of these projects is

$$\frac{(0.1)(66.42)}{1 - e^{-0.1(20)}} = 7.68.$$

The optimal present worth cost is found in the final iteration ($j=3$) to be $W_3 = 72.24$. The whole solution is obtained by tracing back through the tables. In iteration $j=3$, it was found that project $i=2$ should be sequenced last. Thus we go back to iteration $j=2$ to see how projects 1 and 3 should be sequenced (second row). This indicates that of these, $i=1$ should be sequenced last; thus, the optimal sequence is $i=3$, $i=1$, $i=2$.

In each of these iterations, the last column is the equivalent constant annual cost using the projects P. Based on the minimum annual cost approximation for individual projects ($j=1$) we would have chosen project 2 for the initial expansion, which turns out to be the wrong decision. By minimizing the annual cost of pairs of projects ($j=2$) we would have chosen projects 1 and 3 with project 3 undertaken first. This turns out to be the correct answer. //

Table 11.3. Sequencing Problem, Solution by Dynamic Programming

Project subset P	Expansion interval $\tau(P)$	Cost if $i \in P$ is sequenced last			Minimum over i $W_j(P)$	Equivalent annual cost AC using P
		$i=1$	$i=2$	$i=3$		
			Iteration $j=1$			
{1}	0.5	25	—	—	25	51.26
{2}	5	—	43	—	43	$10.93 = AC_1^*$
{3}	5.5	—	—	52	52	12.29
			Iteration $j=2$			
{1,2}	5.5	58.16	65.90	—	58.16	13.74
{1,3}	20	66.42	—	74.46	66.42	$7.68 = AC_2^*$
{2,3}	30	—	76.81	74.54	74.54	7.85
			Iteration $j=3$			
{1,2,3}	35	75.78	72.24	88.16	72.24	$7.45 = AC_3^*$

A jth-order approximation can be applied sequentially, of course, to find the entire expansion sequence. There are different ways in which this could be done, requiring different amounts of computation and yielding different results. For example, having sequenced the first j projects, one could fix their installation times and proceed to find the next j out of the remaining $n-j$, and so on. Alternatively, with more computational effort, one could start with the best initial sequence of j projects, but only fix the *first one* of these, and then apply the jth-order approximation again to the remaining $n-1$ projects. Also, because of the effects of discounting, and because one is usually more interested in the projects that should be undertaken early in the study, one may use a higher-order approximation for the first few projects than for later ones.

As a final computational note about this approximation, the reader may observe that it is not really necessary (and probably not efficient) to use the dynamic programming format for $j=2$ or 3. The numerator of (11.12) can be evaluated quickly for such small j by simply trying all of the possible orderings of the projects in P.

Two other approximations are worth noting for this simple expansion sequencing problem. In the first of these, we create an auxiliary capacity expansion problem of the type we have already studied in Chapters 3–5. We treat the n projects simply as n available capacity expansion sizes; that is, we assume that these projects can be replicated at will. This is solved as a standard capacity expansion problem. The initial expansion is then fixed and that size removed from the list of available sizes. The next expansion is determined by satisfying the remaining demand with the $n-1$ available sizes, and so on. This procedure can be expected to do well when there are many projects to sequence and when nonlinearities in the demand function are thought to be important, which is precisely when a direct sequencing approach is most difficult. In case demand is linear, it easily can be seen that this procedure will lead to the optimal expansion sequence.

Finally, we might consider an approximation scheme based on an approach involving cost of the future (see the Erlenkotter reference cited in Section 10.5). Starting with a backward dynamic programming formulation such as Equation (10.5), we would estimate the cost of all future expansions to be used in the right-hand side. All of the approximations discussed earlier would be potential approaches for making such estimates. This formulation probably would be most useful when there are further complications to consider, such as explicit transportation costs or variable project sizes.

11.2.2 Considering Transportation Costs—Project Timing

As we already have discussed, the project sequencing problem often arises in the context of multilocation manufacturing facilities. It may well be that differences in the cost of transporting the manufactured goods to their markets will influence the sequencing of expansions.

Suppose that as in the simple expansion sequencing problem, there are n potential projects (think of them as manufacturing facilities) of capacity $x_1, \ldots, x_n$ costing $C_1, \ldots, C_n$, but that demand can be broken up into m regional demand functions, $D_1(t), \ldots, D_m(t)$. The production and transportation cost of goods manufacturer by facility i and transported to demand location j are assumed to be v_{ij} per unit. At each point in time, we wish to determine the optimal amounts y_{ij} to manufacture and transport from each facility i to each demand location j. Thus we define

$$V(z,t) \equiv \min \qquad \sum_{i=1}^{n} \sum_{j=1}^{m} v_{ij} y_{ij}$$

$$\text{subject to} \quad \sum_{j=1}^{m} y_{ij} \le z_i, \qquad i=1,\ldots,n,$$

$$\sum_{i=1}^{n} y_{ij} = D_j(t), \qquad j=1,\ldots,m, \tag{11.13}$$

$$y_{ij} \ge 0,$$

where z_i is the amount of capacity currently available at facility i. The first set of constraints says that no facility can produce at more than its capacity, and the second says that all demand is to be satisfied. This optimization is in the form of a *transportation problem*, which is an easy to solve special case of a linear programming problem. Furthermore, using the dual variables, it turns out to be quite feasible to solve parametrically as t is varied. Since we shall not be elaborating further on how to solve the transportation problem, the reader may wish to think of $V(z,t)$ as some given[1] operating cost or congestion cost function such as we have analyzed in Chapters 8 and 9. This transportation cost or congestion cost can be incorporated into the sequencing problem.

We shall show first a version in which the timing of expansions is still determined by running out of total capacity; that is, another expansion is required when $D(t) \equiv \sum_{j=1}^{m} D_j(t)$ exceeds the total capacity installed to date. This is a reasonable assumption if transportation costs are not negligible, but capacity costs are still quite large compared to transportation costs. Then we shall consider the more general case in which timing is an economic decision as well.

In the dynamic programming equation (11.8), suppose we let $W_j(P)$ include the present worth cost of transportation as well as expansion. Then

---

[1] Or computed in a subroutine, say.

(11.8) becomes

$$W_j(P) = \min_{i \in P} \left[W_{j-1}(P-i) + C_i e^{-r\tau(P-i)} + \int_{\tau(P-i)}^{\tau(P)} V(P,t) e^{-rt} dt \right],$$

$$(11.14)$$

where $V(P,t)$ is the transportation cost when the projects of the set P are established and the rest are not. Since this is in essentially the same form as (11.8), it can be solved as indicated in the previous section. Only now, with the added computational burden of the transportation costs, the approximations discussed there become crucial even for moderately size problems.

In the optimization (11.14), we have not included the *timing* of expansions. It may be that some expansions would be triggered by the desire to reduce transportation costs rather than by actually running out of capacity entirely. In fact, if $V(P,t)$ is viewed as a more general congestion cost function, as in Chapters 8 and 9, all expansion would be undertaken for this reason. To incorporate the timing decision, replace $W_j(P)$ by $W_j(P,t)$, where t is the expansion interval for the projects of P. That is, $W_j(P,t)$ is the minimum present worth cost, including transportation, incurred over 0 to t, of optimally deploying the projects of P in that interval. The dynamic program (11.14) becomes

$$W_j(P,\tau) = \min_i \min_{\tau' \le \tau} \left[W_{j-1}(P-i,\tau') + C_i e^{-r\tau'} + \int_{\tau'}^{\tau} V(P,t) e^{-rt} dt \right].$$

$$(11.15)$$

Note that the minimization over τ' is the optimal timing of project i when projects $P-i$ have been established.

The great difficulty with this formulation is that it adds yet another dimension (τ) to an already large state space, making it useless for all but the smallest problems. Fortunately, it turns out that the timing decision in (11.15) can generally be done as a side calculation and need not be included in the dynamic programming state space after all. To see this, we rewrite the integral in (11.15) as an integral from 0 to τ minus the integral from 0 to τ' and rearrange some terms:

$$W_j(P,\tau) - \int_0^{\tau} V(P,t) e^{-rt} dt$$

$$= \min_i \min_{\tau' \le \tau} \left\{ W_{j-1}(P-i,\tau') - \int_0^{\tau'} V(P-i,t) e^{-rt} dt \right.$$

$$\left. + \int_0^{\tau'} [V(P-i,t) - V(P,t)] e^{-rt} dt + C_i e^{-r\tau'} \right\}.$$

$$(11.16)$$

Now observe that τ appears in the right-hand side only as the upper limit of the minimization over τ'. Suppose we *relax that constraint* (i.e., simply minimize over all τ'). Then the left-hand side is independent of the variable τ; and applying the same relaxation to the $(j-1)$st stage, the right-hand side quantity

$$W_{j-1}(P-i,\tau') - \int_0^{\tau'} V(P-i,t)e^{-rt}\,dt$$

is also independent of τ'. Thus the minimization over τ' reduces to

$$\min_{\tau'}\left\{\int_0^{\tau'}[V(P-i,t)-V(P,t)]e^{-rt}\,dt + C_i e^{-r\tau'}\right\}. \qquad (11.17)$$

A necessary condition for τ' to be the minimizing time τ^* is that the derivative be 0, which yields

$$V(P-i,\tau^*) - V(P,\tau^*) = rC_i. \qquad (11.18)$$

This says the project i should be added to those of set $P-i$ when the reduction in transportation cost just offsets the annual cost of project i. This is precisely the timing criterion we found in our study of congestion costs in Chapter 8 [see Equation (8.15)]. Using this timing criterion, the dynamic program (11.15) reduces essentially to (11.14).

The remaining question is whether it is legitimate to relax the constraint in (11.16). If the optimal timing decisions produced by the relaxed problem happen to fall in the proper order (i.e., the expansion time for the jth project in the optimal sequence exceeds that for the $(j-1)$st project, and so on), then they are optimal in the original problem. This is just the general observation that it does not hurt to optimize over a larger set of possible solutions if the optimum turns out to fall within the desired set. If the timing decisions happen not to fall in the proper order, then the solution obtained is not valid, and we are stuck with the full dynamic program (11.15) or, more likely, some approximation method. Fortunately, it turns out that the relaxation procedure is guaranteed to work when $V(P,t)$ is the transportation cost given by (11.13), provided the individual demand functions are nondecreasing over time. In fact, Erlenkotter and Rogers, cited at the end of this chapter, have shown that it is sufficient for $V(P,t)$ to have the following properties.

1. The cost penalty for not using any given project increases over time; that is, for any subset of projects, P, and $i \in P$,

$$V(P-i,t) - V(P,t) \quad \text{is nondecreasing in } t.$$

2. Projects are competitive in the sense that the penalty for not using a given project of some set is greater if there are less other projects in that set; that is, for any subsets of projects Q, P, and i such that $i \in Q \subset P$,

$$V(Q-i,t) - V(Q,t) \geq V(P-i,t) - V(P,t).$$

For practical purposes, we probably would use a criterion such as (11.18) for project timing, possibly modified by heuristic procedures if necessary, whether these conditions are met or not.

11.2.3 Sizing and Sequencing

Suppose, instead of assuming that the projects $i = 1, \ldots, n$ have predetermined sizes x_i, that we allow their sizes to be part of the expansion decision. The dynamic programming formulations of the previous sections could be extended to cover this case, but they probably would not be practical computationally. Instead, we investigate a special case that allows an interesting, and hopefully enlightening, solution formulation.

Suppose we have a single demand (negligible transportation costs) that grows linearly over time and that there are $i = 1, \ldots, n$ projects that can be undertaken in various sizes x at costs $C_i(x)$. Suppose, further, that after these projects have all been established, all further capacity[2] will be provided by means of an alternative technology whose total present worth cost is given by W_F.

The following backward dynamic program solves this problem. Let P be some set of j projects yet to be constructed and $W_j(P)$ the present worth cost of optimally serving all future demand when existing capacity has just exhausted. Starting with $W_0(\text{empty set}) = W_F$, all the $W_j(P)$ can be determined recursively from

$$W_j(P) = \min_{i \in P} \min_x \left[C_i(x) + W_{j-1}(P-i)e^{-r(x/g)} \right]. \qquad (11.19)$$

Note that in the minimization with respect to x, $W_{j-1}(P-i)$ is constant; thus, this minimization is identical to that for our simple capacity expansion problem in Section 4.1. For example, if $C_i(x) = A_i + B_i x$ and x is a continuous variable, then setting the derivative to 0 yields an explicit expression for the minimizing x [see Equation (4.5)].

The computational difficulty of this dynamic program is about equal to that given by (11.8) for the simple expansion sequencing problem. Note that both have the same state space. One could say that we have traded off nonlinear demand, allowed in (11.8), for expansion sizing, allowed in (11.19). Allowing both in a single formulation would multiply the required state space and add greatly to the computational burden. As we already have mentioned in discussing (11.8), the computational burden, when a substantial number of projects is to be sequenced, might already be excessive. Formulation (11.19) suggests that as an approximation, we might want to use our old ploy of *estimating* $W_j(P-i)$ for the right-hand side.

---

[2]Since demand grows forever, all projects would be established otherwise at their maximum size. Assuming a finite total amount of demand results in a much more difficult problem.

11.3 Expansion of Networks

Capacity expansion problems often have a network aspect. Highways, pipelines, electrical power lines, and telecommunications facilities can be viewed as the links of some network. The interconnection of these links can have a significant impact on the capacity expansion problem.

11.3.1 Expansion of a Transmission Network

Suppose that some commodity (automobiles, telephone messages, etc.) is to be transmitted between nodes of a network over the links of that network. Given various point-to-point demands, we wish to determine the optimal schedule for expanding the transmission capacity of the links. That is, we are not given directly the demands for link capacity; these demands are derived from the given point-to-point demands by *routing* them through the network. Since they can be routed only over links having sufficient established capacity, the routing and expansion decisions are interdependent.

In some situations, it makes sense to allow only a *static routing* policy; that is, demand between any two nodes is routed over the same path in the network for all time periods. In that case, the routing/expansion decision must trade off the economy-of-scale advantages of having few links with large demand against the savings of shorter routing with more links. In other situations, we may want to consider *dynamic routing*, that is, allowing demand to be routed over different parts of the network at different times. In this more difficult problem, routing is also influenced by the desire to defer construction of additional facilities. The following example illustrates these effects on a tiny network.

Example 11.7. Consider a communication network of three nodes interconnected by three links of equal length as shown in Figure 11.3. Suppose demand for transmission facilities between any two nodes grows at the rate of 100 channels/year, additional capacity costs $C(x) = A + Bx = 1.5 + 0.005x$, and the discounting rate is $r = 0.1$. If demand is routed over each connecting link (i.e., over the shortest distance in the network), we have three identical simple capacity expansion problems of the type studied in Chapters 3 and 4. In fact this very problem is solved in Example 4.5. The solution with this capacity cost and a growth rate of $g = 100$ turns out to be $x^* = 686$ for a present worth cost of $W^* = 9.93$ for each of the links (assuming unit length since they are all equal). The total cost, therefore, is $3W^* = 29.79$. As an alternative static routing, suppose we eliminate one of the links and route all demand over the two remaining ones. In that case, their demand growth rates would go up to $\bar{g} = 200$. That is, the three capacity expansion problems with $g = 100$ each are replaced with two having $\bar{g} = 200$ each. The optimal solution for this case, also solved in

Example 4.5, turns out to be $\bar{x}^* = 1{,}004$, $\overline{W}^* = 16.52$, for a total present worth cost of $2\overline{W}^* = 33.04$. Since this is more costly, the original minimum distance routing is preferred. Note, however, that the significant economy-of-scale effects have offset to a large extent the extra cost of doubling the distance over which the third demand is routed.

Suppose now that we start with the minimum-distance routing but allow some dynamic rerouting. In particular, how much could we save by initially constructing facilities of size x^* on only two of the links and temporarily routing and third demand over those facilities (at negligible rearrangement cost)? The initial two facilities will exhaust at time $= x^*/200$. Suppose that we install a facility of size x^* in the third link at that time and then expand all links independently afterward. The total present worth cost will be

$$W = 2W^* + C(x^*)e^{-r(x^*/200)} + W^* e^{-r(x^*/100)} = 28.36.$$

The savings of 1.43 over the 29.79 obtained for independent links is due to the deferral of one expansion on one link for about 3 years.

Along with the deferral savings, there are additional savings possible due to economy-of-scale effects. Suppose, when capacity is added to the third link, we add enough to make up for pent-up demand; that is, $x = x^* + x^*/2 = 1029$. The total cost then becomes

$$W = 2W^* + C(1{,}029)e^{-r(x^*/200)} + W^* e^{-r(1{,}029/100)} = 28.12.$$

Finally, what if we also increase the size of the initial expansions on the first two links to take advantage of the larger demand while they are temporarily serving the third point-to-point demand? That is, at time $t = 0$, we install capacity x_1 on two links and serve all demand over those links until $t_1 = x_1/(2g) = x_1/200$, at which time we install $\bar{x} = x^* + x_1/2$ in the third link. All future demands are assumed to be served over the three links independently. The total present worth cost is

$$W = 2\left[C(x_1) + W^* e^{-r(x_1/g)}\right] + C(x^* + x_1/2)e^{-r(x_1/2g)} + W^* e^{-r(x^* + x_1/2)/g},$$

where the first term is for capacity added to the first two links and the other two terms are for capacity added to the third link. This takes on a minimum of $W = 27.83$ at $x_1 = 944$.

To summarize, the best static routing for this network is the minimum-distance routing, which costs 29.79. If we temporarily reroute to defer the initial expansion on one of the links, we can reduce this to 28.36. If we also modify the sizes of the initial expansions to take advantage of the economy-of-scale effects, we can further reduce this to 27.83. If rerouting opportunities are assumed to be available with future expansion, additional savings are possible, but these will be smaller in magnitude due to discounting. //

11.3.2 Mathematical Programming Formulation

Here we consider one systematic approach to analyzing network transmission problems, namely, that of casting them into a mathematical programming format. Unfortunately, the mathematical programs tend to get quite large even for network problems of moderate size. In the next section, we briefly discuss some heuristic solution approaches.

Suppose we are given some network of nodes interconnected by links over which transmission capacity may be provided. Demands for the transmission of some commodity between pairs of nodes are assumed to be known with certainty and are given for each discrete period t by

$D^k(t)$ = total (cumulative) demand at t for transmission facilities between the pair of nodes designated k (demands may be specified between all pairs of nodes, or only between a subset of all possible pairs).

These demands are to be allocated over various possible paths in the quantities

$D_m^k(t)$ = total demand at t for point-to-point demand k that is routed over path m in the network. (We probably would specify some reasonable subset of all possible paths between the nodes, so that we would have a different set of paths for each k.)

Thus,

$$\sum_m D_m^k(t) = D^k(t) \quad \text{for all } k \text{ and } t. \tag{11.20}$$

Demands for transmission facilities along the links now can be found by adding the path demands that include a given link. Let

$D_n(t)$ = demand for transmission facilities in link n at time t

$[\varepsilon_{m,n}]$ = path link incidence matrix. That is, $\varepsilon_{m,n}$ equals 1 if link n is included in path m and 0 otherwise.

Then

$$D_n(t) = \sum_{k,m} \varepsilon_{m,n} D_m^k(t). \tag{11.21}$$

This is the demand for capacity on each link. The capacity expansion problem for each link can now be formulated as in Equation (11.6):

$$\text{minimize} \quad W = \sum_{t,n,q} e^{-rt} C_n^q y_n^q(t) \tag{11.22}$$

$$\text{subject to} \quad \sum_{\tau=0}^{t} \sum_q x_n^q y_n^q(t) \geq D_n(t), \tag{11.23}$$

where for each link n, q indicates the capacity expansion option; x_n^q and C_n^q are the size and cost, respectively, if option q is selected; and $y_n^q(t)$ a zero-one variable which is one if option q is selected.

Example 11.8. Consider, again, the network of Figure 11.3, which was studied in Example 11.7. Suppose now that expansion is to be considered at only two times, year 0 and year 5, and that only the first 10 years of demand must be served with these expansions. The three point-to-point demands are then 500 in the first period and 1,000 in the second. Suppose demand can be routed over the link joining two nodes (designated path $m=1$) or over the other two links (designated path $m=2$). Suppose that capacity can be added on any link in units of 500 costing 4.0 (option $q=1$) or in units of 1,000 costing 6.5 (option $q=2$) and that the cost of expansions in the second period (performed at the beginning of year 5) is discounted at the rate $r=0.1$, giving costs of 3.9 and 2.4, respectively. Then Equations (11.20)–(11.23) can be written as shown in Figure 11.4. Standard integer programming computer algorithms will find optimal solutions readily if the number of integer variables is not too large. Rather than pursuing the optimal solution, we evaluate several solutions that correspond to the solutions of this problem discussed in Example 11.7.

1. Static routing of all demand over its direct link. The reader may check Figure 11.4 to see that this corresponds to setting demand variables at $D_1^k(1)=500$, $D_1^k(2)=1,000$ for point-to-point demands $k=1,2,3$; and $D_n(1)=500$, $D_n(2)=1,000$ for links $n=1,2,3$ (with the rest 0). Using the large expansion ($q=2$) in each link we would have

Figure 11.3. Triangular communication network for Examples 11.7 and 11.8.

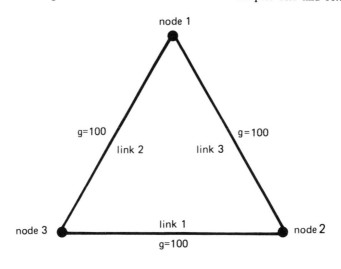

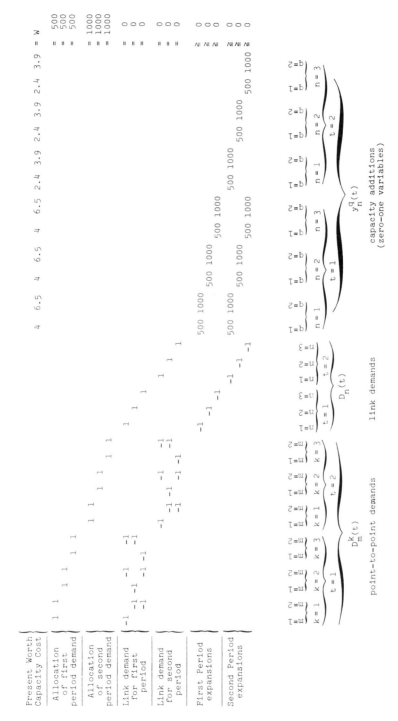

Figure 11.4. Network transmission expansion as a mathematical programming optimization.

$y_n^2(1) = 1$, $n = 1, 2, 3$, and present worth cost $W = 6.5 + 6.5 + 6.5 = 19.5$. If we install the capacity in two increments, $y_n^1(1) = 1$ and $y_n^1(2) = 1$, $n = 1, 2, 3$, the present worth cost turns out to be $W = 4 + 4 + 4 + 2.4 + 2.4 + 2.4 = 19.3$, which is slightly better than installing all of the capacity at once.

2. Static routing over two links (links 1 and 2). In period 1, $D_1^1(1) = 500$, $D_1^2(1) = 500$, $D_2^3(1) = 500$, so that $D_1(1) = 1,000$, $D_2(1) = 1,000$. Similarly, in the second period $D_1^1(2) = D_1^2(2) = D_2^3(2) = 1,000$ and $D_1(2) = D_2(2) = 2,000$. The large capacity increments must be used $y_n^2(t) = 1$, $n = 1, 2$ and $t = 1, 2$. The present worth cost is $W = 6.5 + 6.5 + 3.9 + 3.9 = 20.8$, which is more expensive than the direct routing in case 1 above.

3. Initially route all demand over links 1 and 2 and then reroute to supply each demand over its direct route. The first-period demand variables are the same as for the above case 2, and the second-period demands are the same as for case 1. The present worth cost is $W = 6.5 + 6.5 + 3.9 = 16.9$.

Thus the best of these solutions is the one that uses dynamic routing. Note that we came to the same conclusion in Example 11.7. //

Further complications that may be important in specific applications often can be included by adding more variables and constraints. For example, in telecommmunications networks, it may be costly to *route* demand over some path even if capacity is available. Routing may require physical work activities such as splicing cable pairs (see Section 10.3.1), adjusting certain repeaters, and so forth. We might model this by defining variables

$Z_m^k(t), c_m^k$ —the amount of point-to-point demand

k added to path m in period t at a unit cost of c_m^k.

Similarly, letting $\overline{Z}_m^k(t), \bar{c}_m^k$ be the amount and cost of *removing* demand from path m, we have the additional constraints

$$D_m^k(t) + Z_m^k(t) - \overline{Z}_m^k(t) = D_m^k(t+1), \qquad (11.24)$$

and replace the objective function (11.22) with

$$\text{minimize} \quad W = \sum_t e^{-rt} \left[\sum_{n,q} C_n^q y_n^q(t) + \sum_{m,k} c_m^k Z_m^k(t) + \bar{c}_m^k \overline{Z}_m^k(t) \right].$$

$$(11.25)$$

Of course, any modification such as this will add still more variables and constraints to an already very large mathematical programming problem.

11.3.3 Solution approaches

One possible approach to solving large network capacity expansion problems is to find algorithms that will efficiently solve large mathematical programming problems of the type illustrated in Figure 11.4. For example, the work reported by Charnes et al. cited at the end of this chapter indicates that large gains in computational efficiency may be possible if one takes advantage of the shape of the coefficient matrix (e.g., very sparse, block diagonal, or whatever) and tailors the algorithm so as to use the computer's resources efficiently. Still, such an approach probably will be limited to networks of moderate size and/or to fairly coarse discretizations (e.g., in Example 11.8 we limited ourselves to two time periods and two capacity sizes). This is particularly true if we try to include further complicating factors in the analysis. Suppose, for example, that we try to solve a general network version of the telephone feeder sizing problem of Chapter 10. There we assumed that link demands were determined by a prespecified routing of demand through the network. If the *routing* also were to be optimized, we would have a transmission network capacity expansion problem. Only now, there would be several different *types of capacity* (the different gauges and conduit). Due to the never ending possibility of such complications, we probably would be driven to heuristic and approximation methods even if general-purpose algorithms could be made much more efficient than they are today.

Example 11.7 is illustrative of heuristic approaches to this problem. One typically tries to separate the problem into that of routing the given demand through the network and that of finding the optimal link capacity expansions. For example, one may try to assign some reasonable link capacity expansion cost per unit of demand routed over the link. Then the routing becomes a much easier linear programming problem (no integer restrictions). The solution of this routing problem produces link demands that can be solved as standard individual capacity expansion problems. Based on the solutions of these link problems, we may wish to change our estimates of the linearized link capacity costs for the routing problem. Procedures of this kind tend to be useful in consolidating the demand over fewer links in the network to take advantage of economies-of-scale in equipment costs. Zadeh and Yaged, cited at the end of this chapter, use this kind of approach. Of course, this problem does not have the proper convexity to ensure convergence to anything but a local minimum.

Other heuristics may start with some proposed link capacity expansions and then try very detailed rerouting of demand over time to defer the construction of some of them (see the dynamic routing solution in Example 11.7). Smith, cited at the end of this chapter, discusses such an approach. More sophisticated algorithms would combine various heuristics in sequence or apply them simultaneously.

11.4 Relation to Aggregate Economic Variables

In this section we very briefly point out that the capacity expansion phenomenon, that is, capacity tends to be added in lumps, may be important in various economic problems for which determination of the optimal capacity expansion per se is not the goal.

An illustration of the relation we wish to point out is the feeder cable budgeting problem. A large entity such as a telephone company wishes to estimate how much it will need to spend next year to expand its feeder cable network. Such estimates traditionally are made by relating the budget, based on past observations, to certain aggregate data such as growth in the number of telephones in the area in question. Then the budget estimate is obtained from estimates of the growth variable. This works reasonably well as long as conditions remain static over time.

If conditions *do* change, it may be desirable to try to assess the effect of those changes on the budget. The budget in question actually will be made up of many individual capacity expansion projects. It is therefore quite possible that the budget would be different even for the same growth as last year, for example, due to changes in the economies-of-scale for individual cable installations. Suppose a new type of cable comes on the market that is economically superior to that currently used, provided it is installed in larger sizes (with a larger immediate cost). The budget eventually will be lower with this new technology, but its short-term impact will be in the opposite direction.

Changes in policy (what discounting rate to use, for example) or improvements in the optimization of individual capacity expansions (e.g., the introduction of a new computer program) may also play a role. The effects of such factors on the budget are impossible to assess without some consideration of the underlying capacity expansion problem. Bell and Blum, cited at the end of this chapter, show that estimates of aggregate feeder cable additions can be improved significantly by using a simple capacity expansion model that reflects the effects of changes in the average cable size and the average fill-at-relief.[3]

On a larger scale, economists are interested in studying the expansion of capital, by which they mean productive capacity, in an economy. This is often done by postulating differential equations that relate the rate of capital formation to the output of the economy (e.g., some fraction of the

---

[3]Ratio of demand to capacity at which a shortage is declared and relief is undertaken (e.g., 0.90). See Chapter 10.

output is assumed to be devoted to creating additional productive capacity).

In simple models of capital formation it may be reasonable to ignore the lumpy nature of capacity additions (in the aggregate, the additions may not look very lumpy). A more detailed analysis, however, should take into account the fact that the total capital is an accumulation of individual expansion projects. This is particularly important if one tries to include the effects of business cycles. For example, as the economy recovers from a recession, individual manufacturers may run out of capacity, and hence undertake expansion projects well before the slack productive capacity in the economy as a whole is taken up. Furthermore, if there is little spare capacity as the economy comes out of a recession, there may be a great surge of construction as many individuals expand their productive facilities. This would tend to create more excess capacity than would be suggested by viewing capital as a homogeneous aggregate quantity. It is even possible that lag and surge effects such as these actually may contribute to the creation of business cycles.

Another interesting question is raised by the lumpy nature of capacity additions; that is, who should pay for the excess capacity? Consider a tiny regulated public utility that forecasts a significant growth in the demand for its output. On the basis of this growth it finds that a large capacity addition (e.g., enough for 10 years of growth) would be economically efficient. The regulatory commission sets rates so as to supply the firm with sufficient revenues each year to pay direct expenses and to "pay for capital." Traditionally, capital costs are determined by a depreciation expense and a return on undepreciated capital, both of which are directly proportional to the size of the initial investment. In our tiny public utility, this procedure may create a problem. A *large* investment has been made, but for several years there will be only a *small* number of customers. Thus today's customers can be said to be paying for excess capacity that has been installed not for their benefit, but for the benefit of future customers.

A simplistic solution to this problem might be to allow the investors to earn only on that portion of the plant actually in service at any given time. The difficulty with this approach is that it may well encourage the utility to install capacity in something less than the most efficient expansion sizes.

A better solution would be to modify the way in which revenue requirements are calculated so that all customers, present and future, can be charged about the same amount for the same service. Such a procedure would have to take into account the lumpy nature of capacity expansions, which result in excess capacity. In a large enterprise, the lumps would tend to be smoothed as additions are made to different parts. This effect may still be important if a great deal of expansion is undertaken during periods of rapid growth. The effect may also be important if we try to allocate costs very specifically to the customers who cause those costs rather than aggregating costs over the entire firm.

11.5 Discussion

In this chapter we have looked very briefly at a number of capacity expansion problems: expansion/replacement; location/sequencing; networks; and aggregate economic indicators. Our purpose was to point out that these problems have been studied and to indicate that they can become much more difficult than the simple models that are the main subject of this book. We also tried to show by the examples that an understanding of simple capacity expansion problems could give some insight into these more complex problems.

11.6 Further Reading

The expansion/replacement problem of Section 11.1 has received a good deal of attention. The single-machine case with economies-of-scale in purchase cost is studied by Sinden, cited in Chapter 4, and, for example, by

Stuart E. Dreyfus, A Generalized Equipment Replacement Study, *J. Soc. Indust. Appl. Math.* 8(3), 1960, 4–31.

Hirohide Hinomoto, Capacity Expansion with Facilities Under Technological Improvement, *Management Science* 11(5), 1965, 581–592.

The formulation illustrated in Tables 11.1a and 11.1b in Section 11.1.3 is based on a linear programming version (i.e., demands, costs, and equipment availabilities may change over time, but equipment cost is directly proportional to capacity—no economy-of-scale) studied by Veinott and Wagner, cited in Section 4.5, and

David S. P. Hopkins, Infinite-Horizon Optimality in an Equipment Replacement and Capacity Expansion Model, *Management Science* 18(3), 1971, 145–156.

Much of the investment sequencing discussion of Section 11.2 is based on

Donald Erlenkotter, Sequencing Expansion Projects, *Operations Research* 21, 1973, 543–554,

Donald Erlenkotter and J. Scott Rogers, Sequencing Competitive Expansion Projects, *Operations Research* 25(6), 1977, 937–951,

and Erlenkotter (1975) cited in Section 10.5. A very similar analysis, emphasizing the timing criterion [Equation (11.18)] and plant sizing *given* the expansion sequence is done by

Ram C. Rao and David P. Rutenberg, Multilocation Plant Sizing and Timing, *Management Science* 23(11), 1977, 1187–1198.

Application studies in manufacturing capacity are discussed in A. S. Manne, cited in Chapter 3, and applications in water resources projects, for example, in

Thomas L. Morin and Augustine M. O. Esogbue, Some Efficient Dynamic Programming Algorithms for the Optimal Sequencing and Scheduling of Water Supply Projects, *Water Resources Research* 7(3), 1971, 479–484.

Ronald D. Armstrong and Cleve E. Willis, Simultaneous Investment and Allocation Decisions Applied to Water Planning, *Management Science* 23(10), 1977, 1080–1088.

Network capacity expansion problems (Section 11.3) motivated by the long-haul telecommunications network are studied by

B. Yaged, Minimum Cost Routing for Dynamic Networks, *Networks* 3, 1973, 193–224,

N. Zadeh, On Building Minimum Cost Communication Networks Over Time, *Networks* 4, 1974, 19–34,

R. L. Smith, Deferral Strategies for a Dynamic Communications Network, Working Paper 215, Graduate School of Business, University of Pittsburgh, 1977.

R. A. Skoog, ed., *Telecommunications Networks: Design and Cost Characteristics*, New Jersey, Prentice-Hall, 1981.

The first two papers emphasize the routing of demand over fewer links to take advantage of economies-of-scale in equipment purchase cost, while the third looks at dynamic rerouting to defer the construction of added facilities and Skoog's book provides a comprehensive review of telecommunication transmission networks. The expansion of road networks and electrical power transmission networks, respectively, are studied by

Goran Bergendahl, A Combined Linear and Dynamic Programming Model for Interdependent Road Investment Planning, *Transportation Research* 3, 1969, 211–228,

Kenneth L. Hicks, Transmission Expansion by Branch-and-Bound Integer Programming with Optimal Cost-Capacity Curves, *IEEE Transactions on Power Apparatus and Systems* 93, 1974, 1390–1400.

Dramatic improvements in the solution of large transshipment problems, whose structure is somewhat similar to our transmission network mathematical programs, are reported in

A. Charnes, David Karney, D. Kingman, Joel Stutz, and Fred Glover, Past Present and Future of Large Scale Transshipment Computer Codes and Applications, *Computers and Operations Research* 2, 1975, 71–81.

Although these methods are not directly applicable to our problem, they provide evidence that careful attention to computer implementation can make a tremendous difference in the size of problems that can be reasonably solved.

The feeder cable budgeting problem of Section 11.4 is taken from

W. N. Bell and S. Blum, A Model of Cable Pairs Added at the Main Frame for a Large Entity, *Bell System Technical Journal* 57(4), April 1978, 849–868.

A classic discussion of the effects of the capacity expansion phenomenon on capital spending in the economy is

Hollis B. Chenery, Overcapacity and the Acceleration Principle, *Econometrica* 20(1), 1952, 1–52.

Traditional models of capital formation that do not explicitly consider the lumpy nature of capacity expansion may be found in

J. N. Wolfe (ed.), *Value, Capital, and Growth*, Edinburgh University Press, Chicago, Aldine Publishing Company, 1968.

In Chapter 1 of Wolfe's book, K. J. Arrow's article does consider the durability of capacity via an idealization that disinvestment is not allowed.

A discussion of revenue requirements for the regulated firm may be found in the article by Peter B. Linhart cited in Section 2.11.

Index